GREATER AUCKLAND WALKS

First published in 2021 by New Holland Publishers
Auckland • Sydney

Level 1, Fox Valley Road, Wahroonga, NSW 2076 Australia
5/39 Woodside Avenue, Northcote, Auckland 0627, New Zealand

newhollandpublishers.com

Copyright © 2021 in text: Peter Janssen
Copyright © 2021 in photographs: Peter Janssen
Copyright © 2021 New Holland Publishers
Peter Janssen has asserted his right to be identified as the author of this work.

Group Managing Director: Fiona Schultz
Production Manager: Arlene Gippert
Managing Director: David Cowie
Editor: Duncan Perkinson
Designer: Yolanda La Gorcé
Maps: Adapted from originals by Bruce McLennon/Island Bridge

Front cover image: © Shutterstock
Front cover Inset images From Left to Right: Left: Hunua Falls,
Centre: Auckland Harbour Bridge, Right: Mangawhai Beach

A record of this book is held at the National Library of New Zealand

Janssen, Peter (Peter Leon)
Greater Auckland Walks - Over 200 scenic, historic and hidden walks across the Auckland region

ISBN: 9781869665166

10 9 8 7 6 5 4 3 2 1

All rights reserved. No part of this publication may be reproduced, stored in a retrieval system, or transmitted in any form or by any means, electronic, mechanical, photocopying, recording or otherwise, without the prior permission of the publishers and copyright holders.

While the author and publishers have made every effort to ensure that the information contained in this book was correct at the time of going to press, they accept no responsibility for any loss, injury or inconvenience sustained by any person using this book.

New Holland Publishers places great value on the environment and is actively involved in efforts to preserve it. The paper used in the production of this book was supplied by mills that source their raw materials from sustainably managed forests.

Keep up with New Holland Publishers:

 NewHollandPublishers

 @newhollandpublishers

GREATER AUCKLAND WALKS

Over 200 Scenic, Historic and Hidden Walks

PETER JANSSEN

CONTENTS

DEDICATION 9
INTRODUCTION 11
NORTH 17

1. Mangawhai Cliffs Walkway 18
2. Mangawhai Heads Pa Walks 18
3. Te Arai Regional Park 19
4. Cape Rodney Walkway, Goat Island Marine Reserve. 20
5. Leigh Harbour Walkway 21
6. Ti Point Walkway 22
7. Tawharanui Regional Park 22
8. Scandrett Regional Park Perimeter Loop Walk 24
9. Scotts Landing 25
10. Dome Forest Conservation Area 26
11. Parry Kauri Park 27
12. Pohuehue Reserve 28
13. Mahurangi West Regional Park 28
14. Puhoi Village Lookout Loop Track ... 30
15. Wenderholm Regional Park 31
16. Te Ara Tahuna Estuary Walk, Orewa 32
17. Shakespear Regional Park 33
18. Okura Bush Walkway 34
19. Atiu Creek Regional Park 35
20. Omeru Scenic Reserve 36
21. Library Point Walk, Sanders Reserve Paremoremo 37
22. Paremoremo Scenic Reserve 38
23. Long Bay Regional Park and Long Bay-Okura Bush Marine Reserve 38
24. Awaruku Bush Reserve 40
25. Rata Reserve 41
26. The Fernhill Escarpment 42
27. Manuka and Lynn Reserves Loop Walk 43
28. Campbells Bay to Browns Bay Coastal Walkway 43
29. Centennial Park Loop Walk, Campbells Bay 45
30. Milford Beach to Takapuna and Lake Pupuke 45
31. Smith's Bush/Onewa Domain 47
32. Tuft Crater 48
33. Onepoto Domain 49
34. Kauri Point Beach, Fitzpatrick Bay ... 50
35. Kauri Point Centennial Park/Kendalls Bay/Chelsea 50
36. Le Roys Bush 52
37. Old Birkenhead Walk 53
38. Historic Northcote Point Walk 54
39. North Head Historic Reserve 56
40. Devonport Loop Walk including North Head. 57

CITY 61

1. Hobsonville Coastal Walkway 62
2. Manutewhau Walkway and Moire Park 62
3. Te Atatu Walkway/ Harbourview Orangihina Reserve 63
4. Henderson Creek Walkway 65
5. Opanuku Walkway 66
6. Waikumete Cemetery 67
7. Howlett Esplanade/Waterview Reserve 68
8. Oakley Creek Walkway / Te Auaunga and beyond 69
9. Meola Reef Reserve/Te Tokaroa and Jaggers Bush 71
10. Western Springs Park 72
11. Freemans Bay, Herne Bay, Grey Lynn and Ponsonby 74
12. Auckland Old City 77
13. Karangahape Road and Queen Street. 80
14. Viaduct Basin to St Heliers 83
15. Coast to Coast Walkway 87
16. Historic Parnell 88
17. Mt Eden/Maungawhau, The Withiel Thomas Reserve and Mt Eden Gardens 90
18. Orakei Basin Walkway 93
19. Hobson Bay Walkway 93
20. Kepa Bush Reserve 95
21. Dingle Dell Reserve 95
22. St Johns Bush 96
23. Waiatarua Reserve 97
24. Tahuna Torea Nature Reserve 98
25. Tamaki River Walk from Roberta Reserve to Panmure via Point England Reserve. 98
26. Mt Wellington/Maungarei 99
27. Panmure Basin Walkway 100
28. Highbrook Park and Pukewairiki Crater 101
29. Seaside Park 102
30. Mt Richmond, Mt Robertson and Old Otahuhu 102
31. Hamlins Hill Regional Park/ Mutukaroa 104
32. Old Onehunga 106
33. Cornwall Park and One Tree Hill Domain/Maungakiekie 109
34. Big King, The Three Kings 111
35. Old Mt Albert 112
    The Waikowahi Walkway 114
36. Hillsborough Cemetery and Grannys Bay 115
37. Waikowhai Park, Hillsborough 116
38. Cape Horn Lookout 117
39. Manukau Domain 117
40. Gittos Domain 118
41. Blockhouse Bay Beach Reserve to Green Bay Beach Reserve 118
    Hauraki Gulf 122
    Great Barrier Island 122

ISLANDS 121

1. SS Wairarapa Graves, Whangapoua Beach 123
2. Warren's Creek Track 124
3. Old Lady Track Lookout 124
4. Windy Canyon Track 125
5. Haratonga Coastal Loop Track and Beach 126
6. Kaitoke Hot Springs 127
7. Te Ahumata Track 128
8. Station Rock Lookout 129

5

9. Dolphin Bay Track 129
10. Whaler's Lookout and Johnson's Bay Walk 130
    Kawau Island 131
11. Copper Mine Walk 131
    Tiritiri Matangi Island 132
12. Island Loop Walks 134
    Rangitoto Island 135
13. McKenzie Bay and Lighthouse 137
14. Rangitoto Summit 137
    Motuihe Island 138
15. Motuihe Loop Walk 139
    Waiheke Island 139
16. Matietie Historic Reserve Walk 140
17. Stony Batter 141
    Whakanewha Regional Park 142
18. Cascades Loop Walks 142
19. Pa and Rua Tracks Loop Walk 143
20. Little Oneroa to Palm Beach Coastal Walk 144
    Rotoroa Island 145
21. Rotoroa Loop Walk 146

EAST 149

1. Rotary Walkway, Panmure Basin to Pigeon Mountain/Ohuiarangi 150
2. Musick Point Reserve/Te Naupata.. 151
3. Old Howick from Howick Beach to Stockade Hill 152
4. Mangemangeroa Reserve 154
5. Point View Reserve 155
6. Whitford Path/Wade Walkway, Whitford 156
7. Maraetai Coastal Walkway and Omana Regional Park 157
8. Duder Regional Park 158
9. Clevedon Scenic Reserve 159
10. Waitawa Regional Park 160
11. Tawhitokino Regional Park 161
12. Tapapakanga Regional Park 162
    Mangere Walks. 166

SOUTH 165

1. Mangere Mountain 166
2. Mangere Lagoon 167
3. Ambury Park 167
4. Kiwi Esplanade 168
5. Watercare Coastal Walkway 169
6. Otuataua Stonefields 170
7. Puhinui Reserve 171
8. Otara Creek Reserve, Ngati Otara Park and the Otara Markets 172
9. Weymouth Walkway 173
10. Pahurehure Inlet Walkway 174
11. Conifer Grove Walkway 176
12. Murphy's Bush Scenic Reserve 176
13. Auckland Botanic Gardens and Totara Park 177
14. Mt William Scenic Reserve and Walkway 178
15. Harker Reserve and the Vivian Falls 179
16. Port Waikato Sand dunes. 180
17. Cape Hill Walk, Pukekohe 181
18. Henry Scenic Reserve and Te Ara O Whangamarie Walkway ... 182
19. Hamiltons Gap 183
20. Awhitu Regional Park 184
    Hunua Regional Park 185
21. Hunua Falls 185

22. Cosseys Reservoir Loop Walk 186	24. Wairoa Suspension Bridge Walk 188
23. Wairoa Loop Walk 187	25. Waharau Regional Park 189

WEST 191

1. Waionui Inlet and South Head 192
2. Te Rau Puriri Regional Park 193
3. Rimmer Road Beach Walk 194
4. Okiritoto Stream Walk, Muriwai 195
5. Muriwai Gannet Colony 196
6. Muriwai Lookout 197
7. Mokoroa Falls, Goldie Bush 198
8. O'Neills Bay, Te Henga 199
9. Te Henga/Bethells Beach and Dune Loop Walk 200
10. Lake Wainamu Walk 202
11. Pae o te Rangi Farm Regional Park 203
    Waitakere Ranges Regional Park .. 204
12. Waitakere Dam 205
13. Spragg Bush Loop Walk 205
14. Upper Nihotapu Dam 206
15. McElwain Lookout 207
16. Anawhata Beach 208
17. White's Beach, Piha 209
18. Kitekite Falls 210
19. Tasman Lookout, The Gap and Lion Rock 211
20. Te Ahua Point 212
21. Coman's Track 213
22. Karekare Falls 214
23. Tunnel Point and the Pararaha Valley, Karekare 214
24. Whatipu to Karekare Beach Walk 216
25. Whatipu Caves 217
26. Ninepin Rock and Paratutae 218
27. Omanawanui Track 218
28. Mt Donald McLean 219
29. Manukau Bar Lookout 220
30. Karamatura Falls and Valley 220
31. Lower and Upper Huia Dams 222
32. Arataki Nature Trail 223
33. Arataki Loop Track/Slip Track, Pipeline Road and the Beveridge Track 223
34. Beveridge Track, Arataki Centre 224
35. Exhibition Drive Walk 225
36. Zigzag Track, Atkinson Park, Titirangi 225

GLOSSARY OF MAORI WORDS .. 227

DEDICATION

For Mark Grimmer, for a half a lifetime of good advice.

INTRODUCTION

New Zealand's largest city, Auckland, has an outstanding natural environment. Situated between the Tasman Sea to the west and the Pacific Ocean to the east, Auckland is defined by water. At the heart of the region are two great harbours, the Waitemata and the Manukau, separated by just two kilometres at their narrowest point. To the north lies a third harbour, the Kaipara, one of the largest enclosed harbours in the world.

Flanking the region to the east and north is the Hauraki Gulf, sprinkled with beautiful islands that also protect the city from the worst Pacific Ocean swells. To the south east, the placid, shallow waters of the Firth of Thames are a haven for hundreds of thousands of migratory and aquatic birds. In direct contrast, the west coast lies in the path of the prevailing westerly weather and is infamous for relentless winds, huge swells and crashing surf.

Complementing the two great harbours are two equally impressive parks, the Hunua Regional Park and the Waitakere Ranges Regional Park, both of which were originally set aside as water catchment reserves, but then were greatly expanded in later years.

Under the ground is no less exciting as Auckland is the only city in the world that is located on an active volcanic field that covers an area of 350 square kilometres. This has created one of the world's most unique and iconic urban landscapes that is peppered with over 50 volcanic cones, many in the central city area.

Not all of Auckland is volcanic and Waitemata sandstones and mudstones are a common feature of the Auckland landscape. Light coloured, the rock is very soft making rock falls and small slips common along the cliffs leaving the base littered with broken rock and boulders.

Auckland is blessed with a (usually) equitable climate. Lying on the latitude 36.84 south and influenced by the sea on either side, the region rarely experiences extreme weather. The city has only experienced two very light snow falls in the last 80 years. Rainfall on average is around 1200 mm per year and the sun shines for an average of 2,000 hours per year making it one of the sunniest parts of the country. However, Auckland is a windy place, especially on the west coast. The highest wind gust of 204 kilometres per hour was recorded in February 1992.

Rich soils and a mild, wet climate have resulted in an extraordinary native flora and an equally exceptional fauna. Unsurprisingly, the original environment of the region has been radically altered. Maori cleared the land of most of the natural vegetation on the isthmus and the arrival of Europeans in the nineteenth century did the rest. All the forests in the region have been milled for timber at some point and the balance cleared, originally for farming and later to accommodate a populous city of one and half million people.

For so long isolated from the rest of the world's landmasses, New Zealand became a land of birds. However, its isolation spelt disaster for the avian population with the arrival of people. Since human settlement, 42 per cent or 57 bird species have disappeared forever and many more are endangered. Maori accounted for the extinction of 38 species through hunting and the introduction of the kiore or Polynesian rat. The arrival of Europeans led to the extinction of a further 19 species, pushing many more to the very edge of survival.

Now a thriving multicultural city of over 1.6 million, today Aucklanders are fiercely protective of their extraordinary natural environment and the region is peppered with projects, often initiated and run by locals, that are actively restoring the original habitats.

Kauri Die-back Disease

At first thought to have little effect, kauri dieback disease was first noticed on Great Barrier Island as far back as the in the 1970s. However, it wasn't until after 2000, that lone voices raised concerns about the spread of the disease in the Waitakere Ranges, the area now most effected by the disease. Where it came from, how it got here or even if the disease was always here, still remains unknown.

The pathogen causing the disease, *Phytophthora agathidicida* was only discovered in 2009. Invading the tree's roots, it is now known that this pathogen can sense a kauri, swim towards it and then burrow deep in the tree's roots. There is no cure and all affected trees will eventually die.

By 2014, alarm bells were ringing and drastic action needed. Within the Auckland region most tracks in parks and reserves with kauri were suddenly closed, as it appeared the disease was spread by spores in soil on the bottom of visitors boots and shoes. This had a dramatic impact on the Waitakere Ranges where 80% of the park was closed and to a lesser extent on the Hunua Ranges and other smaller reserves.

Gradually a programme of upgrading tracks and a spraying programme at exits and entrance has allowed some tracks to reopen.

About this book

I'm a firm believer that walks should be enjoyable and relaxing and needn't involve heavy boots, even heavier packs and tasteless food. All walks in this book are under three hours, the vast majority under two and many take less than 30 minutes. Even those of modest fitness can undertake most of them, and nearly all are suitable for family groups. None require complicated maps or special gear, certainly no heavy backpacks or awkward tramping boots. Very rough, overgrown or hard-to-follow tracks have been excluded and most are easily accessible from a main road. As the walks are short and straightforward, some descriptions are correspondingly simple and basic.

Although all the places in the book are close to Auckland itself, some are surprisingly isolated and remote so you can't assume that there is food, petrol and even water. Piha has no petrol and one basic shop; Karekare Beach a car park and toilets only; north of Parakai on the south Head of the Kaipara there is only a café at Shelly Beach. You will need to bring everything for a day trip to Rangitoto Island including water. During summer weekends food vans operate in several locations such as the Hunua Falls and Bethells Beach/Te Henga, but it doesn't pay to rely on them.

Many of the places described in the book involve walking on tracks that vary considerably in quality. How far and for how long you walk is your decision, but some tracks are muddy and rough and comfortable footwear with a good tread is highly recommended. And finally, it rains a lot in Auckland, even in summer, so if you are walking any distance a good waterproof jacket (not just shower proof) is essential.

Walk Grades

The walks are graded Easy, Medium and Hard. Easy are suitable for all ages and family groups and are mostly flat, well maintained and easy to follow. Medium walks require a little more effort with more uphill climbs, but well within the range of average fitness though they do not suit very young children and occasionally the track might be uneven and muddy. Hard means this track is uphill, though the grades and conditions vary considerably from very good with lots of steps to much rougher. Not suitable for very young children and good footwear is recommended.

Times

The times given in this book are for a very leisurely pace. Anyone with good fitness can take 25 percent off the time.

How to get there

Simple maps and instructions are provided on the assumption that the traveller has GPS, a smart phone complete with maps or reasonable paper road and street maps.

Gear

While no special gear is required, Auckland weather is notoriously fickle and track conditions vary considerably, so be prepared. In winter wind and rain can chill you to the bone and in summer the region is exposed to the tail end of tropical cyclones, which can bring high winds and heavy rain, though usually short-lived.

Shoes: Tramping boots aren't necessary. You'll be much more comfortable with a good pair of trainers you don't mind getting dirty, but make sure they have a good tread as tracks are often muddy or have slippery sections over rocks and wooden steps. For summer there are very good, sturdy walking sandals available, with excellent tread. And no, jandals are not great for walking.

Jacket: Invest in a genuinely waterproof jacket. Many are only shower or wind-proof and it rains a lot in Auckland. If you don't want to go to the expense, while heavy yellow plastic coats may not be elegant bush wear, they're cheap and certainly keep the rain out. In wetter seasons, keep a few dry clothes in the car – if you do get wet, you have something warm to change into.

Sun: New Zealand sun is fierce with a high intensity of ultraviolet rays and very short burn times, so it is not surprising that this country has one of the highest rates of skin cancer. In summer you will need a hat, preferably one that covers the back of the neck and the tops of the ears. You will also need to protect your arms either will sunblock or a long-sleeved shirt. Cloudy and windy weather frequently disguises the intensity of the sun, especially on the coast. On the longer walks you might need to take water.

Swimming: Surrounded by water, Auckland has endless beaches, bays and even lakes and small rivers. Drowning was once known as the New Zealand Death and common sense applies here and it is best to cautious, than regretful. This doubly applies to the region's west coast, notorious for its turbulent surf, dangerous currents and treacherous tides. Wherever possible, swim at beaches that are patrolled by life guards, and be extra careful when swimming in unpatrolled beaches.

Security

An unfortunate fact of life is that car burglary is common in New Zealand and some popular attractions even have security guards in the car parks. Short of leaving someone with the car there are a few things you can do to lessen the chances of having it broken into. Most thieves are opportunist so lock your car even on a short walk and double-check your windows are closed (it's easy to forget back windows). Make sure all valuables are out of sight, and if possible, carry your most valuable items with you (wallet, camera, phone, video). Invest in an inexpensive steering lock: this won't stop your car being broken into but will indicate to thieves you are security-conscious and will certainly stop them stealing the car.

Mobile phones

Mobile phones can be very useful if you're lost, but in the deep valley of the Waitakere or Hunua Ranges and on some off shore islands, they don't always have coverage.

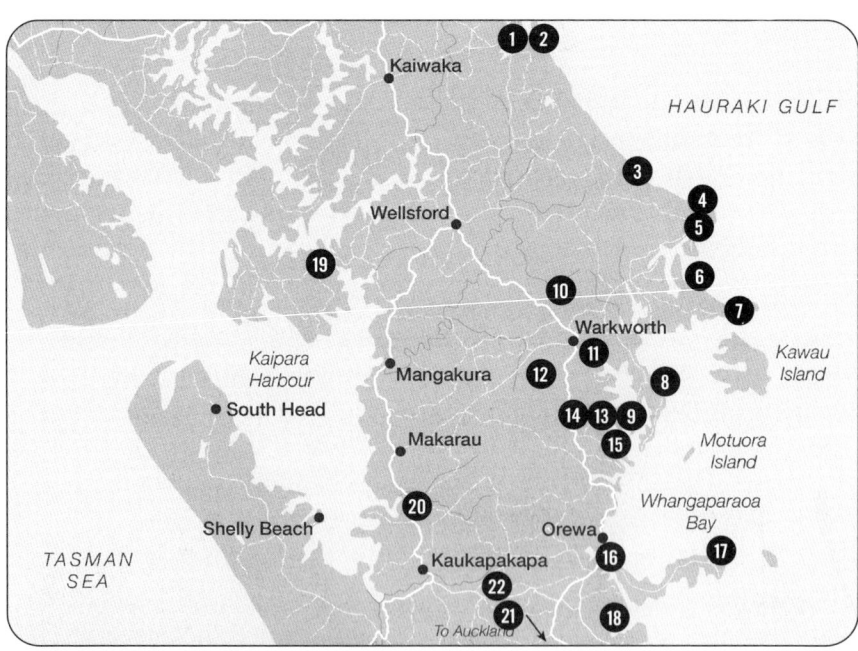
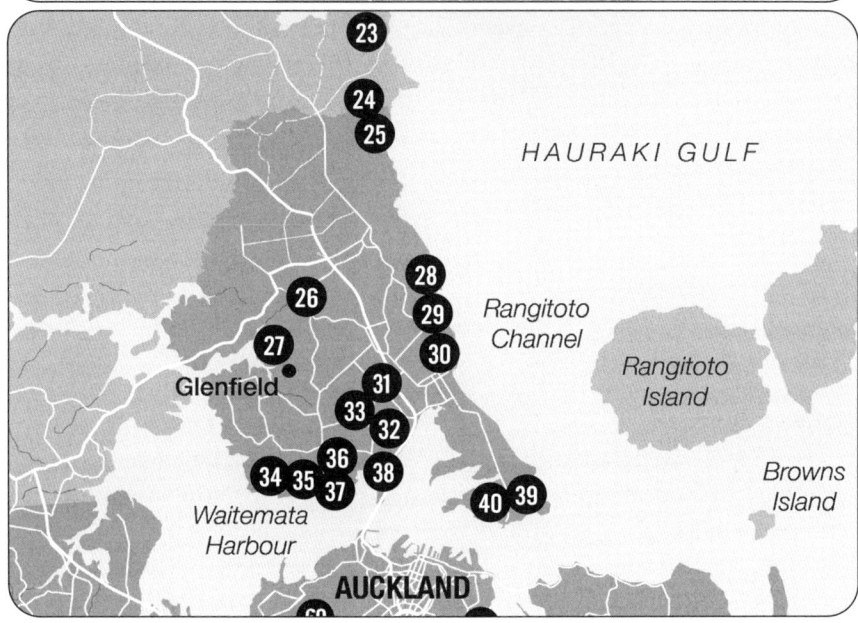

NORTH

1. Mangawhai Cliffs Walkway
2. Mangawhai Heads Pa Walks
3. Te Arai Regional Park
4. Cape Rodney Walkway, Goat Island Marine Reserve.
5. Leigh Harbour Walkway
6. Ti Point Walkway
7. Tawharanui Regional Park
8. Scandrett Regional Park Perimeter Loop Walk
9. Scotts Landing
10. Dome Forest Conservation Area
11. Parry Kauri Park
12. Pohuehue Reserve
13. Mahurangi West Regional Park
14. Puhoi Village Lookout Loop Track
15. Wenderholm Regional Park
16. Te Ara Tahuna Estuary Walk, Orewa
17. Shakespear Regional Park
18. Okura Bush Walkway
19. Atiu Creek Regional Park
20. Omeru Scenic Reserve
21. Library Point Walk, Sanders Reserve Paremoremo
22. Paremoremo Scenic Reserve
23. Long Bay Regional Park and Long Bay-Okura Bush Marine Reserve
24. Awaruku Bush Reserve
25. Rata Reserve
26. The Fernhill Escarpment
27. Manuka and Lynn Reserves Loop Walk
28. Campbells Bay to Browns Bay Coastal Walkway
29. Centennial Park Loop Walk, Campbells Bay
30. Milford Beach to Takapuna and Lake Pupuke
31. Smith's Bush/Onewa Domain
32. Tuft Crater
33. Onepoto Domain
34. Kauri Point Beach, Fitzpatrick Bay
35. Kauri Point Centennial Park/Kendalls Bay/Chelsea
36. Le Roys Bush
37. Old Birkenhead Walk
38. Historic Northcote Point Walk
39. North Head Historic Reserve
40. Devonport Loop Walk including North Head.

1. Mangawhai Cliffs Walkway

 Sand dunes, a wildlife refuge and superb coastal views.

 Moderate ~ Two and half hours return

 How to get there: The beginning of the track is clearly marked from the beach one kilometre north of the Mangawhai Heads Surf Club at the end of Wintle Street.

Forming a broad shallow estuary, the tidal Mangawhai River empties sluggishly into the ocean below a high bluff and is protected from the open sea by a long sand spit. Covered mainly by spinifex and pingao, the dunes of the spit are now conservation land – the 245-ha Mangawhai Wildlife Refuge – and together with the estuary attract numerous shorebirds including Caspian and fairy terns, oystercatchers and New Zealand dotterel. North of the river is Bream Tail, rising to 165 m and noted for massive pohutukawa trees and pockets of native bush.

From the car park by the surf club walk along the beach for about one kilometre when the track is well marked off to the left. An excellent track, the walk starts on a steady uphill climb from the beach and then levels off as it winds along the cliff to Bream Tail. From a viewing platform the coastal views are spectacular coastal, north to Bream Head and in the distant southeast, the Coromandel Peninsula. Directly offshore are the Hen and Chicken Islands and beyond that in the distance Little Barrier and Great Barrier Islands. If the tide is out, you can drop down to the shore and return that way, but this is rocky and uneven in parts and you will need good footwear.

2. Mangawhai Heads Pa Walks

 Great views from two old pa

 Easy ~ 30 minutes return

 How to get there: Both tracks leave from the carpark at the Mangawhai Heads Surf Club at the end of Wintle Street.

If you have neither the time nor the inclination to do the longer Mangawhai Cliffs Walkway, right by the carpark are two very short walks, which are largely ignored by visitors and there is every chance you will have the tracks to yourself.

The Southern Headland track is the shortest and will take just 10 minutes return and has marvellous views directly over the Mangawhai River estuary, the sand spit and south to Te Arai Point and Pakari Beach.

Across the road, Northern Headland track climbs much higher and has more steps but is still not difficult. Here the vista is every bit as spectacular as Bream Tail, looking north along the beach to Bream Heads at the entrance to Whangarei Harbour and taking in the northern islands of the Hauraki Gulf as well as the top of the Coromandel Peninsula. To the south is the sandpit, Mangawhai River with Mt Tamahunga rising above Pakiri Beach.

3. Te Arai Regional Park

 A choice of two magnificent beaches along with great views.

 Easy ~ One hour return

 How to get there: End of Te Arai Point Road (most of this road is unsealed)

Largely undeveloped, Te Arai Point is the only break in the magnificent long sweep of beach that runs from Mangawhai in the north to Parakiri in the south and is the largest expanse of dune country in the Auckland region. Originally cleared of forest by Maori settlers, the area was planted in pines in the 1930s to stabilise the shifting sand dunes and today is the home of the endangered and reclusive katipo spider as well as a vital nesting ground for shore birds, including the critically endangered fairy tern. The katipo spider is New Zealand's only venomous animal but is very shy and bites are extremely rare.

The small regional part of just 50 hectares was considerably enlarged in 2014 by the gift of a further 200 hectares from the local hapu Te Uri o Hau. Popular with surfers, the empty beach of brilliant white sand, is not protected from inclement weather by the islands of the gulf and the beaches experience greater swells and surf than beaches further south.

From the main carpark on the north side of the point it is a short 30-minute one-way walk to the southern beach and from the headland there are stunning views over the beaches and the gulf. Recently plantings of salt resistant native plants are gradually squeezing out the kikuyu grass and blackberry. A tiny cove on the rocky peninsula provides a safe swimming hole away from the open beach. The beach north of the point can be busy on weekends over summer, but both beaches are often deserted the rest of the time. The only facilities are toilets and a small camping ground.

4. Cape Rodney Walkway, Goat Island Marine Reserve.

 Gulf views from this coastal walkway

 Medium ~ First Lookout: 25 minutes return

Cape Rodney Lookout: One hour 15 minutes return

 How to get there: From Leigh follow the signposts to Goat Island, a distance of 3.5km kilometres.

Tiny Goat Island (just one hectare) is at the centre of New Zealand's first marine reserve established in 1975. The narrow channel between the island and the beach teems with marine life including huge snapper, goatfish, blue cod, parore, giant crayfish, red moki and schools of the dramatic blue maomao. The channel and the rocky shores of the island are safe for swimming and snorkelling, although the water can get rough and murky when easterly weather blows in. Goat Island itself is a scientific reserve and while visitors can rest on the rocks, it is prohibited to enter the bush mainly to protect resting sea birds including blue penguins. The Marine Discovery Centre is designed to educate and entertain visitors on the reserve's environment (entrance by fee).

Most people come here to swim and snorkel and far fewer people take the lovely track to the east of the island, and those that do usually only make it as far as the first lookout. Right from the get go, it's all uphill on an excellent track, snaking steeply up to a lookout, a walk that is guaranteed to get you heart racing and is hot work in summer. However, the spectacular views are worth it so you can rest awhile on a wooden seat and take in the vistas north over Goat Island, Pakiri, and Te Arai.

The first steep climb puts most people off continuing further, which is a shame as the second section of the walk is lovely and not so demanding. The track dips through small gullies as it passes through coastal bush and most of the walk is in the shade. Finally, the track ends with another lookout, but this time the views are to the east directly facing Little Barrier Island and Cape Rodney. There is a basic track up to Cape Rodney Road, but it is easier to return the way you came.

This is a very popular spot and there is a lot of pressure on parking, especially on the weekends in summer. Be prepared to park further down the road and walk a bit to the start of the track. As well as toilets and picnic areas, you'll find snorkelling equipment, wetsuits and kayaks are available for hire. A glass bottom boat takes tours for those not so keen on getting in the water.

5. Leigh Harbour Walkway

 Bucolic harbour and estuary walk

 Easy ~ One hour return

 How to get there: Leigh Wharf at the end of Hauraki Road, Leigh

A perfect, small and varied adventure for the little ones or the less able, the walk begins along the shore to the left of the wharf at Omaha Cove, locally known as Leigh Harbour. Initially skirting the rocks (a little tricky right on high tide), the track crosses over a creek and then passes along a small beach in front of old cottages. A bridge crosses over a more substantial tidal creek where stingrays are common in the shallow clear waters and then the track rounds a bush covered bluff to yet another small beach and tidal steam. At low tide you can walk up the stream to Cape Rodney Road, but you will need to have someone pick you up as it is a very long walk back to the harbour.

For a bit of variation on the way back, you can take a basic and steep track over the bluff (which leads to Mt Pleasant Road) and then drops back to the main path, though there are no views.

Parking by the wharf is at a premium and you might need to park a considerable distance from the start of the walk. An alternative is to park in Ferndale Avenue, 50 metres from Hauraki Road and take a flight of steps down to the track.

6. Ti Point Walkway

Glorious walk with ancient pohutukawa trees and coastal vistas

Easy ~ One hour 15 minutes return

How to get there: End of Ti Point Road, 2.2km off Leigh Road, 10km east of Matakana

A hidden gem at the entrance to the Whangateau Harbour, this track follows the shoreline of Ti Point. Meandering through coastal bush remnants, tidal waters lap worn boulders and ancient pohutukawa arch over sandy coves with glorious views over the harbour, Omaha Beach and Tawharanui peninsula. The track is easy and flat, but simply constructed so wear decent shoes and pay attention to where you walk.

Exactly where the track ends is very confusing. You can rock hop around the point (there is a house here) but you will need to be nimble on your feet or you can cross the grass uphill to a stile, from where you can drop down to the shore. There is no exit uphill to Latham Road (from where you could walk back to the start) as this crosses private property. If you don't fancy leaping along the rocky coast, then return the way you came.

7. Tawharanui Regional Park

Endless vistas of the Hauraki Gulf, sheltered beaches and rare native birds

West End Track, Easy ~ One and half hours

North and South Coastal Tracks ~ three hours

Facilities: Two large car parks, toilets, an information centre and camping. The park has walking and cycling tracks.

How to get there: The park is clearly signposted from Warkworth on SH1. The total distance from Warkworth is 26 kilometres, five of which just before the park are unsealed, narrow and winding.

Covering 600 hectares, Tawharanui is Auckland's largest regional park and comprises of a mix of rolling farmland, bushy gullies, tidal saltmarshes and sandy beaches. Covering most of the Tawharanui Peninsula, the vistas from the park out to the Hauraki Gulf are endless, with Little Barrier Island looming to the north and wooded Kawau Island just to the south. In addition, most of the northern shore is protected by the Tawharanui Marine Park. Gently rolling hills make for easy walking, and the open terrain of the park affords constant gulf views from almost every point. The bush areas are quite small with patches of mature and regenerating bush confined to the gullies and coastline. However, the predator-proof fence makes this park a haven for native birds, including kaka that make the journey from Little Barrier Island and Tiritiri Matangi Island. Rare takahe have been introduced to the park and are usually spotted not far from the main car park at Anchor Bay. The park is also home to the only mainland population of Duvaucel's gecko.

Near the entrance to the park is the stunning sweep of Anchor Bay. North facing and sheltered from the south-westerly winds, this beautiful beach is an ideal base for two short walks, though the park is a maze of tracks and there is plenty of scope for those wanting a longer ramble. The dune area behind the bay is roped off in spring to protect the breeding ground of the New Zealand dotterel.

The most popular walk is a combination of the North Coast Track and the South Coast Track which together form a long loop around the entire peninsula. An excellent track, this wanders through bush, along cliff tops and down to the water on the southern side. The walking is easy, though the terrain is undulating with an occasional short steep stretch. It is worthwhile taking a short detour on the Tokatu Loop track to view rare prostrate manuka and to enjoy the spectacular views. This manuka is not a separate species, but a form that has adapted to exposed environments so that it grows parallel to the ground rather than its usual upright habit.

There a several linking tracks between the two coastal tracks, so this walk can be easily shortened.

In contrast the West End Track initially follows the beach, then a short section along the sturdy predator fence and then through wetlands and salt marsh to the car park. You are more likely to see birds on this track.

8. Scandrett Regional Park Perimeter Loop Walk

 A natural amphitheatre encloses this small farm park centred on a pretty beach

 Easy ~ One hour

 How to get there: From SH1 at Warkworth turn into Matakana Road and then immediately right into Sandspit Road. After 5km turn right into Mahurangi East Road and then 6.5km later turn left into Martins Bay Road. The park is 4.5km at the end of this road.

A small park of just 44 hectares, Scandrett Regional Park forms a huge amphitheatre around the old homestead at Scandrett Bay. Occupied from 1864 by the family after whom the bay and part are named, the farm was sold to the Auckland Regional Council in 1998.

Sheltered from the westerly and southerly winds, the old homestead is regularly open to the public, but what is also appealing is that many of the farm's outbuildings still remain. The oldest farm building is the barn dating to 1864 and the old walk-through cowshed and hen house were last in used during the 1950s. The beach is great for swimming especially at high tide.

An easy, well-marked loop walk skirts the perimeter of the small farm through mainly open paddocks with some regenerating bush in the gullies and old kowhai trees clinging to the steeper areas. High cliffs form the eastern and southern boundaries with expansive views of Kawau Island, Tawharanui, numerous smaller islands with Rangitoto, Coromandel and Auckland city forming the backdrop. There are also two old baches available to rent right on the beach.

9. Scotts Landing

 Local history combined with beach and bush

 Easy ~ One hour

 How to get there: Scotts Landing wharf, at the end of Ridge Road, 6km from Mahurangi East Road.

Sheltered waters rich in fish were once vigorously contested by early Maori and the small Manganui/Casnell Island was once a pa site, though the main settlement in the area was across the bay at Sadler Point.

Today the Scott homestead above a small beach is at the heart of this small park, just a short walk from the busy Scotts landing wharf. The homestead dates from 1877, replacing an older house built around 1852 and later destroyed by fire. Unusually the house has strong Georgian influences rather than the more fashionable Victorian style. In the 1970s the Civic Trust Auckland took over the dilapidated building and began a two-decade long restoration.

From the wharf, skirt around the shore to the beach, and after visiting the house, continue along the beach to the island. Best visited at low tide, the shallow water makes the island easily accessible but even a high tide and you can either walk around the rocky shore or clamber up a rough track to the top of the island.

Retracing your steps, cross the grass to a track that begins to the right behind the house. A short walk up hill will take you to another track to the right and this leads out to viewpoint looking east over the Te Kapa River to Mahurangi East. Return to the main track and continue along the ridge which has views both to the east and to the west over the Mahurangi Harbour. The track then emerges on the road where you can walk back to the start but take care as there are no footpaths and the verge is narrow.

For an extended experience, tours of the oyster farms along the river are also on offer.

10. Dome Forest Conservation Area

 Wide vistas from the Dome Lookout in mixed podocarp and broadleaf forest

 Dome Forest Lookout: Easy, One hour return

The Dome Summit: Hard, Two hours return

 How to get there: Take the SH1 for seven kilometres north of Warkworth and the entrance is well marked on the right.

Surprisingly steep and rugged, Dome Forest is a mix of podocarp and broadleaf native bush covering over 400 hectares of native bush of which the highest point is The Dome at 336 metres. One long track, beginning at the car park, runs the length of the reserve and it is very much a track of two halves. Initially the track climbs a narrow ridge, steep in places with many steps and the first impressions of the regenerating forest is a bit disappointing. However, as track levels out along the top of the ridge the trees are much more impressive with fine handsome examples of mature rimu, totara, miro, kawaka, and northern rata. Helpful signage makes identification simple. A feature of the track is the native New Zealand broom, very distantly related to European broom and with similar features such as the long flat leaves.

From the lookout is an extensive view to the south with even the Sky Tower in central Auckland just visible on the southern horizon. The track to this point is in excellent condition but the stretch from the lookout to the nearby summit of the Dome is steep, rough and muddy and more suited to those equipped for tramping. From The Dome there are wide views over the gulf and out to the Hen and Chicken Islands. It takes around an hour for the return walk to the lookout and two hours return walk to the Dome summit.

11. Parry Kauri Park

 Two spectacular kauri trees in a superb forest

 Easy ~ 30 minutes return

 How to get there: South of Warkworth turn off SH1 into McKinney Road and after two kilometres turn right into Wilson Road and the entrance to the park is well sign posted to the left.

Kauri is a very common tree is the Auckland region, and while much of the forest was milled in the nineteenth century, a good number of large specimen trees can still be found. What makes this tiny reserve of just two hectares unique is that kauri is the dominant tree and is the best example of kauri forest in the Auckland region. Right by the car park of the Warkworth Museum, at the entrance to the loop track, is the majestic McKinney kauri, named after the original European landowner, the local Presbyterian minister, Reverend McKinney. Reaching a height of 38 metres, it is almost 12 metres to the first limb with a circumference over seven and a half metres. The McKinney kauri, estimated to be about 800 years old, is the largest kauri tree on the east coast. One of the largest and oldest of New Zealand's 1500 species of snails is the kauri snail/pupurangi. Evolving over 200 million years, these snails can live up to 20 years and have hundreds of tiny teeth that chew up any small creature that happens to cross its path.

Mainly on boardwalk to protect the delicate roots (some steps), this easy track loops through small gullies thick with nikau and ferns and while kauri dominate, there are good specimens of kahikatea, rewarewa, rimu, tanekaha, kohekohe, taraire, karaka and totara, many of which are marked to assist with identification. In the car park near the museum are relics of the early saw-milling days.

12. Pohuehue Reserve

 A pretty waterfall in beautiful native forest

 Easy ~ 30 minutes return

 How to get there: Take the SH1 eight kilometres south of Warkworth.

The short and picturesque walk is to a modest waterfall along the Pohuehue stream. The dominant trees are kohekohe and taraire, two trees confined to the warmer northern areas of New Zealand while the gullies are dense with ferns, nikau palms and rambling kiekie. The native greenhood orchids are common in spring and while rather ordinary to look at, they have an extraordinary and unique pollination method. The lip of the flower is very sensitive to touch and when trigged by a crawling insect, it flips the insect into the flower and traps it there. The only escape is through a small tunnel during which the struggling insect pollinates the plant. After just 30 minutes the lip mechanism resets.

A viewing platform overlooks a small waterfall where the stream tumbles over a five-metre rock face.

While this reserve consists of fine regenerating native bush, it sits adjacent to forestry plantations and farmland which makes a walk on one of the longer tracks an odd experience – beautiful native forest contrasting with cut-over pine forest. Two longer tracks, the Beverley Price Loop Track and the Moirs Hill Walkway are for those who have moderate to good fitness and are prepared for tracks that are rough, steep in places and very muddy in wet weather.

13. Mahurangi West Regional Park

 Beaches, bush and a fascinating old cemetery

 Mita Bay: Hard, 1 hour 15 minutes

Cudlip Point Loop Walk, Easy, One hour return

Te Muri Point and Beach, Easy, Two hours return

Mahurangi Regional Park falls in to three distinct areas. Mahurangi

East is only accessible by boat, whereas Mahurangi West is just a few kilometres off SH1 just south of Warkworth. This western section park also divides into two, with Mita Bay to the north and Te Muri Beach to the south. Particularly appealing is that there are several walk options from the central carpark Sullivans Bay/Otarawao Bay, though the posted times for the walks seem very generous.

The heart of Mita Bay is a small sandy beach backed by large shady pohutukawa and where swimming best mid to high tide and the track. From the end of the car park the track leads off to the left and then almost immediately splits. Take the track going straight ahead which then climbs very steeply to the lookout point with views over the gulf. From there the track drops down very steeply, but fortunately there is a fence to help you down and at the bottom it is just a short walk through bush to the bay.

Overhung with large trees, there is a lovely grassy clearing, though swimming is best a mid to high tide. Leaving the bay, the follows a 4wd track for a long, steep climb up to the road. Walk down the road taking in the great views, passing the link track back to the lookout, and just a few metres on another track to the left winds back down to Sullivans Bay. This return walk from the bay back to the car park is not that interesting so if the tide is low it will be more appealing to walk back via the coastline.

Walking in the other direction from the carpark, the track to Te Muri Beach gently climbs gently up through grassy paddocks to lovely beach and gulf views. To the left a short five minute walks tracks through attractive native bush to a lookout point, though the view is disappointing as it is large obscured by vegetation.

Now the track drops down to Te Muri estuary. At low tide it is possible to rock hop across the small stream, but if you plan wade through the creek in bare feet, go right down to the shore line as the creek is full of rock oyster shells which can inflict a nasty cut.

Once across you have more options. The small graveyard has several old graves dating back to the nineteenth century and to visit will only take 10 minutes return. To stroll to the end of Te Muri beach takes just 25 minutes return and a gentle uphill to Te Muri Point 30 minutes return.

Returning back across the stream you have two options depending on tide. At high tide take the grass track to the left which takes just 20 minutes back to the carpark. Low tide offers the choice of a walk back around the shoreline which takes 30 – 40 minutes. It is not difficult but you will need good footwear and pay close attention to where you place your feet. The numerous rock falls along the coast are testament to the soft silt stone common around the Hauraki Gulf so keep back from the cliff face. Take time to view the extraordinary geometric pattern in the flat rocks by the water's edge; it is hard to believe they are naturally occurring phenomena.

14. Puhoi Village Lookout Loop Track

 Surprisingly appealing bush walk in a location best known for its pub

 Medium ~ 40 minutes return

 How to get there: Domain Rd, over the bridge directly opposite the Puhoi pub.

Feeling guilty about having a beer at the famous Puhoi pub? Well get your shoes on and do this short but not so easy loop walk just across the creek from the pub and have that beer knowing you have burnt off a least few calories. The walk is also a great way to extend a visit to the pub with out-of-town visitors.

It's uphill right from the start, with steps making easier work of the climb through bush in the Puhoi Pioneers Memorial Park. Once the climbing is done, the track levels off along an open ridge with marvellous views over the valley below with seats along the way in case you are really puffed. Eventually the track drops off the ridge a little to the lookout below.

From the lookout it is all downhill on an open grass track, back to start and the pub.

For those wanted a more demanding walk, this track is also the beginning of the Puhoi Track which continues along the ridge and eventually re-joins the Ahuroa Road via a swing bridge over the Puhoi

River at the Remiger Scenic Reserve. If you don't have anyone to pick you up, it is a four and half kilometre walk back to the start and you really will be ready for a drink.

15. Wenderholm Regional Park

 Ancient pohutukawa trees line a sandy beach below native bush

Facilities: Excellent parking, toilets, a huge picnic area and park information

 Lookout: 45 minutes return

Perimeter walk: 2 hours

 How to get there: Take SH1 one kilometre north of Waiwera.

One of Auckland's most popular summer destinations, the 135 hectare Wenderholm Regional Park is the perfect combination of a safe sandy beach, beautiful native bush, a historic homestead and small park perfect for family picnics. Wenderholm (meaning 'winter home' in Swedish), was an earlier name of the historic house built around 1857 and now known as Couldrey House. The house is open from 1 pm to 4 pm on Saturday and Sunday all year round, and every afternoon between Boxing Day and Waitangi weekend (early February). There is a small fee.

Occupying a sandy spit between the languid estuary of the Puhoi River and the open sea, a long narrow park features wide grassy spaces overhung by magnificent old pohutukawa trees and sheltered from westerly winds by a bush-covered headland known as Maungatauhoro. Running along the southern boundary is the Waiwera River and both waterways are very tidal, the banks are lined with mangroves providing shelter and food for numerous small fish and aquatic birds. The Puhoi River is particularly popular with kayakers, an excellent way to experience the mangrove forest and the life it shelters which includes the reclusive fernbird and banded rail. Visitors may even encounter kookaburra as a small colony of these Australian birds still survive in the area from Governor Grey's exotic menagerie on nearby Kawau Island.

The track through the bush begins behind the homestead, initially climbing steadily through mature native bush to a lookout. Tawa, kohekohe, taraire, totara, kowhai, nikau, kahikatea, tawa and rimu are all common, and with efficient predator control the bush echoes to the sound of native birds such as tui, kereru and piwakawaka. From the lookout on top of a crumbly coastal cliff is a fine view of the Hauraki Gulf.

Beyond the lookout the track is rough and frequently very muddy and you will need good footwear if you plan to go beyond the lookout. Dropping down to the estuary of the Waiwera River, the track continues along the river to the road and then back to the beach. An alternative that avoids the noisy road section is to take the track through the middle of the park up to a fine lookout over Waiwera, and then back to the beach on a steep downhill.

16. Te Ara Tahuna Estuary Walk, Orewa

 An urban walk around the wide estuary of the Orewa River

 Easy ~ Two hours

 How to get there: From the Northern Motorway take the Silverdale exit and continue along the Hibiscus Highway towards Orewa. Crossing over the Orewa River, the carpark is directly to the left on the other side of the bridge.

The Orewa River forms a long shallow estuary before emptying into the sea at the southern end of Orewa beach and characterised by numerous side creeks and extensive swathes of low mangroves, this easy 7.5km walk encircles the entire estuary.

This is a walk that has two distinctive faces. On one side is the river, fringed by native and exotic trees and shrubs, and almost empty at low tide. The shallow waters attract a wide variety of aquatic birds, while the shrubbery is home to the occasional quarrelsome tui. Turn the other way and the walk is a tour of contemporary suburb housing ranging from the stylish to the ugly, with parts of the area still under development.

Mainly concrete path all the way, this is shared walkway, but at least here the cyclists are mostly very considerate, and this makes for an excellent winter walk when you are keen to keep your feet dry. Naturally the most attractive sections of the walk are near the sea and at the halfway point, you can take a short detour to Millwater for a coffee. There are numerous toilets along the way, including at the start and at high tide the wharf near the carpark is a popular diving and bombing spot.

The carpark is also used for the Estuary Arts Centre, a café and skatepark.

17. Shakespear Regional Park

 Gulf vistas combine with easy walking and rare birds

 Lookout: Easy, 45 minutes return

Te Haruhi Bay via the Lookout: One hour 15 minutes return

 How to get there: From SH1 at Silverdale just south of Orewa, turn into Whangaparaoa Road and follow the signs to the very end of the peninsula. Park at the car park by the gateway through the predator-proof fence, a short distance south of Army Bay.

Just 40 minutes north of Auckland this 500 hectare park occupies the eastern tip of the Whangaparaoa Peninsula and is a great combination of beach, birds and bush. A mosaic of open paddocks and regenerating native plants, the bush mostly occupies the steep gullies and coastal margins, though there are a number of large old puriri and taraire trees.

The erection of a 1.7-kilometre predator-proof fence in 2010 along with the vigilant eradication of predators just outside the fence, has resulted in an explosion of native wildlife and along with common native birds as pukeko, tui, harrier hawk and kereru, avian visitors from Tiritiri Matangi such as kaka, hihi, korimako and kakariki are not unusual. The fence has allowed kiwi, North Island Robin and White Head to be reintroduced to the park while wading and migratory birds flock to the tidal beaches and wetlands.

The area just north of the park is still Ministry of Defence land, but within the park are several historic pillboxes constructed as part of an elaborate defence network north of Auckland. Pillboxes are low concrete structures, often partially dug into the ground and designed to house machine guns or antitank guns.

Following the Heritage Trail, the walk steadily climbs uphill through a deep bush valley, then open farmland, to the Lookout. The views are superb along the coast to the north, out to the islands of the Gulf and south to downtown Auckland. From here take the Lookout Track downhill to Te Haruhi Bay, a small sandy beach lined with pohutukawa. From the beach, the Lookout Track continues uphill, passing an old shearing shed built around 1900. The track re-joins the Heritage Trail, which then meets the fence, from where it leads back to the car park.

At the entrance to the park is Army Bay. North facing and sheltered from the westerly winds, this sandy beach is the best in the park.

There is good parking at Army Bay and a few hundred metres further on by a small lake. There are toilets at Army Bay and at Te Haruhi Bay on the south shore of the park, as well as a small camping ground and the YMCA have a lodge here.

The park's name is not a spelling mistake, but recalls an early farming family with the surname Shakespear.

18. Okura Bush Walkway

 A very fine grove of mature puriri, wading birds by a river and a historic cottage

 Puriri Grove: Easy, 45 minutes return

Dacre Cottage: Easy, two hours return

 How to get there: Drive north on East Coast Road from its intersection with Oteha Valley Road; after 4.5km turn right into Haighs Access Road. The track begins at the end of the road.

In the early 1850s, Ranulf Dacre, built a small cottage above a sandy beach on Karepiro Bay at the mouth of the Weiti River. While that is unremarkable, what makes Dacre Cottage unique is that was constructed of brick at a time when timber was both plentiful and cheap. The cottage is the highlight of an excellent walk along the Okura and Weiti river estuaries, through stands of fine native bush.

The grove of puriri at the start of the walk is worth a visit in its own right. A handsome native tree, puriri is recognised by its broard spreading habit, glossy leaves and abundance of small purple-red flowers that often carpet the forest floor beneath the tree. Puriri is unusual in that it flowers and fruits all year round. The trunk is short and is often full of hollows and is home to the native puriri moth. This moth is also unusual in that it only lives for 48 hours as it has no mouth and cannot feed and is only active at night.

Beyond the puriri grove, the bush is mainly regrowth with more mature trees and the climber kiekie in the gullies, along with occasional kauri on the ridges. The track, much improved in recent years, then follows the small Okura River, which is home to shore and wading birds, before climbing a small ridge to the cottage. The beach is swimmable at high tide.

Once a quiet spot, the area behind the cottage is now being developed for housing and what once was a peaceful pleasant spot is quiet no longer.

The track continues on to Stillwater, but unless you have transport organised, return the way you came.

19. Atiu Creek Regional Park

 Rolling hills and vistas of the Kaipara Harbour

 Easy ~ One to three hours

 How to get there: From Wellsford, take SH16 4km west to Port Albert Road. Follow Port Albert Road 13km to Wharehine, turn right into Wharehine and 1km later left in Run Road. The park is 4km on the right.

Opened in 2008, the rolling hills of this farm park covering 843 hectares is one of Auckland's largest regional parks and one of the few places that provides good access to the shores of the enormous Kaipara Harbour.

Given to the city by immigrant Swiss couple Jackie and Pierre Chatelanat, this was the largest block of land donated to the city since John Logan Campbell's gift of Cornwall Park in 1901.

Laced with easy walking tracks, most of the park is open farmland and is still an actively working farm. Bush reserves cover a third of park, mainly in the gullies and along the shore hilly and open nature of the park allows for endless vistas over the harbour, Oruawharo River and the tidal Atiu Creek after which the park is named.

There is something for everyone here. Numerous well-formed interconnecting tracks make for easy walking from an hour-long rambling to a complete circuit of the park which will take up to three hours. As well as walking there are also cycling and horse-riding options available, but the coastline is tidal and not suitable for swimming.

In addition to off-road parking, toilets, excellent information boards, there is also camping and holiday cottages to let

20. Omeru Scenic Reserve

 Two pretty waterfalls amongst stately totara trees

 Easy ~ 40 minutes

 How to get there: Take SH 16 for eight kilometres north of Kaukapakapa and the reserve is well marked on the right (1.5 kilometres north of the Kaipara lookout).

Located at the confluence of the Omeru and Waitangi streams and this reserve is a combination of bush and open grass and is an ideal spot for a family picnic. Two small waterfalls just a short distance apart are the main attraction of this 14-hectare reserve, gifted to the local council by politician Sir Basil Orr in 1971.

The larger of the two falls on the Omeru Stream tumbles over two rocky cascades dropping about six metres in a series of pools which are popular swimming holes in the summer. Nearby two smaller waterfalls on the Waitangi Stream feed into small pools fringed with the climber, kiekie. The two creeks join a short distance downstream and on the junction point is the site of a major pa (also called Omeru) with much of the earthworks still visible. Not far downstream the creek joins the Makarau River, a tributary of the Kaipara Harbour. The reserve continues much further upstream and is dominated by fine totara trees along with regenerating kauri, rimu, titoki and tree fuchsia.

From the car park it takes less than the 10 minutes to walk to the falls on an easy track and a ramble around the entire reserve will take around 40 minutes. Just south of the reserve is a great lookout point over the Kaipara Harbour.

The spacious grassy areas are perfect for picnics and barbeques and the free range chooks in the carpark will delight visitors and children.

21. Library Point Walk, Sanders Reserve Paremoremo

 Upper harbour views, an old pa, and the Magic Faraway Tree

 Easy ~ 30 minutes

 End of Sanders Road, off Merewhira Road, Paremoremo

This 41ha reserve is best known for its extensive mountain bike tracks, but it does have an appealing short walk, very much worth a detour if you are in the area. This track is for walkers only, the other longer track is shared with mountain bikers.

The location on the north side of the Upper Waitemata Harbour and adjoining Paremoremo Creek is one unfamiliar to most Aucklanders and initially is hard to work out just where you are. From the substantial shelter and toilets, the track runs down to Library Point to an old pa site, perfectly situated on a high bluff to watch the comings and goings on the harbour, though now only the protective ditch is visible.

Saving the best for last is The Faraway Tree and without giving too much away, this carved tree will delight both the very young and not so young.

If you are a dog owner there is also a large area for dogs off leash.

22. Paremoremo Scenic Reserve

 The perfect bush water hole

 Easy ~ 20 minutes return

 How to get there: On Brookdale Road (an extension of Paremoremo Road, 1km past the entrance to Auckland Prison, Paremoremo

It might be a short walk but if you have energetic youngsters this is the place to go. From the parking area cross over the bridge and immediately you are plunged into jungle-like bush, dense with nikau palms and thickets of supplejack.

An excellent track follows Paremoremo Stream until you reach a short flight of steps with a wooden handrail. A few metres past this, and before you climb the next set of steps, a rough track leads off to the right. Scramble down the bank and rock hop across the stream and up the opposite bank to the fence line. Follow the fence to the left until you reach the swimming hole, it is impossible to miss. Two rope swings, along with a tyre swing hang out over a deep pool in the stream. Return when the young ones are exhausted. The bank is steep, and the water is very deep, so it is not really suitable for the very young.

23. Long Bay Regional Park and Long Bay-Okura Bush Marine Reserve

 Auckland's most popular regional park

 Easy ~ Two hours return

 How to get there: Exit the Northern Motorway (SH1) at Oteha Valley Road, turn right all the way to the East Coast Bays Road and then turn left.
Head north along East Coast Bays Road to Glenvar Road and turning right continue down Glenvar Road for 4km. Turn right into Beach Road and the Park entrance. Buses also run from the city directly to the park.

This beautiful coastline on the north fringe of the city is Auckland's most popular regional park. Encompassing coastal habitats ranging from sandy beaches through rocky headlands to tidal creeks, the 111-hectare park is complimented by a 980-hectare marine reserve offshore.

Long Bay itself is a magnificent sweep of beach backed by sand dunes which are undergoing extensive restoration using native pingao and spinifex. To the north, the park follows the crumbling coastal cliffs of Waitemata Sandstone bisected by narrow streams which are being restored as wetlands, while the northern border is the estuary of Okura River.

From the main carpark at Long Bay the walk heads north and you will be guaranteed endless panoramic views from the cliff tops both along the coast and out to the islands of the gulf. Near the beginning of the walk is the homestead built in 1863 by George Vaughan and substantially extended after his marriage to Margaret in 1877. The appearance of the house today is that of the house in the 1890s and the family farmed there until 1965 when part of the land was purchased for the regional park.

Beyond the historic homestead, the coastal walkway winds and dips over hills and headlands and passes a number of small bays and beaches, finally terminating at the Okura River. Off this excellent track, used by pedestrians and cyclists, a number of side paths explore wetlands and regenerating bush.

At low tide it is possible to walk part of the way back along the coast, ideal for exploring the plants and creatures that inhabit the tidal zone, though it slippery in places. With the aquatic life gradually returning now the area is protected as a marine reserve, dolphins are becoming regular visitors.

Long Bay attracts one and a half million visitors each year and the main beach is very popular for family and group picnics, especially in summer weekends and particularly on Sundays. Most visitors to the park only come to for the main beach and far fewer do the coastal walk to the north but if you want to avoid the crowds try and visit during a week day or during the off season.

24. Awaruku Bush Reserve

 Ancient trees and a secret glow worm dell
 Easy ~ 30 minutes

A popular local reserve, this small patch of bush was preserved when the area was developed in the late 1960s to protect several very old trees. Kahikatea is the main tree, the largest of which is over 20 metres tall and more than 650 years old but other trees include kohekohe, puriri, rewarewa, tanekaha and towai. Nearly matching the kahikatea in age if not size is one huge puriri, said to be over 500 years old. The understory is thick with nikau, kiekie and ferns. Excellent signage helps with the identification of native trees.

Within the reserve is a tiny quarry abandoned in the early 1900s as the stone was not suitable for roading and today is a damp grotto dripping with water and lush with mosses and ferns, the perfect environment for the New Zealand glow worm. You will need a torch to visit the glow worms as at night it is very dark in the bush.

There isn't a map at the entrance or any other direction signage in the reserve, but it is small and impossible to get lost on the maze of short tracks.

Easily combine with the nearby Rata Reserve for a pleasant outing.

How to get there: From Glenvar Road in Torbay, turn into Awaruku Road where the entrance is clearly marked on the right.

25. Rata Reserve

 A haven for the increasingly rare Northern rata tree

 Easy ~ 30 minutes return

 How to get there: The reserve has several entrances and one of the easiest to find is on Fitzwilliam Drive off Glenvar Road.

Pohutukawa grabs all the limelight as one of New Zealand's few spectacular flowering trees, leaving its very near cousin, the rata largely forgotten. Being the favourite food of the glutinous possum hasn't helped the rata's profile as possums can completely destroy a mature rata tree in just a few years.

Here at the Rata Reserve on Auckland's North Shore a good number of large rata are flourishing in this small reserve at the head of steep gully. Rata is easily recognisable by their long stringy bark, narrow trunk and small leaves. Northern rata usually, but not always, start off life as an epiphyte high above the forest floor. The plant then sends roots down the host tree's trunk to search for soil. If there are several roots, they may enlarge, coalesce and eventually encapsulate and strangle the host tree. The mature tree generally grows to height of around 25 metres. Covered in crimson flowers, rata, like pohutukawa, flowers in early summer and December is a good time to visit here.

As well as rata trees there are good specimens of kahikatea, kanuka and miro, several huge puriri, with a wild understory of kiekie, nikau and ferns. At the bottom of the reserve is a tiny wetland lush with raupo. There are no maps or signage, though there are helpful plaques to identify trees. The track forms a loop around and gully and the reserve is small so you won't get lost.

Awaruku Reserve is just a short way down the hill and can easily be visited in the same outing.

26. The Fernhill Escarpment

 A magnificent grove of totara trees in a forgotten reserve

 Easy ~ One and half hours

 How to get there: At the end of Vanderbilt Parade there is a small carpark. The track starts at the white post across the park. There is no parking at either Bush Road or Albany Highway, so it is not easy to start at these points.

The Fernhill Escarpment is a steep hillside on the north-east bank of the Oteha Stream and runs from Albany village centre through to Tawa Drive. Most people know the escarpment as 'the short, steep section' when driving on Bush Road.

Very few people bother to visit this reserve, yet it has some of the most impressive native trees in the Auckland area. The dominant tree is totara and they certainly do dominate as these trees are not only huge but some are estimated to be up to 800 years old. Along with the totara are impressive examples of kahikatea and tanekaha. What is even more appealing is that the track runs both side of Lucas and Oteha streams, making this an ideal loop walk. The streams are impressive after heavy rain.

The condition of the tracks has been improved but it is fairly basic, and locals have added a few helpful 'bridges' to cross smaller side creeks.

Starting at Brookfield Park at the end of Vanderbilt Parade, walk across the grass to the white post where you will find the track just inside the trees. Turn left and follow the creek downstream where is runs behind part of the Massey University Campus. There is a concrete crossing point but continue downstream to Albany Highway and cross the stream here, turning right immediately after crossing the bridge. A large police notice advising not to use the track at night is hardly reassuring, but it is a comfortable walk during the day.

Now continue upstream all the way to Bush Road where you cross over the bridge, turn right and walk about 50 metres to find the track to continue back to the starting point.

27. Manuka and Lynn Reserves Loop Walk

 An 800-year-old kauri is the highlight of this easy loop walk

 Easy ~ One hour

 How to get there: End of Manuka Road, Bayview, North Shore

Very much a local walk, these delightful reserves are barely known outside the suburb of Bayview but are home to one of Auckland's most impressive kauri trees.

Start the walk at Manuka Reserve at the very bottom of Manuka Road where there is a boat ramp, toilets and a grassy park. From here the path leads upstream along Upper Hellyers Creek through regenerating bush with views over the tidal stream to dense bush on the Greenhithe side (more attractive at high tide). Eventually the track reaches Lynn Reserve, which straddles both sides of Lynn Road. Cross over the road through a typical suburban park with a children's playground and toilets. Beyond the park, a track enters a small gully and then follows a picturesque stream overhung with nikau palms and fern trees and enclosed by substantial kauri, puriri, tanekaha and kahikatea. Eventually track splits and at this point veer to the left towards Morriggia Place. A little further on is a magnificent single kauri tree, estimated to be around 800 years old and with a diameter of over two metres, is said to be the largest kauri on the North Shore. Retrace your steps for a short distance and exit the bush on to upper Lynn Road. Turn left up the road and then 100 metres on right into Manuka Road and back to the start point.

28. Campbells Bay to Browns Bay Coastal Walkway

 Urban coastal walk over clifftops and along sandy beaches

 Medium ~ One and a half hours one way

 How to get there: End of Huntly Road Campbells Bay Beach

It is not hard to see why this is such a popular walk with locals. Linking several smaller beaches and coves, the walkway combines beach walking with more vigorous cliff top paths with constant views both along the coast and out to the island of the Hauraki Gulf.

Beginning along the beach at Campbells Bay, the path skirts a low rocky point to meet with Mairangi Bay beach and then continues along the cliffs to Murrays Bay. This cliff top section of the walk has suffered erosion with a short detour along local roads, but most people use the rocky path at the bottom of the cliff. Although the cliffs are not particularly high, the rock here is soft siltstone and the small slips and sizeable rockfalls are testament to the instability of the terrain.

These cliffs are an easy lesson in Auckland's peculiar geology. Waitemata siltstones are a common feature of the Auckland landscape. Mostly consisting of mudstone and sandstone, these were formed in the vast Waitemata Basin from material eroded from Auckland's oldest volcanoes that lay to the west. Today this stone is most noticeable in the tall crumbling cliffs of the Waitemata Harbour, the off-shore islands and the northern shore of the Manukau Harbour. The broad tidal rock shelves at the base of the cliffs and long reefs are also composed of Waitemata siltstones along with greywacke. The rock is very soft and fractures easily so small slips and rock falls are common along the cliffs, the base of which are usually littered with broken rock and boulders.

From Murrays Bay the track continues along the undulating clifftop, dropping down to Rothesay Bay before rising again on the last segment to Browns Bay. If you don't fancy walking back the same way, you can catch a bus to Takapuna which goes back along Beach Road to Campbells Bay. A low tide it is possible to walk back along the base of the cliffs, but your will need to have good footwear and nimble feet.

29. Centennial Park Loop Walk, Campbells Bay

 Secluded bush walks and hidden WWII fortifications

 Easy ~ One hour

 How to get there: There is parking in the reserve, but it is easier to park on Beach Road, Campbells Bay. The Beach Road entrance to the park is between numbers 182 and 186.

This hidden park of over 70 hectares was set aside as a reserve to commemorate the centennial celebrations in 1940 and the Remembrance Avenue of pohutukawa date from this time. Occupying a broad valley, a maze of tracks meanders through a mixture of exotic and native tree, enthusiastically maintained by a band of local volunteers.

From Beach Road enter the park and follow the Avenue of Memorial Ave up to the left and then take the Mamaku Track along the boundary to the Kohekohe Track off to the right. This track enters the most attractive part of the park, following a small stream dense with kiekie, ferns, supplejack and nikau. A short sidetrack leads to the a tiny pillbox, a reminder of the coastal defence system set up during the World War Two. The Tui Track and Magnolia Walk will take you back to the beginning.

30. Milford Beach to Takapuna and Lake Pupuke

 Fine city beaches, coastal views and lava flows.

 Easy ~ 45 minutes

 How to get there: Milford Reserve, end of Craig Road, Milford or from the boat ramp carpark at the end of The Promenade, Takapuna Beach. The track begins in front of the camping ground.

Linking two of the North Shore's most popular beaches, this walk offers a glimpse into Auckland's dramatic volcanic park and combined with nearby Lake Pupuke makes this a very enjoyable family outing. This description starts at Milford beach but of course it can be easily done in reverse. At very high tide you are likely to get your feet wet.

Begin at the beach at Milford, an easy sandy start to this walk, though right on high tide the water laps the sea wall and it can be a bit tricky keeping your feet dry. At the end of beach hop up on to the raised footpath and follow this all the way around to Thornes Beach, a small sheltered beach, great for swimming. Beyond Thornes Beach, the path becomes uneven and you will need decent footwear to do a bit of rock hopping, though there is nothing too difficult.

One of Auckland's oldest volcanoes, Lake Pupuke erupted around 140,000 years ago in at a time when the sea level was much lower and the coastline was beyond Great Barrier Island. Today the lake is Auckland's only remaining freshwater crater as unlike most other local craters, Pupuke eruptions included lava as well as ash and thereby created a solid crater wall, even though it is just 200m from the sea. The lake comprises of two craters covering 104 hectares, is 55 metres at its deepest point and relies entirely on rainwater and runoff with no stream outlet.

The resulting lava flow from the lake is much more visible than other mainland craters as it is exposed along the coast between Milford and Takapuna beaches and especially between tiny Thorne Bay and the boat ramp at Takapuna. At Thorne Bay water from Lake Pukupe bubbles up from cracks in the lava, more visible at low tide. In particular look out for trees casts and moulds. These casts form when lava flows over and encases a fallen tree. The heat of the lava burns the wood and when the lava solidifies, it forms a hollow cylindrical cast of the tree trunk looking somewhat like a rock cannon. At the Takapuna boat ramp car park, a whole kauri forest of lava tree moulds is exposed at low tide.

At the camping ground at Takapuna turn right up the Promenade and then right into Hurstmere Road and continue walking for about a kilometre to Henderson Park on the left which leads down to the lake. From here a track follows the lake to the boat club and beyond that through Sylvan and Kitchener parks which have a grove of very fine old puriri. Exit the park at Pierce Ave and return to Milford Beach.

31. Smith's Bush/Onewa Domain

 A botanical gem in the heart of Auckland's North Shore

 Easy ~ 30 minutes

 How to get there: Smith's Bush is part of Onewa Domain and the entrance is off Northcote Road just near the intersection with Akoranga Drive.

Most Aucklanders' experience of Smith's Bush is a quick glimpse of native trees as they whizz along the Northern Motorway. Life has been tough for this tiny bush remnant and its existence has always been precarious. Milled for the best timber, the reserve was devastated by the creation of the motorway in the late fifties which cut right through the heart of the bush and further reduced with the recent widening of the motorway for the bus lane. On the eastern side of the motorway only a narrow sliver of trees survive. Despite this Smith's Bush still remains magnificent.

Smith's Bush is a botanical curiosity. Located on high ground, the bush is dominated by kahikatea, a tree that favours low lying swamp land, and most of kahikatea are not more than 100 years old indicating that they are more recent colonisers. Dispersed among the kahikatea are much older puriri, one of which has five huge trunks, and, oddly for a coastal area, there are no pohutukawa or kauri.

Once inside the bush, the rumble of the nearby motorway does not detract from the bush experience. An extensive boardwalk protects the fragile forest floor and guides the visitor through the ancient trees which also includes taraire, kohekohe, mahoe, tawa, karaka, matai and totara.

The circular walk only takes 20 or so minutes and is further enhanced by an excellent brochure available at the entrance which both locates and details the native flora.

32. Tuft Crater

 One of Auckland's oldest volcanic craters now filled by tidal water and mangroves

 Easy ~ 40 minutes return

 How to get there: Access Tuff Crater end of the domain from St Peters Street or McBreen Avenue, Northcote; access Onepoto Domain from Sylvan Avenue.

The series of eruptions that created Lake Pupuke also included two craters just north of the Auckland Harbour Bridge. Tuft and Onepoto craters are just 200 metres apart, separated by a narrow ridge created by debris thrown up by the explosion. Then the climate was much warmer with lower sea level and the Waitemata Harbour a river valley so both craters were originally small fresh water lakes. As the climate gradually warmed and the ice caps melted, the sea level rose, flooding both craters.

Tuft crater (also known as Tank Farm) is largely intact and is surrounded by a 35-hectare reserve. At high tide water pours through a narrow channel from Big Shoal Bay, flooding the crater so that only the tops of the mangrove trees visible above the water. Extensively replanted with native vegetation as part of a major restoration plan by the Forest and Bird Association, the association has also undertaken a massive weeding programme and impressive progress has been made to completely restoring the crater. Today the reserve is home to 100 native plants and 40 bird species including the rare banded rail.

On the headland below McBreen Avenue is a small but impressive grove of large kohekohe along with kowhai, puriri and pohutukawa. Kohekohe is unusual for a New Zealand tree in that the flowers grow from the trunk and branches, a feature not uncommon in tropical trees. Unfortunately, kohekohe is a favourite food of possums which feast on the leaves, fruit and flowers.

Easy tracks follow the shores of the crater and there is a long-term plan for a bridge over the entrance to create a circular walk.

At the eastern end of the reserve is a footbridge over the busy Northern Motorway, that leads directly on to the tidal marshes that are designated a 'site of special wildlife interest' (there is no track). The motorway has protected the tidal flats and sand banks from predators. Despite the constant noise from the motorway, it is the haven for shore birds including banded and New Zealand dotterels.

This walk can be easily combined with the Onepoto crater via access on Exmouth Road

33. Onepoto Domain

 Easy

 Bush and wetland walk 20 minutes

Perimeter walk, 40 minutes

 How to get there: Sylvan Ave, just off Onewa Road.

In contrast to Tuft crater, Onepoto has not fared so well and is now highly modified. Photographs from the early twentieth century show the larger Onepoto crater full of water at high tide and very similar in size and shape to Tuft crater. Much of the crater rim became a quarry in the 1950s to provide fill for the construction of the Northern motorway and in 1975 the crater was filled to provide sports field. The only water remaining is a small, dirty duck pond popular with model boat enthusiasts.

However, in recent years things have improved and now the remaining north-east crater wall has been replanted and is a pleasant mixture of native and exotic trees. Below the trees a small wetland has been restored and is crossed by a substantial board walk.

Along with the sports fields there is a huge children's playground and a picnic area making this an ideal stroll for the very young.

34. Kauri Point Beach, Fitzpatrick Bay

 Lovely hidden cove and beach best at high tide

 Easy ~ 20 minutes return

 How to get there: End of Balmain Road off Waipa Street, Chatswood.

First consult your tide tables before setting out for Kauri Point Beach, unless of course you are just walking the dog or feel like a pleasant stroll. At high tide this is a lovely swimmable beach in a hidden cove just 10km from central Auckland. Officially this is Fitzpatrick Bay in Kauri Point Domain but ask locals directions to Fitzpatrick Bay and you are very likely to receive blank stares. Most people know this bay as Kauri Point Beach in Balmain Domain; in the end it's all the same place. Only accessible on foot, it's an easy 10-minute walk from the end of Balmain Road through regenerating bush to a large swath of grass above a small sandy beach. Facing south west, it's a bit exposed to westerly winds but it also captures all the heat of the sun late in the day. The shallow water is ideal for small children and as this is also a dog park, so your pooch can run around and swim all it likes. Parking is very limited at the end of Balmain Road so you might have to walk a bit to the start of the track.

35. Kauri Point Centennial Park/Kendalls Bay/Chelsea

 A loop walk through reserves on Kauri Point on the shores of the Waitemata Harbour

 Medium ~ One hour

 How to get there: Well sign posted entrance on Onetaunga Road opposite Bragato Place, Chatswood.

Kauri Point Centennial Park is at the heart of this loop walk at Chatswood and can be easily combined with all or part of the following three walks.

Originally known as Shark Bay, Kendalls Bay is a shallow sandy inlet just west of the Chelsea Sugar Works and directly opposite Meola Reef. Set aside as a reserve in 1888, the native bush had mostly been cleared by early Maori settlers and then milled for timber by Europeans and planted in pine trees. Today the park comprises of native species typical of regenerating forest such as kanuka, tanekaha, coprosma and ferns. Behind the beach is a small wetland.

Three Maori pa (settlements) overlook the bay as sharks were highly prized as a food source and such areas were jealously guarded and protected. Today bronze whaler sharks are still very common in the deeper channels that run closer to the north shore of the harbour.

As the name of the park suggests, there are substantial stands of young kauri growing along steep ridges and here they grow in association with hard beech, a tree more commonly found much further south. The ridges are bisected by equally steep gullies and this route is for the fitter and more adventurous.

Start this walk at the entrance on Onetaunga Road, opposite Bragato Place where the track drops down to the beach which is swimmable at high tide with grassy areas ideal for a picnic. Walk to the other end of the beach where the track climbs back up the hill with steps on the easier sections. An unmarked side-track leads out to one of the old pa sites which has a magnificent view over Meola Reef and Te Atatu peninsula.

Once back on the road, walk downhill where a more basic track cuts back into the bush and follows the cliff top to a sealed driveway that leads down to the sugar refinery. Take a short detour to the left to the view the old Managers House (this is private property so be respectful). Continue down to the main road and turn left over the bridge where another track begins immediately to the left off the carpark. It is a very pleasant, quiet walk initially along Duck Creek and then up through bush where eventually the path emerges on to Ravenstone Place and a five minute walk back to the start.

36. Le Roys Bush

 A local treasure of hidden gullies, a waterfall and lush wetlands.

 Grade: Easy ~ Time: 45 minutes

 How to get there: Le Roy's Bush has numerous entry points including off Onewa Road, Le Roy Terrace, Valley Road and Hinemoa Street in Birkenhead; access Little Shoal Bay Reserve via Council Terrace, Seaview or Winding Avenues. There is good parking off Council Terrace by the bowling club at Little Shoal Bay.

Le Roys Bush in the heart of Birkenhead lies at the heart of this North Shore community. In the early 1970s, when the Birkenhead Borough Council continued to dump fill in the wetland behind Little Shoal Bay, locals took action by sitting in front of the bulldozers and eventually persuaded the council to extend the older reserve to include the tidal wetland behind the bay.

The reserve dates to 1918 when Edward Le Roy purchased the steep upper valley that ran up from Little Shoal Bay and over the years acquired smaller pieces of adjacent land, actively planting native trees as well as waterlilies in three ponds he created. On Edward's death in 1947, local people raised money to buy the bush area and over time yet more parcels of land were added and today three reserves, Le Roys Bush, Lutners Bush, and Little Shoal Bay Reserve together total just over 22 hectares.

Like a partly completed jigsaw puzzle, the reserves snake up the main valley, branch out into side gullies and climb over steep hillsides with numerous entry points. While locals are very familiar with the bush, the excellent tracks are confusing to the visitor, but just continue uphill and eventually one track or another will lead either left to Hinemoa Street or right to Onewa Road.

Through the heart of the reserve runs the stream, Te Wai Manawa, which forms a substantial wetland of raupo and native grasses behind Little Shoal Bay, while much further up the valley is a small picturesque waterfall. Milled in earlier years, there are fine examples of native trees including kauri, miro, taraire, puriri, kohekohe, tawa, mahoe and totara while the stream is home to native fish including giant and banded kokopu and the long-finned eel. Copper skinks and geckos also make the bush their home along with numerous native birds.

37. Old Birkenhead Walk

 Bush, cafes and a historic sugar refinery

 Medium ~ One hour

 How to get there: Park on Council Terrace, Little Shoal Bay, Northcote Point

From the carpark walk pass the playing fields down the access road to the bowling club where the track up through Le Roys Bush begins to the left. The reserve can be very confusing to visitors with numerous side-tracks that either head up to the left to Hinemoa Street or right to Onewa Road, but either way you won't get lost. Essentially head up hill to the waterfall and then take the left-hand track to emerge onto Hinemoa Street near the library. If that was confusing enough you are now in Highbury, also known as Birkenhead. Originally Birkenhead was the small collection of shops much further down Hinemoa Street, while this area called Highbury, but in recent years the two names have become interchangeable. Continue west along Mokoia Road, through the Highbury shops, turn left into Colonial Road and walk down hill to the Chelsea Sugar Refinery.

Halfway down Colonial Road is a group of original workers cottages built in 1909 and like the refinery itself, constructed from bricks made on site. Just before the bridge at the bottom of the hill, a track leads off to the right and if you are in a mood for a longer walk see previous entry.

At the heart of this 37 hectare Heritage Park is the Chelsea Sugar Refinery, which began operating in 1884 and is still a working factory today. The visitor experience centre opened in 2018 and together with factory tours, café and baking school, has quickly became a very popular destination on the North Shore.

From the refinery veer to the left and take the track around the shoreline, passing through a pretty Chelsea Bay before climbing steeply up Telephone Road to Rugby Road and back to Hinemoa Street and the heart of old Birkenhead. The café on the corner, once a butcher's shop still retains the old tiles and butcher's hooks hanging from the ceiling. Turn right along Hinemoa Street and after 300 metres turn into Whanganella Street and a little further on left into Tizard Street where at the end a path leads down through the trees to the wharf. The Birkenhead Wharf was first built in 1882 and today is a busy ferry terminal to the central city. Walk back up Hinemoa Street, right in Wakanui Street and then right again into Maritime Terrace and back to the start.

At Shoal Bay look across to Birkenhead Point where you will notice a large group of tall palm streets and old trees. These are all that remain of the eccentric Clement Wragge's dream to turn Birkenhead Point into "the glens of charming Tahiti."

38. Historic Northcote Point Walk

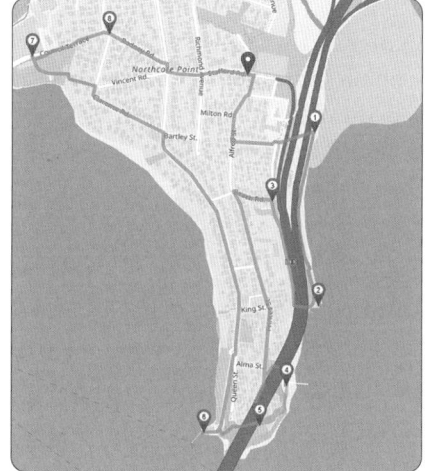

A secret tunnel, a stroll under the harbour bridge, a historic pub and an arthouse theatre all on one walk

 Easy ~ One hour

 How to get there: Stafford Park on Denby Lane just off Stafford Road, the first exit after the bridge going north

Once the busy main highway north, today Northcote Point is better known for the Bridgeway Theatre, historic pub and the award-winning Engine Room Restaurant. From Stafford Park walk back along Denby Lane to Stafford Road where directly opposite is a walkway that

will take you to Alfred Street. Walk south along Alfred Street and turn left into Tennyson Street where at the end of this street you will spy a tunnel under the motorway. To the left is the former Harbour Bridge Toll Plaza building which once overlooked a row of toll booths stretching across the motorway and now a police station. Enter the underpass, taking time in the very middle to shout out loudly and enjoy the superb echoing qualities of this tunnel, emerging at the other side right at the water's edge with superb views of the central city.

From here walk along the path to the dinghy lockers and the Sulphur Beach boat ramp, though the beach has been largely destroyed by the piles of the motorway above. If the tide is very low you can scramble along the shore to the Golden Hole, though you will need good footwear and nimble footing. Otherwise walk up to Princes St and continue south for 600 metres before turning under the motorway to small boatyard. Both the beach and the name Golden Hole take their names from a sulphur works which operated briefly on the beach in 1878. Pause for a moment, pretend the motorway is not towering above you and take in the bucolic maritime scene from the boat yard to the city.

Returning to Princes Street continue under the harbour bridge to Northcote Point itself. It is another world under here as hundreds of vehicles thunder just a few metres above your head. Old villas still stand on the edge of the point, as they did before the bridge was built in the late 1950s. Quotes from famous New Zealand writers wrap around the bridge piles, each quote progressively longer as the piles grow taller.

Right on the point is the site of the Onewa pa marked by a carved pou and the tell-tale defensive ditch cutting at right angles across the point. Immediately to the right is number one Queen Street, built in 1901 from a single kauri log from the Trounson forest north of Dargaville.

Follow the steps down to the wharf (the first wharf was built in 1856), now carrying commuter passengers, but once bustling with cars, trucks and passengers making their way on the main road north. Walking north along Queen Street on your right is the historic Northcote Tavern, built in 1882, where inside the walls are lined with old photos of the Point, when Queen Street was lined with small shops taking advantage of the passing trade. With careful observance many of these shops still exist but are now houses.

Further along Queen St is the iconic Bridgeway Theatre built in 1927 as the Onewa Picturedrome, though now known for featuring art house films, while directly across the road is the award winning Engine House Restaurant, occupying the old post office. Turn left into Clarence Road, passing the old police station at number 11 (built 1913) before taking a narrow path alongside the driveway at number 52 down to Little Shoal Bay. Once the site of a Maori village, the small bay also housed the local gas works and is now home to small pleasure boats.

Turn right up Council Terrace and up to Rodney Road passing the fine Masonic Lodge built in 1912 and back to the intersection of Queen and Stafford Road, taking in the historic Methodist Church opened in 1901 and back to Stafford Park.

39. North Head Historic Reserve

 Wide views over the Waitemata Harbour from this sea-fringed volcanic cone with fortifications including tunnels and gun emplacements

 Easy ~ One hour

 How to get there: The main vehicle entrance is at the end of Takarunga Road, Cheltenham. North Head is about a 20-minute walk from Devonport Wharf.

Justifiably famous for its splendid gulf, harbour and city views, the North Head reserve occupies the ancient volcanic cone of Maungauika which erupted 50,000 years ago. Although there is evidence of occupation and cultivation of the rich volcanic soil, this hill was not fortified by Maori in pre-European times and nearby Takarunga/Mt Victoria was the main pa for the area.

As early as 1836 a pilot station was established at the foot of North Head. In 1885, in response to the Russian expansion into the Pacific, the government set about building three batteries to protect the city from an imminent attack (the explosion of Mt Tarawera in 1886 was initially thought to be the beginning of a Russian bombardment). The underground tunnels and the oldest buildings on the summit, a cookhouse and barracks, still remain from this period.

Further fortifications were added during both the First and Second World Wars and the reserve has excellent signage including original photographs of the defence positions. The south battery is still intact. It features one of the few disappearing guns left in the world; although it is no longer working, it was designed to be loaded underground, raised and then fired, thereby protecting the men servicing the gun.

Most visitors just walk from the car park to the disappearing gun to take in the view but is well worth taking more time to explore the area. The cookhouse on the summit (open 8.30am to 4pm) has a collection of old photos and shows a short video, while there are extensive rooms and tunnels just below the summit on the eastern side.

A track around the base of the cone leads to small sea caves and a sheltered sandy cove suitable for swimming (also accessible from Cheltenham Beach over the rocks). North Head is also a popular spot for a bit of rock fishing, as the main channel runs close to the shore at this point.

40. Devonport Loop Walk including North Head.

 An easy walk from the ferry taking in the best of the North Shore

 Easy ~ Two hours

 How to get there: Devonport Ferry Terminal at the end of Victoria Road

Standing sentinel over the entrance to the Waitemata Harbour, North Head is a great spot to take in city and Gulf views as well as catch up on Auckland's military history. Although the old volcanic cone is the highlight of this walk and can be done separately, the walk described is a great outing in Devonport.

Starting from the Devonport ferry wharf walk along King Edward

Parade towards North Head. Devonport is easily accessible by a short ferry trip from downtown Auckland and there is plenty of parking in the area if you come by car. At the end of the Parade at Torpedo Bay veer right to the Torpedo Bay Naval Museum. This small modern museum details New Zealand's navy history, its free and has a lovely café. Behind the museum take a stroll out on the wharf and visit the boat shed with its collection of small boats including an old whaler.

If the tide is right walk for 50 metres over the rocks just to the left of the boat shed to the base path. The rocks are a bit slippery and at high tide you will get your feet wet so if that doesn't appeal retrace your steps and walk around to Takarunga Road, the main entrance to the reserve.

After exploring North Head (see the previous entry) stroll along lovely Cheltenham beach, an excellent and safe swimming beach at mid to high tide (it is very shallow at low tide). At the end of the beach walk up to Vauxhall Road and walk left for 200 metres and then turn right into Albert Road. Continue 500 metres to the base of Mt Victoria to the old cemetery.

Over the centuries the area, valued for its warm fertile soil and excellent fishing grounds, was fiercely fought over and occupied by numerous iwi. Around 1793 Te Haukapua (Torpedo Bay) saw several bloody clashes between Ngati Paoa and Ngapuhi, culminating in the defeat of Ngati Paoa. Although victorious, Ngapuhi did not settle permanently and returned north. Conflict between the two iwi continued in a long series of battles until 1828, when the great Ngapuhi fighting chief Patuone married Takarangi, the sister of Te Kupenga, a Ngati Paoa chief. Patuone moved to the area when he was gifted land at Takapuna and when he died in 1872, aged 109, he was the first person to be buried on the slopes of Mt Victoria.

Walk through the cemetery and after visiting the grave of Patuone, make your way up to the track that winds its way up to the top. There are numerous rough tracks circling the hill and these can be a bit muddy and slippery in winter.

Typical of hilltop pa, the summit of Takuranga is crowned by a series of wide terraces that once would have supported houses and been encircled by protective palisading. Fortifications built in the nineteenth century, and extended during WWII, have erased or damaged the Maori earthworks at the very top.

As expected, the views from the top over Auckland, the North Shore and the sea are impressive. Return down the road that will take you down to Devonport where you can grab a well-deserved drink and food in numerous cafes in the main street. Particularly appealing is the grand Edwardian Esplanade Hotel near the wharf.

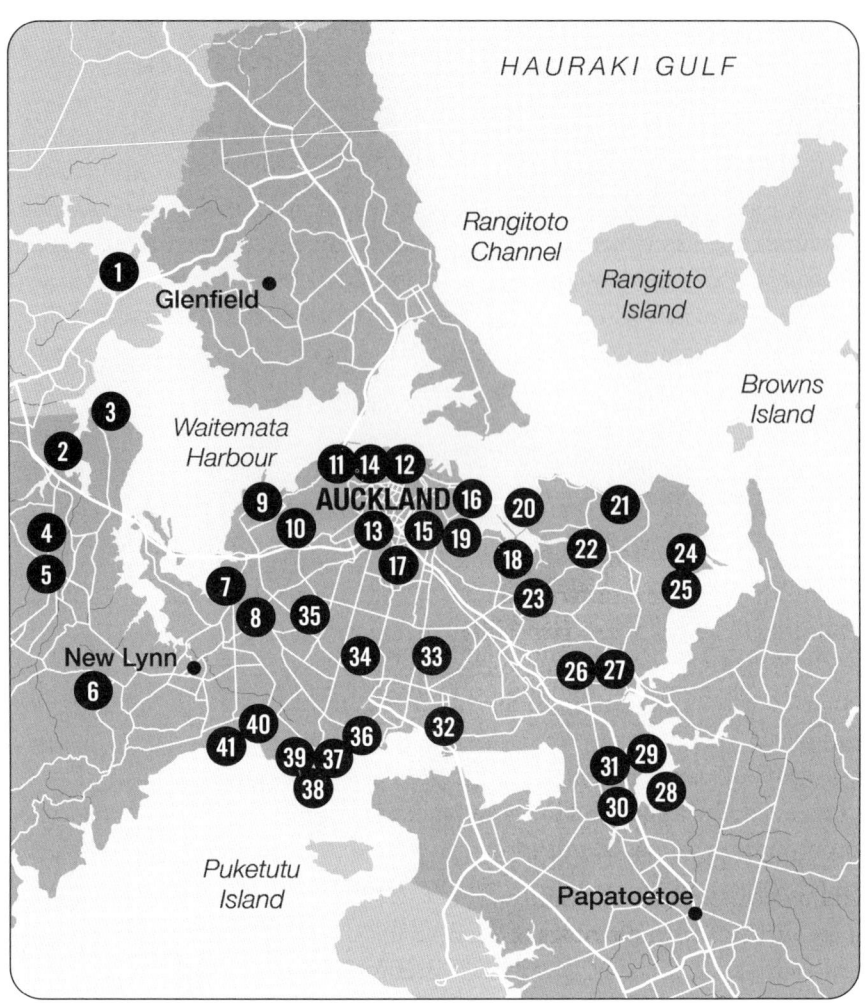

CITY

1. Hobsonville Coastal Walkway
2. Manutewhau Walkway and Moire Park
3. Te Atatu Walkway / Harbourview /Orangihina Reserve
4. Henderson Creek Walkway
5. Opanuku Walkway
6. Waikumete Cemetery
7. Howlett Esplanade/Waterview Reserve
8. Oakley Creek Walkway / Te Auaunga and beyond
9. Meola Reef Reserve/Te Tokaroa and Jaggers Bush
10. Western Springs Park
11. Freemans Bay, Herne Bay, Grey Lynn and Ponsonby
12. Auckland Old City
13. Karangahape Road and Queen Street.
14. Viaduct Basin to St Heliers
15. Coast to Coast Walkway
16. Historic Parnell
17. Mt Eden/Maungawhau, The Withiel Thomas Reserve and Mt Eden Gardens
18. Orakei Basin Walkway
19. Hobson Bay Walkway
20. Kepa Bush Reserve
21. Dingle Dell Reserve
22. St Johns Bush
23. Waiatarua Reserve
24. Tahuna Torea Nature Reserve
25. Tamaki River Walk from Roberta Reserve to Panmure via Point England Reserve.
26. Mt Wellington/Maungarei
27. Panmure Basin Walkway
28. Highbrook Park and Pukewairiki Crater
29. Seaside Park
30. Mt Richmond, Mt Robertson and Old Otahuhu
31. Hamlins Hill Regional Park/ Mutukaroa
32. Old Onehunga
33. Cornwall Park and One Tree Hill Domain/Maungakiekie
34. Big King, The Three Kings
35. Old Mt Albert The Waikowahi Walkway
36. Hillsborough Cemetery and Grannys Bay
37. Waikowhai Park, Hillsborough
38. Cape Horn Lookout
39. Manukau Domain
40. Gittos Domain
41. Blockhouse Bay Beach Reserve to Green Bay Beach Reserve

1. Hobsonville Coastal Walkway

 Aviation history combined with upper harbour views

 Easy ~ One hour, 15 minutes

 How to get there: Begin at the wharf at the end of Hobsonville Point Road.

The Hobsonville Coastal Walkway feels like an afterthought; even the confusing signage looks temporary and lost in this vast new suburb of intensive housing occupying the old Hobsonville air force base. Part of the problem is that there is still a lot of building going on here, so the area is not fully developed and hopefully it will get better in the future as this has the potential for a being a great urban walk. Linking several historical sites, information boards tell the story of the base from its inception in 1929 at a time when Hobsonville was on the isolated outer reaches of Auckland city. Key buildings have been preserved and for aviation buffs, this will be a good afternoon outing. The other surprise are the views of the upper harbour with the high bush-clad hills of Greenhithe and Beach Haven just across the water, while to the south the Waitemata opens out like a giant lake with Mt Albert on the horizon.

Easy walking on hard surfaces, the loop walk around Hobsonville will take a bit more than an hour and is ideal on a sunny winter's afternoon when keeping your feet dry is probably more important than view. A ferry service runs from central Auckland and takes 45 minutes.

2 Manutewhau Walkway and Moire Park

 A tidal waterway, sports fields, bush and a marvellous view of Auckland city

 Easy ~ One and half hours

 How to get there: West Harbour Drive between numbers 109 and 111, opposite Garcia Place, West Harbour

Possibly not worth a special trip but this is a very pleasant walk if you are in the area.

From West Harbour Drive walk down the path where a bridge crosses over the tidal, bush-lined Manutewhau Stream. Turn right over the bridge and follow the track up stream. There are numerous side-tracks which lead up to the sports fields of Moire Park, but if you are walking upstream with the creek on your right, you won't get lost. Continue through the low bush until the track emerges on to Moire Road, cross over the road and the track continues on the other side.

Initially a bush track, after a few hundred metres the path emerges into a broad grassy park that runs between the stream and local houses. After about 15 minutes the path crosses over Oriel Street and into Saint Margarets Park, followed by the Flaunty Reserve and finally over Fitzherbet Ave and into Fitzherbert Reserve and the highlight of this section of the walk. Here on a high open hilltop are marvellously unique views of Auckland city. Spread out before you is the upper Waitemata harbour, the leafy inner suburbs, the harbour bridge, downtown Auckland and beyond that Rangitoto Island. After taking in the views make your way down Sumich Place to Moire Road from where it is a short walk back to the start on West Harbour Drive.

3. Te Atatu Walkway/ Harbourview/Orangihina Reserve

 Aquatic bird paradise with expansive views of the Waitemata Harbour and downtown Auckland

 Grade: Easy ~ One hour

 How to get there: There are numerous points of entry to the walkway around the peninsula. Chapman Strand is at the end of Chapman Road, Harbour View Beach Reserve is at the end of Harbour View Road, and the Peoples Park entrance is opposite Gloria Avenue. There is off street parking and toilets at both Chapman Road and Harbour View Beach Reserve.

During the 1950s, the extension of the north western motorway gave easy access to the Te Atatu peninsula from the central city resulting in a housing boom on the huge area of flat land. Previously cleared for farming, very little native vegetation survived and even that was confined to the coastal margins, but today the peninsula has one of the largest remaining wetlands in the Auckland area and a superb coastal walkway. Mostly following the shoreline, the walkway, flat all the way, links the tidal bays with small patches of bush and the substantial wetland of the Orangihina Reserve. Even though the bushy sections are tiny, native birds such as tui and piwakawaka are common.

Starting from the Chapman Reserve on the western side of the peninsula, the path follows the broad estuary of Henderson Creek, characterised by wide mudflats, tidal creeks, and swathes of mangrove forests, shell banks and shallow beaches. Plentiful crabs, cockles, worms, shrimps and mud snails attract many coastal and wading birds, including godwits, stilts, oystercatchers, kingfishers, shags and herons.

Strolling around Orukuwai Point and down the eastern side of the peninsula, the walkway follows the estuary of the Whau River where it empties into the Waitemata Harbour. From the path there are wide views to the east, especially spectacular when the sun is rising over the city (the Maori name Te Atatu means 'the dawn'). The shallow waters are rich with fish including flounder and grey mullet. Here the walkway enters the Harbourview/Orangihina Reserve and continues to the Harbour View People's Park.

Along this stretch of the shore are the wetlands and although invasive weeds are a problem, coastal natives such as giant umbrella sedge, karo, saltmarsh ribbonwood and coastal tree daisy are all well established. A combination of tidal flats, salt marsh, estuary and freshwater wetlands, the area is home to migratory, coastal, wading and freshwater birds. The rare New Zealand and banded dotterel and fernbird are found here, while the deeper freshwater ponds are the ideal habitat for the kokopu, a native fish. Alongside nearby Pollen Island Reserve, this area is one of the most important coastal habitats in the Auckland region.

The walkway also passes several historic homesteads built in the late nineteenth century, though these are not open to the public.

While the Te Atatu Walkway almost encircles the entire Te Atatu peninsula north of the motorway, the stretch between Chapman Strand on the Henderson Creek estuary and the Harbourview/Orangihina Reserve is by far the most attractive. The downside is that parts of the walkway are also used by cyclists and the start and finish points are a good 45 minute walk apart.

4. Henderson Creek Walkway

 History, nature and art stretch out along a tidal estuary

 Easy ~ One hour one way.

 How to get there: Falls Park Henderson or end of Flanshaw Road.

Now a quiet backwater, Henderson Creek was once a busy waterway linking west Auckland to central Auckland, when the alternative road trip via Mt Albert and New Lynn was slow and difficult. The walkway follows the Creek from the North Western Motorway up stream to Falls Park, just beyond the junction with the Opanuku stream where a small waterfall prevented further navigation up the broad tidal creek.

In recent years the banks of the steam have been extensively replanted in native trees and the shared cycle/foot path links several grassy parks and historical sites. Starting at the northern end, the walkway is sandwiched between the creek, local houses and suburban roads. Nearer central Henderson is the International Walkway of Trees featuring dozens of trees from around the globe, same labelled, others not. Nearby is an intriguing local sculpture, which as first glance appears to be upright mini surfboards, but are colourful representations of inanga or whitebait. Further upstream is Tui Glen Reserve which was New Zealand's first motor camp. Opened in 1924 as the Tui Glen Motor Camp and Amusement Park, the riverside jetty was a popular spot for launching small boats and kayaks on the creek. Today within the park is a huge children's playground, along with a small cottage, built in 1908 and typical of the modest workers' homes in the Henderson area.

Beyond Tui Glen the walkway ends at Falls Park, which is notable for the Falls Restaurant housed in the historic Falls Hotel built in 1873 and relocated to this site in 1996. Adjacent Cranwell Park was once part of

Thomas Henderson's original farm and developed as an orchard by Ben Cranwell around 1900. At the northern end of this park is Delta Point, the meeting place of the Henderson Creek and Opanuku Stream and the location of an important wharf linking Henderson with Auckland.

5. Opanuku Walkway

 Glorious native bush in the heart of Henderson

 Easy ~ 25 minutes

 How to get there: There several entrances to the walkway but the main one is Henderson Park on Wilsher Crescent.

A path begins over a bridge at Henderson Park and wends its way up Opanuku Stream along short boardwalks through spectacular native bush. Dominated by massive totara and enormous kahikatea, there are also old titoki, karaka, a huge cabbage tree, kowhai overhanging the stream, groves of silver fern and several large kauri. Without a doubt it is one of the finest remnants of native bush in the urban area and a small glimpse of what lowland forest in the region must have been like before the arrival of people. Unfortunately, the section linking the walkway with Border Road is now closed and you will need to return the way you came.

On the other side of the creek is a shared walk/cycle way and while this walk is nothing special it is worth visiting the extensive collection of flax varieties, most of which are named along with details of their various uses.

6. Waikumete Cemetery

 Death, design and solitude in New Zealand's largest cemetery

 Easy ~ Allow at least one hour

 How to get there: 4128 Great North Road, Glen Eden or a ten-minute walk from Glen Eden Station on the Western Line. Gates are opened at 7.30 am and closed at 6 pm (winter) and 8.30 pm (summer).

New Zealand's largest burial ground, the Waikumete Cemetery is a vast graveyard covering over 100 hectares. First opened in 1886, Waikumete, became Auckland's main cemetery in 1908. The oldest section is along Glenview Road as the main access to the cemetery for both the dead and the living was by the railway line to Glen Eden. Burials in the old part were divided by religion and even today the cemetery has distinct Jewish and Muslim burial grounds.

Unidentified passengers from the 1979 Air New Zealand Erebus crash are buried in a site near the main entrance and marked by a memorial with the names of those buried here and those not recovered from Antarctica. Another memorial in the form of a granite slab marks the Holocaust memorial next to the Hebrew Prayer House and buried at the base of the memorial is an urn of ashes taken from the Auschwitz Concentration Camp. Mausoleums are uncommon in New Zealand cemeteries but Waikumete contains many of these, mainly for Dalmatian families from West Auckland, including two fine examples belonging to the Corban and Nobilo winemaking families. In contrast to the elaborate mausoleums are the large number of unmarked graves of the victims of the 1918 influenza who collectively have one granite memorial.

Today the main entrance is off Great North Road recognised by a strikingly stylish crematorium. Designed in 1943, the crematorium wasn't built until 1952 and is an unusual combination of Art Deco and Modernism.

Paths and roadways wind around and over the low rolling hills with the graves interspersed with gardens and trees making for a surprisingly enjoyable walk whether to enjoy the unusual landscape or to contemplate the more serious side of life and death.

7. Howlett Esplanade/Waterview Reserve

 A mangrove forest just a short distance from the central city.

 Easy ~ 45 minutes

 How to get there: The two main entry points, one to the Waterview Reserve on Herdman Street; the other to Howlett Reserve on Howlett Street.

At Waterview the Oakley Creek finally joins the wide estuary of Whau River as it empties into the harbour west of Point Chevalier. Long a dumping ground and highly polluted, the waters of both the creek and the river have considerably improved over the past decade with control of industrial waste on the Whau River and restoration of Oakley Creek. Despite the recent construction of the motorway interchange, an excellent track runs along the tidal mouth of the creek and around to the languid mangrove forests of the Whau River estuary. Walkways now link the Howlett Esplanade and Waterview Reserve with the Oakley Creek Walkway and cross under the motorway passing through a small wetland to join up with the Eric Armishaw Park and Walkway in Point Chevalier.

For most folk this is as close as people can get to the Pollen Island/Motu Manawa Marine Reserve. Tens of thousands of motorists pass by this 500-hectare marine reserve each day with little thought to the unique environment flashing by. Home to rare birds and plants, Pollen Island has managed to survive through very tough times but in 2005 the entire area was put under the control of the Department of Conversation and the reserve today is considered to be one of the best salt marsh and mangrove habitats on the Waitemata Harbour.

A fringe of mangroves just beyond the main island protects the fragile banks from being battered by waves in the open harbour. Although consisting mainly of cockle shells and occasionally flooded by very high tides, the highest points of the shell banks are home to grasses, sedges and small shrubs including manuka and coprosma. Sheltering behind the high banks are extensive mangrove swamps and salt marshes. This complex environment of tidal creeks, sand banks, mudflats, salt marsh, shell banks and shrub land hosts a rich and varied flora and fauna. Oddly enough, the motorway makes access very difficult and to some extent protects the area from human activity, dogs, cats and other predators.

Birdlife flourishes here, from the most common such as pukeko, kingfisher and white-faced heron through to the shy and endangered spotless crake, fernbird and banded rail.

8. Oakley Creek Walkway / Te Auaunga and beyond

 The largest waterfall on the Auckland Isthmus

 Easy ~ 45 minutes

 How to get there: There are numerous access points to the creek, though it is easier from the eastern side of the creek, especially from the Phyllis Street Reserve off Springleigh Avenue, where there is good parking and toilets. The Western Line from the city stops at Mt Albert, a short distance from the walkway.

The longest waterway on the Auckland isthmus, the Oakley Creek begins life in Hillsborough and then drains water from the volcanoes Mt Roskill, Three Kings and Mt Albert and finally enters the Whau River at Waterview.

Driven by local initiatives the creek between New North Road and the outlet has undergone a radically transformation with extensive restoration and replanting of native plants. Today the water runs much cleaner and the bush walk along the creek attracts locals and visitors alike. The section of the walkway between the Phyllis Street Reserve and the motorway interchange at Waterview is by far the most attractive part of the walkway, the highlight of which is the Oakley Creek Waterfall, the largest waterfall in the Auckland urban area. Water cascades six and half metres over a basalt lava flow into a small pool and after heavy rain can be very spectacular. The waterfall and other deeps pools along the creek attract swimmers in the summer, though the water quality is very questionable. Above the falls there are several small rapids over old lava flows and throughout the regenerating bush are lava boulders, a constant reminder of the area's dramatic volcanic past.

Despite the intensely urban surroundings with houses pushing close to the water, the bush along the creek is home to native birds such as tui, piwakawaka, and in the creek itself can be found eels, inanga, kokopu and freshwater mussels. The creek becomes tidal near the motorway where it joins the Waitemata Harbour by the Waterview/Howlett Reserve. At this point you can come up to join Carrington Road walking past the original main block of the Auckland Asylum, a handsome Victorian brick building, constructed of pale yellow bricks and opened in 1867.

An outing along the creek can be extended via the walkway which connects to the Waterview/Howlett Walkway (see the previous entry) or north under the motorway and through a small wetland to Walker Park in Point Chevalier. Western Springs Park is just 10 minutes' walk away.

From the other end at the Phyllis Street Reserve, the walkway extends another four kilometres to Walmsley Park in Mt Roskill. The upper reaches of the creek east of New North Road were once a wide swamp, but work projects in the 1930s reduced this section of the creek to little more than a large drain of polluted water. Recently developed and landscaped, this section has vastly improved, the creek is no longer a drain, but a small pretty stream rushing through lava boulders, along banks densely planted in native trees, with all-weather paths, attractive footbridges and boardwalks.

9. Meola Reef Reserve/Te Tokaroa and Jaggers Bush

 An old lava flow with a lively Maori legend.

 Easy ~ 45 minutes

 How to get there: Take Meola Road and between Westmere and Point Chevalier follow the clearly marked signs to the reserve. There is limited off street parking, toilets and plenty of space for a picnic.

Meola Reef is the exposed section of ancient lava flow 11 kilometres long that originated from the Mount Saint John eruption around 28,000 years ago. Virtually cleaving the harbour in two at low tide, the lava flow ends just 500 metres from the hills that are now the suburb of Chatswood. At time of the eruption, the harbour was a wide river valley and it was the cooling waters of the river that finally stopped the lava. The two main creeks in the area, Meola and Motions creeks are kept apart by this huge lava flow.

Maori tradition tells two different stories to account for the long rocky reef that snakes almost all the way across the Waitemata and known to Maori as Te Tokaroa (long rock).

The first story concerns the patupaiarehe, who are frequently described as fairy people, a description that implies a certain degree of cuteness, when in fact patupaiarehe were usually belligerent and unfriendly, not only to humans, but frequently to each other. Long ago two patupaiarehe iwi who lived in the deep, wet Waitakere bush clashed one night on the shores of the harbour just west of Te Rae (Point Chevalier). The losing side was gradually pushed back to the shore and with their route back to Waitakere cut off, decided that they would make their escape by building a bridge of loose rocks to the other side of the harbour. Covered by water at high tide, this causeway would confuse their enemies as to where they had escaped. Hauling heavy rocks, their stone bridge creeping ever deeper into the harbour, the patupaiarehe forgot about the dawn until suddenly the sun rose over the eastern horizon. With the bridge incomplete, the patupaiarehe were trapped forever and turned to stone by the sun's rays; some even say that the tree branches sticking out from the lava reef are the gaunt bones of those caught by the sun.

A similar story, but this time involving humans and with a happier ending, involves a siege of a pa on the summit of Owairaka (Mt Albert). The people trapped in the pa escaped by a lava cave that ran from the northern slopes of the pa to Te Wai Orea (Western Springs lake). From there they fled to the coast where they picked up rocks, built a causeway and crossed over to safety on the northern side of the harbour.

This is an easy, flat loop walk through open grass fields and regenerating coastal vegetation. Towards the exposed reef the track ends and mangroves give way to oyster-covered rocks. You will need very good, strong footwear if you intend to walk out any distance onto the reef itself. This is best done at very low tide and is much more difficult than it looks from a distance.

As this is a short walk, it can be combined with a stroll through Jaggers Bush, a small area of regenerating bush on the eastern slope above Meola Creek. The entrance to the bush is just across the road from the carpark.

10. Western Springs Park

Birds galore on these inner-city springs

Easy ~ 45 minutes

How to get there: Great North Road, Western Springs with parking either on the road or by Western Springs Stadium. Toilets and picnic areas but bring something to sit on as there is bird poo everywhere.

Best known for its large lake and shallow ponds, this large city park is also one of the region's most important reserves for aquatic birds. Including both native and introduced birds, the number of species is surprising: black swan, geese, pukeko, cattle egret, Australian coots, mallard duck, teal, shovelers, paradise ducks and two rare native birds, the dabchick/weweia and New Zealand scaup/papango. There is a downside to all these birds, and that is the sheer quantity of bird droppings. You will need to think twice before you let the kids "run free" (certainly not barefoot) and if a picnic is planned, pick your spot carefully and prepare to be invaded by geese and swans.

Developed in 1875, the lake held spring water in a water reservoir to supply the rapidly growing city. It was given the name Western Springs to differentiate these springs from those in Domain which was the original water supply for the city. As the city continued to grow, the water supply came increasingly from new reservoirs in the Waitakere Ranges and by 1928, Western Springs became redundant. The area remained undeveloped and an eyesore until after the Second World War, though the zoo had been established in 1922.

Today Western Springs is a marvellous park with paths meandering around the large lake and numerous smaller ponds and wetlands. It is very easy walking, ideal for the little ones and pushchairs and allow about 45 minutes to amble around the park. When crossing the small bridges keep an eye out for eels as both native long-finned and short-finned eels are common here, along with the native fish, the banded kokopu. On the western side of the park by the zoo are picnic tables, a children's playground and a small Japanese garden, a gift from Auckland's sister city Fukuoka.

Beyond the entrance to the zoo is Motions Road from where another track follows the Meola Stream, through the Pasadena Reserve to the Point Chevalier shopping centre. For a longer walk turn right along Motions Road to Jaggers Bush and the Meola Reserve.

11. Freemans Bay, Herne Bay, Grey Lynn and Ponsonby

 A fascinating stroll through Auckland's historic inner suburbs.

 Easy ~ Long Loop walk: Easy, three hours

Short Loop walk: Easy, two hours

 How to get there: Begin Victoria Park, Freemans Bay.

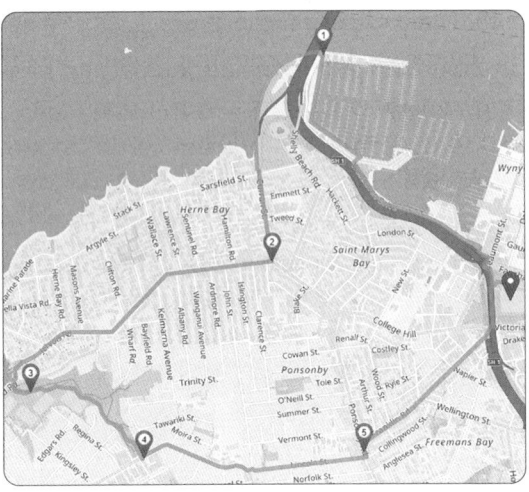

Reclamation of Freemans Bay began in 1873 and by 1901 the bay had vanished, primarily used as boat yards. In order to create a healthy open space for the crowded and poor neighbourhood, the reclaimed land was opened as Victoria Park in 1905 with London plane trees planted around the perimeter, many of which still flourish today. The historic caretaker's cottage on the northern eastern and now a café and bar, dates from the time the park was established. Bisecting the heart of the park is the motorway flyover, opened in 1962, while underground is the Victoria Park Tunnel opened in 2012.

Cross over Fanshawe Street at the intersection of Beaumont Street and enter the boat yards. Freemans Bay was always a centre of boat building since the 1840s and in the 1880s nine shipyards were operating here and today maritime related industries still flourish.

Take the walkway along the shore of St Marys Bay, pausing to admire the handsomely carved wooden seat along with an old anchor and steel buoy and on to Westhaven Marina, the largest in the southern hemisphere and accommodating up to 2000 boats. Established in the 1940s the marina is home to four yacht clubs are based here, as well as the Ponsonby Sailing School and the Auckland Dragon Boat Club.

Past the marina the walk continues under the Auckland Harbour Bridge (1959), the construction of which completely obliterated St Marys Bay. Once under the bridge walk up Curran Street pass the Point Erin Pool, opened in 1962 and located within a pleasant park on a high bluff above the harbour. Further up Curran Street on the right is elegant Ponsonby Primary school, and main building dating from 1921.

At the top of Curran Street turn right into Jervois Road and stroll down past smart shops, trendy cafes and restaurants including Andiamo, one of Auckland's longest running Italian restaurants. On the other side of the road, between Wallace St and Clifton Road, are a series of stylish 1930s art deco apartments.

Continue right to the end of Jervois Road, passing the Empress Gardens Chinese Restaurant, specialising in Cantonese cuisine since 1981 and walk down the stairs to Cox's Bay. Cross over the road into Cox's Bay Reserve, a mixture of sports grounds and park, though both the tidal stream and the bay are pretty smelly at low tide. However, the stream improves as the path meanders through replanted native trees to Hukanui Reserve and through to Richmond Road.

For the short loop walk continue left up Richmond Road for 600 metres to Lincoln Street and stroll up to Ponsonby Road, re-joining the last part of this walk at Franklin Road.

For the full loop walk cross over Richmond Road into Westmoreland Street West and continue to the end where an obvious walkway leads through the houses to Sackville Street and cross over in to tree-lined Hakanoa Reserve. At Hakanoa Street turn left into Cockburn Street and 50 metres on turn right into Dryden Street and walk 200 metres up to Grey Lynn Park.

Once a dairy farm along the upper course of Cox's Creek, this park was developed when the area was opened for housing in the 1880s. It is home to one of Auckland's oldest Rugby League clubs, the Richmond Rovers, and hosts the popular Grey Lynn Festival every December. A popular feature is the small collection of contemporary sculptures.

Walk through the park to Williamson Ave and walk up to Ponsonby Road past the old Ponsonby Fire Station, originally built in 1889 as the Newton Borough Council Chambers and Fire Station and now a restaurant.

Cross over Ponsonby Road and into Western Park, easily recognised by the sculptures of buried historical buildings. Opened in 1879, this is one of Auckland's oldest parks, and many of the old trees in the park date from this time. Walk through the park downhill, past the playground and exit at Beresford Street West. Continue along to Hepburn Street and turn right and down to Wellington Street, from where you walk up to Franklin Road and turn left. Lined by huge plane trees planted in the 1880s, the street is now best known for its spectacular display of Christmas lights.

At Ponsonby Road turn right and stroll along one of Auckland's best-known streets, famous for its fashionable shops and smart cafes to the Russell Street. Directly opposite are two iconic eateries, the Turkish Café and Café Cezanne, barely changed in both look and style since they opened in the early 1980s.

The next intersection is Three Lamps and the heart of old Ponsonby. On the corner of Ponsonby and Jervois Road is the old Glue Pot Tavern, closed in 1994 and now apartments and shops. A pub existed here since 1870, but in 1939 the old pub was totally renovated and renamed the DB Ponsonby Club Hotel. From the late 1960s through to its closure, it was one of Auckland's most famous live music venues, hosting both local and overseas performers including The Rolling Stones. Apparently, the pub acquired its nickname The Gluepot by unhappy housewives whose husbands were "stuck in the glue pot".

Directly opposite is the iconic old Ponsonby Post Office built in 1912 and out front is the city's only surviving underground men's toilet. Opposite the Post Office is the Leys Institute and Library, opened in 1905 as a "Mechanics' Institute for the 'rational recreation' of the local working class.

Continue down College Hill Road, to The Cav gastro pub on the corner of Wood Street. Built as the Suffolk Hotel in the late 1860s, the pub has a wide terrace facing the city with fantastic views especially at sunset.

Turn into the side streets and here you will find a combination of old cottages, council flats and contemporary apartments, now typical of this area. Once a down-at-heel working-class suburb, after a typhoid outbreak in the 1950s, the city council demolished large areas of old wooden houses, replacing them with modern flats and houses.

Cross over Franklin Road, past the Bird Cage Tavern, originally the 1886 Rob Roy Hotel and finally wander through the old gas works, once Auckland's first real street market, and now a mix of upmarket restaurants, professional offices and boutique shops.

Central Auckland, Historic Walks

At a casual glance central Auckland is a city of modern high rise with little to offer in the way of historic buildings but tucked away are some architectural gems and this walk features over 35 listed heritage buildings. For easy of navigation the city has been divided into two walks which can be easily done together. A further and much longer walk covers the waterfront and Tamaki Drive to St Heliers.

12. Auckland Old City

 Meander through the historical heart of old Auckland

 Easy ~ One hour

Fed by a spring in Myers Park, the Waihorotiu Stream ran down to the sea along a gully that is now Queen Street to Horotiu Bay, and on either side of the stream were two headlands, Point Britomart and Point Stanley. It was on high ground of Point Britomart that both Maori and Europeans settled, with the original pa near the High Court building. Shortland Street was the heart of the colonial settlement and today many of the Auckland's oldest and most important historic buildings are in this area.

The walk begins at the Britomart Railway Station in Queen Street, originally opened in 1912 as the main Post Office, the building is in the Imperial Baroque style. Directly over Customs Street is the Dilworth Building in the striking Stripped Classical style, opened as an office building in 1927. The original plan was for two identical buildings on either side of Queen Street, creating a grand entrance to the city. On the left at 34 Queen Street is the Strand Arcade, originally two buildings, the L shaped arcade opened in 1929.

Turn left into Shortland Street, the city's original and current commercial centre. The South British Insurance Building, at 5 Shortland Street, one of Auckland's tallest buildings when it opened in 1929, was also at the time ultra-modern and heavily influenced by the Chicago style of architecture. Just up the street, Debretts Hotel on the corner of High Street was originally built in 1841, rebuilt in 1860 and completely remodelled in the Stripped Classical style in 1926. Renamed Debretts in 1959, the hotel is noted for its Art Deco interior. The 1YA Radio Station, at 74 Shortland St was a purpose built, state-of-the-art radio station constructed in 1936 in the Romanesque style and without any external windows.

Detour right into Bankside Street to this lone survivor of a modest four-roomed workers dwelling built in 1884 and unusually built of concrete and not wood.

At the top of Shortland Street is Emily Place in the centre of which stands the Churton Memorial erected in remembrance of the first vicar of St Pauls Anglican Church. An earlier memorial and the old church were demolished when the area was excavated to provide fill for harbour reclamation below the point. Once the heart of the colonial settlement, this small park is now best known for its huge pohutukawa trees.

Turn right into Princes Street and on your right at number 19 is The Northern Club, which started life as a hotel in 1867. Shortly afterwards it became government offices, and finally two years later became, and still remains The Northern Club, Auckland's oldest gentlemen's club, though women have been admitted since 1990.

Turn left into Waterloo Quadrant and walk down to the intersection of Parliament Street, the name of which is a reminder of Auckland's brief period as New Zealand's capital city from 1841 - 1865. In this street are Corner Courteville, Middle Courteville and Braemar House, three fine examples of early twentieth century flats built for professional city dwellers.

Continue down Waterloo Quadrant to Anzac Ave where on the corner is the Auckland High Court, one of Auckland's earliest and grandest buildings. Constructed between 1865 and 1868 in the fashionable Gothic Revival style - especially appealing are the carved heads of local dignitaries, Maori rangatira and royalty. Diagonally across from the High Court is St Andrews Presbyterian Church, built in a simple style in 1850 of local basalt and Auckland's oldest surviving church.

Cross the road and enter the grounds of Old Government House, built for the Governor of New Zealand in 1856 when Auckland was still the capital, and continued as the Governor's Auckland residence after the government moved to Wellington.

Left into Princes Street and on the corner at number 19a is the old Synagogue. Combining Moorish and Romanesque elements, the synagogue was opened in 1885 and continued to be in use until 1969 when the congregation moved to a larger building. On the same side of Princes Street is a row of five merchant houses, built in the late nineteenth century when this street was Auckland's most desirable address. Across the road and impossible to miss is the University of Auckland's Old Arts Building. Designed by American architects and opened in 1926, this building was highly controversial at the time, and criticised for being inappropriate for a university and not English enough. An important feature is the original use of New Zealand motifs in the decoration.

Cross back over the road into Albert Park. Originally the site of the pa Te Horotiu, in 1845 the Albert Barracks were established and substantially fortified in the 1860s. Taken over by the council in 1879, it became a public park and still retains a strong Victorian flavour. Particularly notable are the statues of Queen Victoria and Sir George Grey, the elegant band rotunda and the quaint caretaker's Lodge. The park has several important and rare trees, including massive Moreton Bay figs and a very rare Ombu tree, a native of Argentina.

Exit Albert Park down into Kitchener Street to the Auckland Art Gallery. Originally the city library, this building in the French Renaissance style, was opened in 1887 and finally became a dedicated art gallery in 1971.

Cross Kitchener Street into Khartoum Place and down the steps to Lorne Street, through the Suffragette Memorial. Composed on 2000 tiles, the memorial was opened by the Irish President Mary Robinson in 1993 to mark the 100th anniversary of women's suffrage in New Zealand.

Turn left into Lorne Street, left again into Wellesley Street and walk up the hill to Symonds Street to St Pauls Church at 28 Symonds Street. Auckland's original Anglican church, the first building on this site dates from 1841. Built in the Gothic Revival style, the current church was opened in 1895 and the planned tower was never completed.

13. Karangahape Road and Queen Street.

 Two of Auckland's most famous shopping and entertainment thoroughfares.

 Easy ~ One hour

 How to get there: Corner of Symonds Street and Karangahape Road

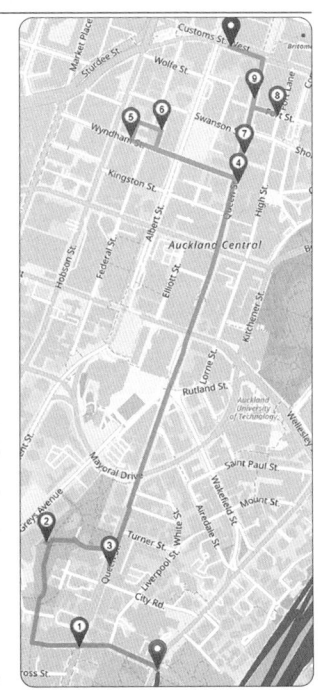

These two streets formed the old centre of Auckland's commercial district. Karangahape Road was the city's most important retail destination where all the great department stores were located and frequently described as New Zealand's Oxford Street. Queen Street linked the business and retail centres and was the focal point for entertainment, commerce and shopping.

Begin this walk at Grafton Bridge on the

corner of Symonds Street and Karangahape Road and which was at the time of opening in 1910, an engineering masterpiece of contemporary concrete construction.

Below the bridge and stretching along both sides of the road is the Symonds Street Cemetery, opened in 1846 when this area was on the outskirts of town. Common at the time, the cemetery is divided into different religious denominations, including Presbyterian, Roman Catholic, Anglican with the distinctive Jewish section directly across the road. Many notable people are buried in the cemetery including New Zealand's first Governor, Captain William Hobson, whose grave is located between Grafton Bridge and the on-ramp to the Southern Motorway.

Karangahape Road (more usually known as K'Rd) was originally the main thoroughfare leading west out of the city and by the early and mid-20th century, the street had become Auckland's premier shopping street. When the motorways destroyed much of the housing in the area, the street declined, with the grand shops closing to be replaced by strip clubs, dodgy bars and street prostitution. Now high-rise apartments are changing the street yet again and today there is a mix of eclectic shops, lively cafes, stylish and not so stylish bars, but also a good deal less sleazy.

Rendalls at 184 K'Rd built in 1904, was the city's leading clothing and drapery store and a little further on at number 244 is the fine George Court department store opened in 1926 and modelled on Selfridges in London. Closed in 1993 and converted into apartments, this handsome building still dominates the street skyline.

Cross over the road to another great survivor, the elegant St Kevins Arcade at 183 K'Rd. Opened in 1924, and home to tailors, dressmakers and photography studios, the arcade is little altered after nearly 100 years.

Linked to St Kevin's arcade by a flight of stairs is Meyer's Park, formerly an overgrown gully, turned into a park in 1915, and named after former mayor, Arthur Meyer. It was Meyer who provide the funds for a playground and the stylish 1916 Kindergarten building. A feature of the park is a full-sized statue of Michelangelo's Moses, imported by Milne and Choyce Department store in 1971 and gifted to the city in 1973. One of a pair, the other statue was the naked David which the city declined on the grounds of 'good taste.'

From the park exit go past the Kindergarten into Upper Queen Street. Directly opposite are a row of original nineteenth century shops, while on the right is the old Theosophical Society Hall, built in 1923 and is now home to the White House brothel. Further up at 429 Queen Street is the imposing Auckland Baptist Tabernacle built in the classical style and opened in 1885.

Stroll down Queen Street to Aotea Square. Flanked by the Town Hall and the Aotea Centre, the square was opened in 1979 as a space for markets, open-air concerts and festivals. Visitors enter the square from Queen Street, through the magnificent Waharoa Gateway by sculptor Selwyn Muru. Next to the gateway is the 2003 bronze statue by Toby Twiss of former mayor Sir Dove Myer-Robinson, more usually known as just "Robby."

The Auckland Town Hall was opened in 1911 and the Great Hall, inspired by the Gewandhaus, in Leipzig Germany, not only seats over 1500 people, but also boasts internationally renowned acoustics. On the opposite side of the square The Aotea Centre designed by Ewen Wainscott, was opened in 1974, with the main Kiri Te Kanawa Theatre seating over 2,000.

Further down Queen Street on the corner of Wellesley Street is Civic Theatre opened in 1929 as New Zealand's first purpose-built picture. Today the Civic is the largest surviving atmospheric cinema in Australasia famous for the eclectic interior style that ranges from the Indian-influenced foyer to the dramatic Moorish auditorium.

Directly opposite is the Smith & Caughey's Building, Auckland's leading upmarket department store, opened in 1929 and designed in the Chicago School style by renowned architect Roy Lippincott.

Continue down Queen Street and detour up Wyndham Street to the impressive Cathedral Church of St Patrick and St Joseph. Established under Bishop Pompallier in 1848, prolific Auckland architect Thomas Mahoney designed the new and enlarged cathedral opened in 1907.

Retrace your steps back to the Shakespeare Hotel, on the corner of Wyndham and Albert Streets. This fine late Victorian corner hotel built in 1898, is one of the few inner city's hotels to survive and is fortunate not only to retain the original exterior, but also many interior features including kauri floors, old sash windows and a fine wooden staircase. It was designed by Edward Mahoney and Sons who were also responsible for the Catholic Cathedral and other nearby pubs including the Empire, Albion and The Birdcage.

Return back to Queen Street and detour across the road to Vulcan Lane, once a lane that bordered the waterfront and had such a reputation for street walkers and bookmakers that it became known as Vultures Lane. Now a street of smart shops, it is best known for two fine old hotels, the Occidental, built in 1870 and the Queen's Ferry, opened much earlier in 1858.

Back to Queen Street and a final left turn into Customs Street to the Customs Building. This is yet another local building attributed to architect Thomas Mahoney, but neither a church nor a pub, but a fine customs house in the French Renaissance style and now housing sophisticated shops.

14. Viaduct Basin to St Heliers

   A coastal walk from city to beach.

   Easy ~ Two hours

With detours, three and half hours

   How to get there: Viaduct Basin, Quay Street, downtown Auckland

This long walk, with detours, takes in a long stretch of Auckland's busy waterfront along Quay Street and Tamaki Drive. If you are up for an even longer walk (an extra 30 minutes) you can begin under the Auckland Harbour bridge walk into the city, picking up this walk at Viaduct Basin and taking all the detours.

Viaduct Basin, now the heart of the city's entertainment district, was not so long ago a small harbour for fishing boats. After winning the yachting America's Cup in 1995, the basin was transformed into a base for the successful challenge in 2000. The Basin is also the location of the New Zealand Maritime Museum housing exhibits from the first Polynesian explorers to the contemporary.

From the Basin take a short detour to the Tepid Baths, built in 1914 on the site of a dry dock previously used for swimming and still retaining its delightful Edwardian style.

Return to the waterfront and walk around Princes Wharf lined with restaurants, hotels and apartments. Opened in 1929, the wharf hosted Auckland's ocean-going liners and is still today the main passenger terminal for cruise ships.

Rising above Auckland's main ferry terminal is the striking 1904 Ferry Building, designed in the baroque style by Alexander Wiseman using sandstone and brick on a base of Coromandel granite.

Detour One, Queens Wharf, 20 minutes. The wooden Queen Street Wharf was first built here in 1852 but was replaced by a much larger concrete structure at the beginning of the 20th century. Container shipping made its position as the city's main wharf redundant, sparking a long and sometimes acrimonious debate regarding a new purpose for the prime waterfront location.

Eventually after much controversy over a venue for the 2011 Rugby World Cup, The Cloud was hastily built as a hospitality and party zone. However, the unique building won over the affection of many Aucklanders, and what was meant to be a temporary building, is still standing. A historic warehouse, Shed 10 has been retained.

At the end of the wharf and equally controversial, is an artwork by Michael Parekowhai. The Lighthouse is based on a full-scale model of a 1950s state house, which is viewed through the windows and door.

Return to Quay Street and follow the highly decorated cast-iron red fence, erected in between 1913 – 1923 to improve security.

Past the iconic red fence is Auckland's main container port, though the earlier Bledisloe Wharf was built in the 1930s to handle consignments of frozen meat for export. Converted into a container wharf, the first ship carrying containers, arrived in June 1971.

Detour Two, Parnell, 20 minutes. Cross Quay Street into the Strand and turn left into Gladstone Road with a great view over the container port and walk up the road into Dove Meyer Robinson Park, better known as the Parnell Rose Gardens. After strolling through the 5000 rose plants, walk down to tidal Judges Bay and walk towards the Parnell Pool. On the grassy slope above is the tiny wooden St Stephens Chapel, built in 1857. At the pool a public walkway passes the 1950s glass mosaic mural by James Turkington and then crosses back to Tamaki Drive.

At Gladstone Road, Quay Street becomes Tamaki Drive with the next point of interest, the Parnell Pool, just over the road. Opened in 1914, the saltwater pools were designed in the fashionable Lido style by Hungarian architect Tibor Donner and are still a popular destination today.

Past the pool, the walk passes the huge tidal basin of Hobson Bay on the right with pleasure boats swinging with the changing tide.

Detour Three, Paratai Drive, 15 minutes. Cross the road and right on the corner is a path marked by a white handrail leading up the hill to Paratai Drive. At the top, turn left and stroll along the crescent above the bluff, admiring the grand houses overlooking the sea. At Okahu Street turn left and drop down to Okahu Bay.

Pokanoa Point has long been associated with boating, first developed as boat mooring area with a haul-area in the mid-1940s, as well as the base for the Royal Akarana Yacht Club, Coastguard, Auckland Sailing Club and the Waitemata Rowing Club.

Okahu Bay has always been the main village for Auckland iwi Ngati Whatua and the area was extensively redeveloped in 1952 with the construction of new houses above the flat ground by the bay. Today only the Orakei Domain Church and Urapa remain near the beach and the reserve is now known for its popular Waitangi Day concerts.

At sea level on Bastion Point is Kelly Tarlton's Sea Life Aquarium, one of Auckland's main tourist attractions, created in 1985 by diver Kelly Tarlton. Utilising an old storm water and sewerage system, the underground aquarium now houses 2,000 fish, including sharks and stingrays as well as penguins. While you are here, take a walk out to sea on the Okahu Bay Wharf.

Detour Four, Bastion Point, 20 minutes. Walk up the road to the Savage Memorial to Bastion Point home to Ngati Whatua o Orakei for 300 hundred years. The striking Orakei Marae with its main house Tumutumuwhenua occupies the high ground and was in 1977 the scene of a long occupation when the government planned to sell off land that it had acquired many years before for public works. Most of the land was eventually returned to the iwi.

On the bluff is the tomb and memorial garden for Michael Joseph Savage, the country's first Labour Prime Minister. Designed by Tibor Donner and Anthony Bartlett, the memorial was opening in 1943 and has spectacular views over the city and the Gulf.

Return to Tamaki Drive and walk past the Tamaki Yacht Club established in 1937. Over the road and embedded in the cliffs are a series of small pillboxes built to the defend the harbour during WWII, which is all that remains of Fort Bastion, originally constructed in 1886 in response to the "Russian Scare."

Offshore is Bean Rock Lighthouse, built in 1871 and the country's oldest wooden light. It is also the only surviving cottage-type lighthouse where the lighthouse keeper lived in three rooms; a living area including a kitchen, a bedroom and a long-drop toilet open to the water below.

Rounding the point, the next stop is Mission Bay, crossing over the footbridge into Selwyn Reserve. Directly on the right and now a café, is all that remains of the Melanesian Mission established here to train missionaries. The enterprise was a disaster and after the outbreak of dysentery in 1863-64 which killed 14 students, the mission at Auckland was closed and shifted to Norfolk Island. Today only the distinctive dining hall, with its volcanic stone walls and shingle roof remains.

In the heart of the park is the glorious Trevor Moss Davis Memorial Fountain. Built of Sicilian marble, water gushes out of the central statue of three bronze sea monsters. At night the fountain is brightly lit by colourful lights and on hot summer day, children convert the fountain into a paddling pool.

Directly across the road is the elegant art deco Berkley picture theatre opened in December 1937, while further along the bay are the Garden Court Flats built in 1936. Designed by Surrey Alleman in a rather severe art deco style, one of the selling features were "airtight garbage tin cupboard under sink bench with outside ventilators."

Around the next point is Kohimarama, the longest beach and the least developed of the waterfront bays.

The final stop is St Heliers Bay, named after the fashionable resort Saint Helier in Jersey, and here there are plenty of eateries or if you prefer, a simple picnic under the huge Moreton Bay fig trees on Vellenoweth Green. At St Heliers, you can catch a frequent bus back to the city or take Detour Five.

All beaches are swimmable, but considerably more enjoyable on a high tide.

Detour Five, Achilles Point, 30 minutes return. From the beach walk up Cliff Road for about 900m to a marvellous lookout point over the islands of the gulf from Achilles Point.

15. Coast to Coast Walkway

 A 16km hike across Auckland, from the Waitemata Harbour to the Manukau shore

 Easy ~ Three hours

 How to get there: Ferry Building, Quay Street Auckland

Starting at the Ferry Building on the Waitemata Harbour, the walk links some of Auckland's most famous landmarks; Auckland University, The Domain, Mt Eden/Maungawhau, Maungakiekie, Jellicoe Park and eventually reaches the Manukau Harbour at Onehunga. At the same time the trail also meanders through back streets and hidden parks and while 16 kilometres might sound a long way, the variety of landscapes will provide plenty of interest to make you forget how far it is. The walking is easy, though both Maungawhau and Maungakiekie involve steep but short climbs. The final leg of the walk finishes at the restored Onehunga lagoon on the Manukau Harbour.

It is the perfect walk for the fitter first time visitors to the city but even if you are a long time Auckland resident, this walk will still provide you with pleasant surprises and is ideal on a sunny winter's day when more challenging walks are muddy and wet. If you are lured by the prospect of coffee and cake along the way, you will be surprised that the walk manages to avoid any cafes until you exit Cornwall Park on to Manukau Road near Royal Oak. However, should substance become essential you can do a short detour after Mt Eden to Olafs Artisan Bakery Café in Stokes Road or to Eve's Pantry on Manukau Road opposite the Logan Campbell statue.

The signage along the way can be erratic in parts, so if you are not familiar with Auckland streets, make sure you have a good map on your phone or print one out. At Onehunga regular bus and train services run back to the city centre.

16. Historic Parnell

Historic buildings and hidden parks.

 Easy ~ One hour

 How to get there: Begin the walk on the corner of Parnell Road and St Stephens Ave – a local map will come in handy.

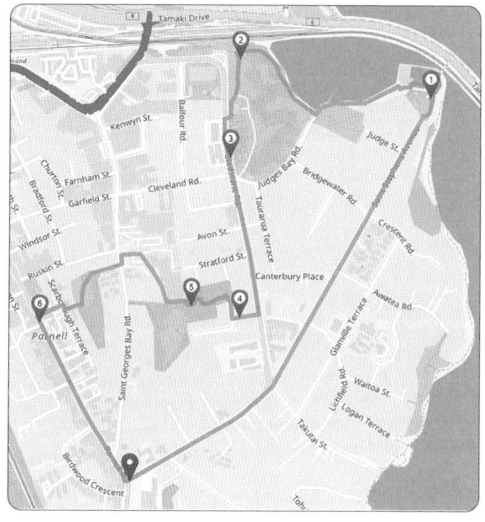

Start at St Mary's in Holy Trinity Cathedral on Parnell Road. Built entirely of timber between 1884 and 1897 by Benjamin Mountfort in the Gothic style, St Mary's has been described as 'one of the finest of all wooden churches in New Zealand.' Originally on the other side of the road, the church was moved to its present site in 1982.

From St Marys cross over to Bishopscourt at 8 St Stephens Ave. Designed by Frederick Thatcher and built between 1861 and 1863, these beautiful wooden buildings are grouped around a central courtyard. Originally built for Bishop Selwyn, Bishopscourt is still the residence of the Anglican Bishop of Auckland and, as such, is not open to the public.

Continue to the very end of tree-lined St Stephens Ave and go down the steps towards the waterfront. Halfway down, just before the bridge over Tamaki Drive, turn left. This path takes you past the Parnell Baths. Originally a tidal swimming pool enclosed by a rock wall, the Parnell Baths is Auckland's only saltwater pool. The building was awarded a Gold Medal in 1958 by the New Zealand Institute of Architects and still features a stylish stone-and-glass mosaic that graces the front of the building.

Continue along the edge of Judges Bay. On the left on a small rise is the historic St Stephen's Chapel. This picturesque small chapel was built for the signing of the Constitution of the Anglican Church of New Zealand in June 1857. Designed by Fredrick Thatcher, the wooden building was used as Bishop Selwyn's semi-private chapel and today functions as a local church.

From Judges Bay take the steps up the hill through Sir Dove-Myer Robinson Park to the lookout over the sea and the city. From here turn around and walk through the Parnell Rose Gardens, famous for their spectacular display of roses in the summer.

Exit left from the gardens and continue walking up Gladstone Road for about 500 metres, then turn right into Alberon Street, and right again into Alberon Place. At the end of this short street take the flight of steps straight ahead that leads down through dense nikau bush to Alberon Reserve. This lovely park edged with palm trees is almost unknown to anyone other than locals and is a surprise haven in the middle of Parnell. Take the path out of the park to the right, climb up to St Georges Bay Road, and turn right then left into Scarborough Reserve, another pretty park hidden in the small valley below Parnell Road. Take the exit to the right out of this park which leads up to Parnell Road itself. Turn left back up Parnell Road to return to St Mary's.

On the left at 350 Parnell Road is Hulme Court. Built in 1843 in the Regency style, this is reputed to be Auckland's oldest building on its original site. Later purchased by Colonel Hulme, after whom it is named, it was used as Government House during the 1850s and was also at one time the home of Bishop Selwyn. The original bluestone walls have since been plastered over, but the hipped slate roof is original.

17. Mt Eden/Maungawhau, The Withiel Thomas Reserve and Mt Eden Gardens

 An extinct volcano with a distinct crater, great views over Auckland city and a magical love story.

 Medium ~ Allow two hours

 How to get there: Parking on Puhi Huia Road between Mt Eden Road and Clive Road

Auckland city's highest volcano at 196 m Mt Eden/ Maungawhau (mountain of the whau tree), is a perfectly formed cone with a very distinctive crater and one of the most popular viewing points over the city. Maungawhau, like so many of Auckland's volcanoes, was an important pa and the evidence of terraces, house sites and kumara pits is very clear. The mountain was also the home of Puhihuia and the story of her love for Ponga is one of the great Maori love stories.

Long ago the people of Maungawhau were in conflict with the people living at Awhitu on the Manukau harbour, and even though they were related, they could not agree on who had the rights to the rich shark-fishing grounds at Puponga on the southern side of the Manukau.

To resolve the conflict the local people invited the Awhitu people to the pa to resolve their differences. Among the visitors was Ponga, a brave warrior, but one of the lesser chiefs who fell in love with the beautiful Puhihuia the minute he set eyes on her. The two secretly met and decided not to part. However, Puhihuia was admired by many others of considerably more mana than Ponga, so the couple eloped and Ponga returned home with Puhihuia. When they reached Awhitu the chief was horrified and, realising that serious trouble lay ahead, insisted that

Puhihuia return immediately to her people. However, when they saw that Puhihuia had not been kidnapped and was deeply in love with Ponga, they allowed her to stay despite their deep misgivings.

Meanwhile back at Maungawhau, the pa was in turmoil and a similar argument raged between those who wanted to fight and bring back Puhihuia and those who deeply wished to prevent war. While the men discussed and prevaricated, Puhihuia's mother decided that immediate action was required and together with a large group of other women, they dressed as warriors, boarded their waka at Onehunga and set out across the Manukau for Awhitu to bring back Puhihuia.

Standing on a high cliff, Puhihuia and Ponga nervously watched as the waka of Maungawhau drew near. As the waka came close Puhihuia recognised her mother and quickly realised that the warriors were in fact all women. Against Ponga's wishes she went down to the shore to confront the women and one by one in hand-to-hand combat the valiant Puhihuia, driven by her love for Ponga, defeated each of her opponents. Impressed by the strength of her love for Ponga, the people of Maungawhau relented and a great feast blessed the marriage of Puhihuia and Ponga and brought peace between Maungawhau and Awhitu.

In the 1820s Ngapuhi tribes with their newly acquired muskets invaded the area and the local population fled south, most of whom never returned, leaving the isthmus largely depopulated. In 1840, Maungawhau was part of 3000 acres that Apihai Te Kawau traded to the Crown to establish the settlement of Auckland.

In January 2016 the summit of the mountain was made car and bus free and the walk up the mountain is now quieter and a good deal more pleasant. While the old road is a walkway, an easy gradual climb to the top, it is a good deal more satisfying to take the numerous tracks that wind up and around the mountain, though some are uneven and quite steep.

Return to Clive Road and walk down to Mountain Road and turn right. After about 400 metres turn into Withiel Drive and walk down the drive a few metres to a tiny bush reserve on the left, a botanical gem in the heart of the city. For a start, it is extraordinary that this tiny park of less than one hectare even survived given its location. The reserve was part of the garden of Professor Withiel Thomas, biologist, geologist and educationalist at Auckland University. It was gifted to the city by his son in 1948.

Lava forests once covered over 5,000 hectares on the Auckland isthmus but today less than 29 hectares remain, most of it unprotected. The basalt lava landscape is a tough place to grow anything; there is very little soil and plants must survive in pockets of humus built up by leaf fall. In addition, the landscape is very free draining and therefore extremely dry. Despite this, plants and animals do thrive. Karaka, pohutukawa, mahoe, puriri and titoki all manage to grow to a good size and, more remarkably, there are many delicate ferns that shelter in damp crevices. The trees bring birds such as tui and kereru and 24 species of land snails have been recorded in the nearby Government House gardens.

The lava rock walls common in the inner Auckland suburbs are reminders of where many of the rocks from similar lava forests end up. Once you step off Withiel Avenue into the bush, the first impression is of an incredible jumble of rocks. The short loop walk picks its way through a rocky gully through which tough native trees push their way skyward. The reserve is not marked but the track is easy to find once you are looking for it and the walk only takes about five minutes.

Return back to Mountain Road and turn left and walk about 100 m to Omana Ave on your right and walk to the very end of the no exit street.

Eden Garden was established in 1964 in a former quarry and the gardens are reputed to have the broadest collection of camellias in Australasia, as well as an extensive collection of subtropical vireya rhododendrons, clivias and hibiscus. In addition to the gardens there is a very pleasant café, and ideal end to your outing.

18. Orakei Basin Walkway

 A pleasant stroll around an old volcanic crater

 Easy ~ 45 minutes

 How to get there: Orakei Road, entrance to the car park is 400 metres from Ngapipi Road where there is off-street car parking and toilets

This impressive explosive or maar crater erupted around 85,000 years ago throwing up a broad tuff ring along which Orakei, Kepa and Upland roads now run. Originally a freshwater lake, the 700 metres wide basin became tidal at the end of the last Ice Age when ocean levels rose. The water level is controlled by sluice gates which ensure that the high water levels keep the basin free of mangroves.

An excellent level track, almost three kilometres long, rings the entire basin with an attractive boardwalk along the railway line (constructed in 1925) which cuts off the basin from the Purewa Creek. A bridge over a side creek is a great place to see shags and heron up close as they roost and preen on a huge old tree overhanging the water. White-fronted terns frequent the basin to feed in the shallow water. The trees surrounding the basin are a mixture of natives and exotic trees with most intensive recent plantings of natives.

Can easily be combined with the following walk if the tide is favourable.

19. Hobson Bay Walkway

 Bird haven in sight of the central city

 Easy ~ One hour 45 minutes (tide dependent)

 How to get there: Thomas Bloodworth Park, Shore Road, where there is parking. toilets and a playground. Orakei Station if you come by train.

In direct contrast to the circular Orakei Basin directly across the road, Hobson Bay is a broad, shallow, tidal inlet fed by shallow creeks and lined with mangroves. In 1925, a railway line cut right across the bay and in 1926 Tamaki Drive effectively cut off the bay from the sea, leaving a narrow gap through which the tide flowed. Earlier in 1914, a sewer pipe was opened to dump the city's sewage into the sea (though today, it is where Kelly Tarlton's aquarium stands). All this resulted in the bay silting up, becoming much shallower and allowing mangroves to flourish where they had not grown previously (the pipeline was replaced by an underground tunnel in 2010.)

Located just a short distance from the central city that has brought intense urban development around the bay, Hobson Bay is an important habitat for coastal birds. The shores of the bay are thriving roosting and nesting grounds for the pied shag as well as the feeding ground for various aquatic birds, and a resting place for birds traveling between the Hauraki Gulf and Waitakere Ranges.

The walk around Hobson Bay is a mixed bag but makes for an intriguing view of the inner city. Starting at the Thomas Bloodworth Park the walkway along the eastern shore is a combination of boardwalk, muddy path, chunks of concrete and is best done between mid and low tide (preferably on an outgoing tide) as it is not accessible at high tide. Weaving around small coves, under old trees and below crumbling cliffs, the walkway runs out at the Awatea Reserve where you will need to head up to Awatea Road and then turn right into St Stephens Ave. At the end of the avenue a set of steps drop down past the Parnell Pool to the waterfront. This popular pool was once a simple affair, enclosed by a rock wall and filled by the high tide.

From the pool continue walking east along the waterfront and turn right into Ngapipi Road and past the old boat sheds to a small park where an information board and a short section of the old pipeline tells the fascinating story of Auckland sewage works. Turn right into Orakei Road and over the entrance to Orakei Basin. If you intend to include the Orakei Basin walk, cross over the road at this point.

Here the Hobson Bay Walkway drops down to another boardwalk which transverses a mangrove forest awash at high tide. On Shore Road, the walkway branches off on yet another board walk, past St Kentigern's School and back to the start.

20. Kepa Bush Reserve

 The largest bush reserve on the Auckland Isthmus

 Easy ~ 40 mins

 How to get there: The main entrance is off Kepa Road between numbers 251 and 253 which leads to a very pleasant grassed picnic area with tables. Another entrance is off Colenso Place. You can also park at the Eastridge Shopping Centre.

A little over 13 hectares, Kepa Bush is the largest bush remnant on the Auckland isthmus and runs from Kepa Road to Pourewa Creek. Most of the forest is regenerating, but there are some mature examples of pohutukawa, taraire and kohekohe. In recent years weed clearance and predator control have ensures that many native species are now recovering, including the native tree fuchsia (a favourite food of possums), though the recovery is hampered by the lack of large trees nearby.

Established as a reserve in 1962 when the Auckland City Council acquired the land from St John's College, Kepa Bush has an excellent network of well signed posted tracks with only the occasional muddy patch. Several lookout points give views over the bush and towards the city.

21. Dingle Dell Reserve

 An oasis of secluded bush gullies

 Easy ~ One hour

 How to get there: There a number of entrances, the main one is off Dingle Street where there is parking on the road, a large picnic area, toilets and good signage at the start of several tracks.

Although established as a reserve as early as 1880, it wasn't until the 1930s that native tree planting began (most of the mature bush on the Auckland isthmus had been cleared in pre-European times.) Today this small reserve of just nine hectares is a pleasant bush oasis in suburban St

Heliers. Bisected by a number of streams, the deep wooded gullies are dense with fern and nikau while on drier slopes totara, miro kahikatea, rimu, kohekohe and tanekaha all flourish – it is very easy to feel hidden away here. Despite the distance from other reserves, tui, piwakawaka and riroriro have made a home here.

There is a mix of easy walking paths covering 5.5km through native bush with views of the sea, harbour and Mt Victoria and North Head.

22. St Johns Bush

 Beautiful native trees and bush with a stream and a mighty Kauri tree

 Easy ~ 30 minutes

 How to get there: The main entrance is on the corner of Ripon Crescent and Worcester Road, St Johns.

This tiny five-hectare reserve in suburban St John's is a surprising bush remnant containing around 160 native plants. The bush on a steep hillside was originally set aside by the first Bishop of New Zealand, George Selwyn and his wife Sarah, with the aid of landscaper, Henry Appleyard. Together they set about restoring the bush as well as planting exotic trees on the margins. Some of the oaks in the reserve are over 170 years old.

After years of benign neglect when the reserve became overrun with invasive weeds, today St John's Bush is a much loved, quiet oasis containing some very large puriri and pohutukawa trees which, in this forest location, are drawn up to the light and grow as tall forest trees rather than their usual spreading habit. One kauri tree is estimated to be 150 years old. Even kaka make their way to this reserve on their journey from reserves on Tiritiri Matangi and along the coast to the bushy gullies of the Waitakere Ranges.

What makes this reserve especially attractive is the excellent signage throughout, not only identifying native trees, but drawing attention to native insects such as weta and the giant native centipede.

23. Waiatarua Reserve

 Auckland's largest urban wetland and home to both water and bush birds.

 Easy ~ One hour

 How to get there: Main entrance is on Grand Drive near the intersection with Abbotts Way where there is parking and toilets.

Covering 20 hectares in the heart of urban Auckland, the large wetland that makes up most of the reserve has had a difficult history. Created by a lava flow 9,000 years ago from nearby Mt Wellington, the area was originally the only freshwater lake on the Auckland isthmus. It was known to Maori as Waiatarua and in European times, St John's Lake. A hair-brained scheme in 1929 saw a tunnel dug under Remuera which drained the entire lake into the Orakei Basin, a disaster for both the basin which became clogged with silt, and the lake which completely disappeared.

In recent years, considerable effort by both the council and local action groups has made significant progress in restoring the wetland, if not the original lake. Today the reserve – the largest urban wetland restoration project in the country – is a mixture of native and exotic trees on the fringes with wide swathes of mown grass and in the centre of the reserve, a wetland. Recent changes to the storm water control in the area has allowed the wetland to expand and new plantings of native trees and shrubs are much more sympathetic to the environment.

Today, wildlife is gradually making a comeback here. Tui, riroriro and piwakawaka frequent the bushy margins, while duck and black shag find a happy home in the dense rushes and grasses of the swamp. The native butterfly, the Red Admiral, can also be spotted flitting about the bush margins while the still waters are home to the native short-finned and long-finned eels.

The easy flat loop walk around the park will take about one hour. It is also a dog-friendly walk.

24. Tahuna Torea Nature Reserve

 Native birds thrive in this combination of bush and sand spit.

 Easy ~ One hour return

 How to get there: The main entrance is at the end of West Tamaki Road, Glendowie

Hugging the estuary of the Tamaki River, the 25 hectare the Tahuna Torea Nature Reserve is a reserve of two distinct parts. The first area by the car park is a mix of coastal vegetation, tidal creeks, lagoons and saltmarsh, and is home to a wide range of birds including ducks, shags and pukeko. The bush track behind the wetland is well worth a detour. With excellent plant identification signs and the trees still relatively small, it is easy to get a close look at the leaves and flowers, something more difficult with mature trees.

In complete contrast, the other part of the reserve is a long tidal spit of sand and shell jutting far out into the Tamaki Estuary, the preserve of wading birds such as stilts, godwits and oystercatchers.

Initially the walk is a combination of track and boardwalk, providing easy dry walking at any tide. However, most of the spit is underwater at high tide, so if you want to walk this section check the tides, with the walk best planned on an outgoing tide. If the tide is low you can cut directly from the car park to the spit, but you'll need good footwear as the tidal flats are muddy and littered with sharp oyster shells.

25. Tamaki River Walk from Roberta Reserve to Panmure via Point England Reserve.

 A coastal walk that can be easily combined with the Tahuna Torea Reserve

 Easy ~ Two hours

 How to get there: Roberta Reserve entrance is on the corner of Roberta Avenue and Riddell Road, Glendowie, while Panmure access is at the eastern end of Kings Road

Although just 15 kilometres long, the Tamaki River extends from the Hauraki Gulf deep into the heart of the Auckland isthmus where it is just two kilometres from the Manukau Harbour to the west. The river has four main arms, Otahuhu, Otara, Pakuranga and Middlemore creeks which are all very tidal and characterised by narrow muddy channels lined with mangroves. On the other hand, the mouth of the river is very wide with sand banks, small shelly beaches and high crumbling cliffs.

Industrial development and urbanisation have heavily compromised the natural environment of the river, but a greater awareness of conservation is gradually making an impact with significant sections being gradually replanted in native trees and shrubs. The waterway is home to a surprising number of birds and aquatic life. The Tamaki Path is a walking and cycleway that connects Ngati Otara Park in Otara with Tahuna Torea Reserve in Glendowie.

Beginning at Roberta Reserve in Glendowie, the walkway passes through the Tahuna Torea and Wai O Taiki Nature reserves before reaching the huge Point England Reserve with its wide expanse of sports fields. From there the path continues passing through three more reserves all with their own character: Riverside, Dunkirk and Mt Wellington War Memorial Park. Along the way, there is no shortage of playgrounds, picnic spots and toilets, and once you reach the Panmure Yachting and Boat Club it is a short stroll along Kings Road to the Panmure Shopping Centre. Unlike its busy counterpart on the eastern shore of the river, this walk attracts far fewer people and yet it is just as appealing.

26. Mt Wellington/Maungarei

 Bulky, big and with impressive views

 Medium ~ 45 minutes

 How to get there: Parking and toilets on Mountain Road, opposite Monaco Place, Panmure

Bulky and tall at 135m, Maungarei is one of Auckland's most distinctive volcanoes and also one of the youngest - erupting just 10,000 years ago (only Rangitoto is more recent.) Occupied by Ngati Paoa, the mountain top became a formidable pa in the 17th century, supporting a population of around 2000, and today substantial terracing remains on the eastern side. Marred by extensive quarrying, much of the cone's lava fields have disappeared and the southern slopes have been completely been sheared off and are now steep cliffs. In 1963 a large water reservoir was built into the crater to supply the rapidly expanding suburbs and is still in use today. More recently most of the old exotic trees have been removed so now the mountain looks very bare, as the native seedlings planted to replace the big old trees will take years to flourish.

Despite this, the mountain is a magnificent place to visit and it is a surprisingly easy walk to the top especially now that cars no longer can drive to the summit. A rough but not difficult track winds around the deep central crater and as expected the views are superb. The old quarry prevents walking around the base, but the summit is far more interesting walking.

This is an excellent companion walk to the Panmure Basin walk as the two volcanic craters couldn't be more different and they are only a 15 minute walk apart.

27. Panmure Basin Walkway

 A tidal lagoon in a volcanic crater

 Easy ~ 45 minutes

How to get there: There are numerous entry points to the crater but the Panmure Domain at the end of Cleary Road is the easiest.

Although highly urbanised, the walk around the Panmure crater is an ideal family outing as it is completely flat with picnic areas, a playground, toilets, good parking and only takes about 45 minutes. It is a good walk to combine with nearby Maungarei/Mt Wellington

Erupting 28,000 years ago, the circular Panmure Basin is an excellent example of a maar volcano, an explosive volcano that produced ash rather than lava. Originally a freshwater lake, the ash ring around the volcano has eroded away and as the climate warmed and the oceans rose, the crater filled with sea water to create the tidal lagoon we see today. Recently discovered and hidden under a thick layer of mud is a small scoria cone from a later eruption. Both shags and whiteface heron roost and breed here.

This is a great walk with young children as there are plenty of places to park around the crater, toilets and several children's playgrounds.

28. Highbrook Park and Pukewairiki Crater

 The river, ponds, gardens and an ancient crater

 Easy ~ 30 minutes

 How to get there: Take the Highbrook exit off the Southern Motorway and head east along Highbrook Drive. The entrance to the park is off to the left by the river, but pay attention as it is easy to miss.

Highbrook Park is a large park hugging the river terraces of the Tamaki River and Otara Creek along the Waiouru Peninsula. The park is basically split into two by busy Highbrook Drive, though there is a pedestrian crossing for easy access between the two sections. Along the Tamaki River, the park is narrower, with a path that twists and turns following the river and passing deep ponds enclosed by native plants and home to aquatic birds, expertly landscaped by the international designer Peter Walker.

Across the river, the area where Panama Road reaches the water, is a wide tongue of old lava flow from another volcano. A small scoria crater, McLennan Hills volcano was just 45 metres high before it was quarried away until it completely disappeared.

The Otara Creek section is more open and encompasses the Pukewairiki crater. One of Auckland's oldest volcanos, Pukewairiki erupted around 130,000 years ago and now contains a small mangrove swamp and salt marshes. It is only filled at high tide.

This park attracts very few visitors. The path is largely flat and perfect for both walking and cycling with a family with good parking, toilets and a small playground.

29. Seaside Park

 A quiet hidden park on the banks of the Tamaki River.

 Easy ~ 30 minutes

 How to get there: The very end of Princes Street East, Otahuhu

Just minutes off the frenetic Southern Motorway this quiet park occupies a broad flat peninsula in the Tamaki River and is home to community groups and sports clubs. A pleasant track follows the water, winding through old exotic trees, under planted with coastal native shrubs. Dog friendly and with plenty of space to picnic, fly a kite or throw a ball, the two kilometre path also meanders through a short section of native bush, dominated by salt resistant ngaio with a short track past a small lagoon and down to a side creek.

30. Mt Richmond, Mt Robertson and Old Otahuhu

 Volcanic cones, magnificent old trees and surprising historical monuments

 Easy ~ One and half hours

 How to get there: There are several entrances but the two main entrances are off Great South Road, just north of Portage Road (easy to miss) and off Mt Wellington Highway, near New Brighton Road Otahuhu.

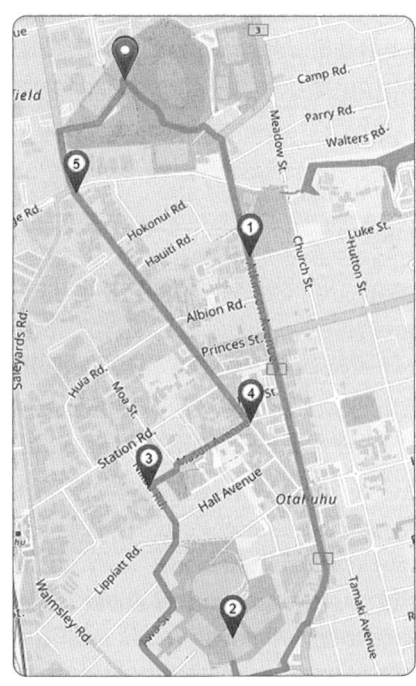

Just north of central Otahuhu is Mt Richmond/Otahuhu, an old

volcanic cone comprised of a complex of craters, lava cones and tuff rings which have been substantially altered over the years. Two separate parts of the old crater are now sports fields and the north western section was quarried over a long period, but it is still well worth a visit.

Of strategic importance to Maori settlers, the hill overlooked the main portage route between the Otahuhu Creek, off the Tamaki River, and the Mangere Inlet on the Manukau Harbour. In the 15th century, the northern chief Tahuhu-nui settled in the area, and it is from this man that Otahuhu takes its name. Terraces, house sites and kumara pits are still clearly visible today.

A great place to explore, a series of rough tracks cross and encircle the rugged cone which rises up to 50 metres and holds a small secondary crater with its own tiny lava dome. Massive old trees dot the slopes including Moreton Bay fig, London plane, Southern magnolias, though unfortunately the beautiful grove of olive trees has been cut down. It is steep in places and it will take around 30 minutes to scramble around the reserve.

Exit the reserve on to Atkinson Ave and head south. Immediately you cross Portage Road, which follows the original Maori portage route, while just to your left is Otahuhu Creek where waka were hauled out of the water. A little further on is the beautiful kept Otahuhu Cemetery with the oldest part furthest from the road.

Continue down Atkinson Ave, through a mixed of commercial and residential buildings to the Methodist Church. Little of the old historic Fencible settlement established by British and Irish soldiers in the 1860s remains, as the area became very industrialised in the early 20th century, but this lovely wooden church built in 1880 somehow survived. A further 100 metres, on a busy intersection, are two of Auckland's most important war memorials.

Most striking of these is the soldier riding a rearing horse set on a high plinth above the rushing traffic. Unveiled on Anzac Day 1928, the bronze statue of a New Zealand mounted rifleman is a tribute to all those who served in the First World War and was gifted by local businessman Alfred Trenwith. Right behind this statue is a much older and simpler memorial, the Nixon Monument. Highly unusual as few monuments survive from this era, this stone obelisk was erected to Marmaduke Nixon and other soldiers who died at the battle of Rangiaowhia in the Waikato during the New Zealand Wars.

Cross the road and walk down into the playing fields of Sturges Park and Mt Robertson. Like Mt Richmond, this small hill is a volcanic cone that erupted around 40,000 years ago. Originally a large maar crater with a high tuff ring and lava dome, a pa name Te Poutu a Raka was established on the high ground. However, over the years the area has been highly modified with very little of the pa remaining and the main crater turned into a sports field.

From Sturges Park continue on to Nikau Road and take a narrow pathway to the right which leads to Mason Ave, past a fine Anglican church constructed of honey coloured Huntly brick in 1928 and on to the main street of Otahuhu, Great South Road. One of Auckland's most diverse communities, this vibrant shopping centre is famous for its eclectic mix of Polynesian, Asian and European shops and eateries.

31. Hamlins Hill Regional Park/Mutukaroa

 A quiet sanctuary of bush and farmland in the heart of industrial Auckland.

 Easy ~ One hour

 How to get there: The entrance, off Great South Road near the intersection with Sylvia Park Road, is easy to miss so get in the left-hand lane early.

Sandwiched between industrial Penrose and urban Otahuhu, and bordered by two very busy roadways, it would be easy to dismiss this small regional park as having little to offer. Covering 48 hectares, the park is a combination of rolling grassy hills and patches of regenerating bush, Hamlins Hill is the largest non-volcanic hill on the Auckland Isthmus. There are traces of a small pa site overlooking the portage between the Tamaki River and the Manukau Harbour and today the park consists of two small section of Auckland's oldest European farms, Hamlin's Farm to the south and Penrose Farm to the north. Remains of an old rock wall and part of a hawthorn hedge are still to be found on the old Penrose Farm and on the slopes of the highest point, Hamlins Hill, are two old Holm oaks (an evergreen Mediterranean species Quercus Ilex), but it is a mystery as to when the oaks were planted or by whom.

Largely farmland, steady replanting of native trees over the last 20 years has seen the gullies and steep land gradually returning to bush. Despite the open nature of the park, predator control has resulted in a surprising number of native birds including fantail, tui, waxeye, paradise ducks and white-faced heron. There are few places in Auckland, let alone in the heart of industrial Penrose, that you can watch a harrier hawk glide effortlessly over grassy fields looking for its next meal. Cattle graze in well managed paddocks and, used to people, they will come very close to have a peek at the visitors.

Two loop tracks, one to the top of the small hill and another through the farmland will take about 30 minutes each. In wet weather, the paddocks can be very muddy and you need to come with wearing your gumboots or waterproof boots.

Hamlins Hill, open to the winds from every direction, is a popular place to fly kites and dogs on a lead are welcome.

32. Old Onehunga

🏔 Onehunga town and around, warts and all
🚶 Easy ~ Three hours

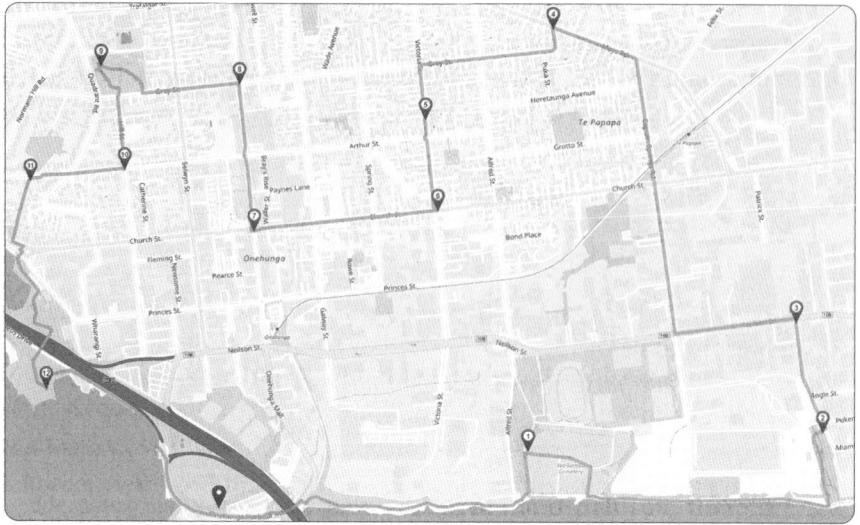

It would be fair to say that this is not the most picturesque walk in Auckland city, but on the other hand it must be one of the most varied outings on the isthmus. An important portage point for Maori, it was from Onehunga that Puhihuia and Ponga eloped over the Manukau to Awhitu, and from where Puhihuia's female relatives set out to bring her back home.

During the nineteenth century, Onehunga was Auckland's main port but it was eventually eclipsed by Waitemata Harbour's ability to handle larger ships. An expanding industrial based maintained Onehunga's economy well into the 20th century and along with neighbouring Penrose is still one of Auckland's important commercial hubs.

Begin this walk at the Orpheus Reserve on the restored Onehunga foreshore where there is plenty of parking and toilets. It is hard to believe that Onehunga was once a popular beach resort with a direct tramline attracting weekend crowds to the sandy shores. However, the rise of industry, while vital to the local economy, resulted in heavily polluted water, killing off both the sea life and the visitor trade. The construction of the South Western motorway severed Onehunga's connection to the sea, but recently both the lagoon area and the waterfront along the Manukau Harbour have been considerably improved and while not pristine, now attract visitors to the cycle paths, walkways and the extensive children's playground.

Walk south along the seafront to the port (the path runs right along a busy road at one point.) Coastal shipping came to an end here in 2016 and today the port is home to a small fishing fleet and a storage area for containers. There are plans to redevelop the area to include more housing. Right across the road from the wharfs is one of Auckland's oldest pubs, established in 1865 as the Manukau Hotel. Now renovated, the old double fireplaces and fine kauri floors were uncovered and restored. Decorated in an appropriate nautical theme, the bar features historic photos of old Onehunga including other local hotels long gone.

Tearing yourself away from the pub, continue under the motorway to the Manukau Foreshore Walk which follows the tidal Mangere Inlet almost as far as Otahuhu. Detour around the Waikaraka cemetery opened in 1890 and the burial place of Prime Minister David Lange. The volcanic stone walls for the cemetery and adjoining Waikaraka Park were built in the 1930s as a work scheme for the unemployed.

At Miami Parade detour away from the foreshore into the heart of industrial Onehunga. Miami Parade must be one of Auckland's most misnamed streets as this is the least attractive section of this stroll. At Neilson Street turn left and head towards Captain Springs Road. At 275 Neilson Street is the former factory of the Onehunga Woollen Mills built in 1886 and famous for producing fine quality blankets and travel rugs. At Captain Springs Road detour to the left and visit the Auckland Potters Studio at number 96. This long-established studio has a display of pottery as well as items for sale.

Walk up Captain Springs Road to Grotto Street and detour to Hochstetter Pond between numbers 26 and 40. Although it looks like a crater it is in fact a collapsed lava lake from the Mt Smart eruption which was mined for diatomaceous earth with the foundations of the mining operation are still visible. The 'pond' forms a small but deep depression surrounded by loose rocks and is being gradually cleared of weeds and replanted in native shrubs. This tiny wetland is home to the rare wetland sedge Carex subdola.

While today the housing in this area is decidedly modest, these high slopes with expansive views over the harbour attracted two brothers, William and Thomas Kemp who built extensively in the area including two very fine villas at 16 Mays Road and 177 Grey Street. From here walk down Victoria Street towards Church Street, passing the only surviving Fencible cottage at number 111. Built in 1847, this is one of Auckland's oldest surviving buildings and this tiny house once accommodated two families. Turn right into Church Street which true to its name features the local landmark of the Church of Our Lady of the Assumption (1889, spire added 1903).

Onehunga Mall (originally Queen Street), the town's main street, defies description and is an eclectic mix of budget businesses, a large outlet centre, local shops and smart cafes that accurately reflects the varied demographics of modern Auckland. At the lower end of town, the old Carnegie library (built 1912) is now a gastro pub, while further up the street at number 303, Scotlands, the fine Victorian house of Dr William Scott is now a Thai restaurant.

Continue up Onehunga Mall and turn left into Grey Street and Jellicoe Park. Originally known at the Green Hill Reserve, the park features the only surviving blockhouse, once part of a string of such fortifications designed to protect the city by an attack by Maori in the 1860s. That attack never came and in the end it was the British who moved south to begin the war in the Waikato. A careful inspection of the brick walls on the south side of the building reveals a single vertical brick at regular spaces in the exterior walls. These were originally the loopholes from which the muskets were fired. Two other buildings also on the Onehunga site are Laishley House, built in 1856 and originally situated at 44 Princes Street, Onehunga, along with a replica Fencible House, built in 1959. In 1921 the park was renamed after the then Governor General Viscount

John Jellicoe.

From the park, head downhill to Arthur Street and back over the motorway to Orpheus Reserve.

33. Cornwall Park and One Tree Hill Domain/ Maungakiekie

 Outstanding pa site, spectacular trees, superb views and a small farm in the middle of the city

 Easy ~ Perimeter walk: One hour 30 minutes

Inner loop: One hour

 How to get there: The main entrance to the park is off Green Lane West, Greenlane.

Justifiably one of Auckland's most popular attractions, these two adjacent parks not only attract visitors to the superb views from the summit (182 m), but also as a place to picnic and enjoy the company of the farm animals.

An extinct volcano with a substantial and distinctive crater, Maungakiekie (mountain of the kiekie, a native vine related to the tropical pandanus), was home to a substantial Maori population supported by the rich volcanic soil. Abandoned as a pa around 1750, the terraces, kumara pits and house sites on the higher slopes of the hill are clearly visible.

One Tree Hill was part of a parcel of land acquired by the Crown in 1847 as a Domain and in 1901 John Logan Campbell gifted to Auckland the adjoining land to the north which is now known as Cornwall Park. Campbell is buried on the summit next to the obelisk and today both parks cover 220 hectares.

The tree after which One Tree Hill is named has itself had a turbulent past. Originally a totara tree, 'Te Totara i Ahua', stood on the summit. It was cut down in the nineteenth century – though at this point the story becomes murky. One version goes that the tree was cut down by a settler for firewood; however, according to two other sources, the totara had already disappeared and it was a pohutukawa that was cut down.

Yet another variation of the same story says that the tree was cut down by a drunken European in an act of sheer vandalism; while yet another version says that the tree was cut down by workmen protesting the lack of food rations.

John Logan Campbell tried to replace the native tree on the summit, using pines as a shelterbelt; but while the native trees failed to take hold, two of the pine trees flourished. One of the pair was cut down in 1960 with no fuss, leaving just the single tree to match the name. It was this lone tree that was attacked by a Maori activist in 1994. The tree was later removed by the Auckland City Council because it was unstable. It wasn't until 2016, that a small grove of pohutukawa and totara were finally planted on the summit with the expectation that one tree will eventually become dominant.

Cornwall Park is noted for its mature trees including the avenue of oaks and the olive grove situated above the picturesque cricket ground. Acacia Cottage, Auckland's oldest surviving building, was moved to the park in 1920. Built in 1841, it was originally situated in Shortland Street in the city where it was occupied by John Logan Campbell and his business partner, William Brown. Now restored, the house contains period furniture, and is open to the public.

Operating as a working farm, the parks are the ideal place to get up close and personal with the cattle and sheep which, used to the presence of people, are calm and quiet and will allow you to get very close. Spring is a particularly popular time to visit to see the new-born lambs.

The park is laced with paths. Being both gardens and farmland, it is open and impossible to get lost. The inner loop which follows the road and takes in the steep climb to the summit will take an hour and a quarter and this is the best viewpoint for visitors to grasp the complex geography of Auckland city as both harbours are clearly visible. Far fewer people tackle the more basic tracks around the perimeter, though runners find the cross-country paths appealing. Most visitors do not realise that the actual main entrance to Cornwall Park is on Manukau Road just to the north of Alexandra Park, easily recognised by the enormous fountain and statue of John Logan Campbell. Beyond the statue, a long drive lined with magnificent puriri trees leads to Greenlane and the entrance to the park proper. The perimeter walk begins either to left or the right over stiles and will take about one and a quarter hours.

34. Big King, The Three Kings

 Last peak standing with a fascinating geological history

 Easy ~ 30 minutes

 How to get there: Duke Street, Three Kings, just off Mt Eden Road where there is off street parking and excellent information

Erupting around 28,000 years ago, the Three Kings/Te Tatua-o-Riukiuta volcanic field was once a miniature representation of volcanic activity in the Auckland area. The three largest cones were High King (135 metres), Big King (133 metres) and East King (120 metres.) Located between Mt Albert Road and Landscape Road, the largest marr crater on the Auckland isthmus was 200 metres deep and 800 metres wide and contained more than 10 small scoria cones. The eruption resulted in huge lava flows running north-west for three kilometres and lava caves can still be found underground today.

Extensive quarrying has all but obliterated the volcanic landscape and today just Big King is left and even that has a large water tank on the summit. Not a large park and maybe not worth a long trip to visit, it is nevertheless a lovely place for a stroll if you are in the area.

35. Old Mt Albert

 Surprising architecture, a streamside stroll and outstanding views

 Moderate ~ One hour

 How to get there: Corner of Mt Albert Road and New North Road, Mt Albert

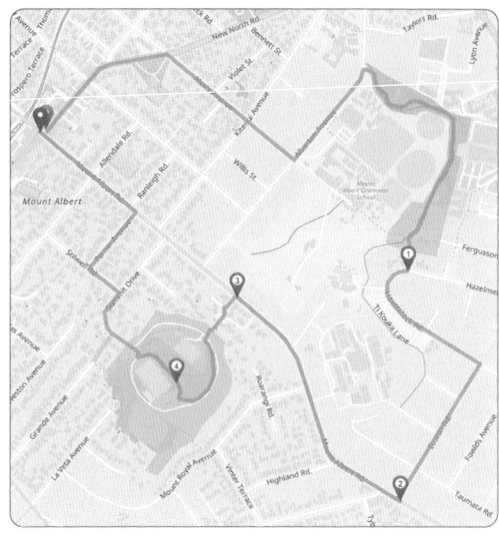

Centred on the volcanic cone of Mount Albert/Owairaka, the rich soils attracted early Maori settlers and in the nineteenth century, the area became a very fashionable as a place where wealthy Aucklanders had large country houses, the best known of which is Alberton. In the 1920s and 30s the suburb rapidly developed to accommodate the growing population and was linked by busy tramlines to the central city.

Combining historic streets, Meola Creek and the mountain itself, this walk provides plenty of variety.

Beginning at the Mt Albert railway station, walk north along New North Road passing striking Art Deco buildings at 866, 858 and 826 New North Road. On the corner of Alexis Avenue is Ferndale House dating from 1865 and typical of the Victorian country houses that still exist in the area, often tucked in behind newer houses. Directly opposite Alexis Ave is the historic Methodist Church, the heart of which, recognised by the vertical wall cladding, was built in 1866. Turn right into Alexis Avenue lined with numerous examples of the Californian Bungalow, very popular in the 1920s and particularly prevalent in Mt Albert.

At Alberton Ave turn left past Mt Albert Grammar School, opened in

1922. The façade is decorated with numerous examples of bound bundle of sticks motif indicating strength through unity. The school still has a small farm, a reminder that this was a rural area when the school was built.

About 300 metres down Alberton Ave, the Roy Clements Treeway begins to the right.

Skirting Meola Creek, the Roy Clement Treeway is mostly raised boardwalk over marshy ground behind Mt Albert Grammar School. Native plants such as kahikatea, cabbage trees and flax flourish in the damp ground, despite the highly urban nature of the immediate area. The Three Kings Aquifer, part of the larger Greater Western Springs Aquifer bubbles up in a small wetland along the treeway. Groundwater percolates over many years through the volcanic rock from the Three Kings area, running into Meola Creek as very clear, clean fresh water. The spring is to the left of the boardwalk going south and is signposted. The creek itself begins at the base of nearby Mt Albert/ Owairaka and was once an overgrown weedy wasteland until the 1990s when local teacher Roy Clements initiated a project to clean and replant one kilometre of the creek. While not pristine, both the creek and the surrounding area have improved enormously.

The southern end of the walkway is Kerr Taylor Park and from here it is a bit of detour to get back on to Mt Albert Road. From the park turn right into Haverstock Road and follow the road around to Euston Road, turn right and walk 500m to Mt Albert Road. Again, turning right walk past the Mt Albert Research Centre for Food and Plant Research, a seven storey building constructed in the 1970s to house the DSIR (The Department of Science and Industrial Research.)

A little further on 100 Mt Albert Road is Alberton, one of Auckland's best-known historic houses. With fine views north over the city, the house was built in 1863 at the heart of a 500 acre country estate for the Kerr-Taylor family and is now open to the public.

Continue west along Mt Albert Road to Toroa Terrace and turn left to walk up the mountain via a steep but short path to the road the encircles the top of the mountain.

Erupting over 30,000 years ago, this was one of the largest volcanic cones in the Auckland area, but extensive quarrying has reduced the mountain to half its original size. It was on this maunga that Wairaka and her followers settled after she left the Whakatane area to avoid an arranged marriage. It was Wairaka who broke the tapu on women paddling waka and saved the waka Mataatua from being swept out to sea, an action reflected in the name Whakatane "to act like a man".

Now car free, the mountain has fantastic views in every direction over the city. The archery field is not the crater, but an old quarry. From the mountain stroll down Summit Drive to Mt Albert Road and back to the shopping centre which appears odd as only one side of the street has old buildings. The side of New North Road alongside the railway line was once a small shunting yard with a branch line up to the mountain to a quarry.

The Waikowahi Walkway

The broad Manukau Harbour with its narrow entrance to the Tasman Sea is a huge tidal basin 20 kilometres wide with a particularly wild and dangerous bar at the mouth. In contrast to the low lying land that characterises most of the Manukau shoreline, the coast to the north is surprisingly rugged. While still very tidal, high unstable cliffs of mud and sandstone and steep gullies have restricted development. In several places, local councils very early on created reserves on the coast. While these reserves were commonly planted with exotic trees, native trees were also preserved particularly in the gullies and today large pohutukawa and puriri are common all along this coastline. In more recent years, restoration projects replanting native trees and shrubs have considerably enhanced the shoreline reserves.

The Waikowhai Walkway links over a dozen parks and reserves stretching 10 kilometres west from the Onehunga foreshore and there are long term plans to extend the walkway right out to the Manukau Head. However, significant proportions of this walkway rely on access at low tide where access is via muddy bays or over slippery, shell-encrusted rocks so both good balance and strong shoes are a necessity. The links between the parks, especially important at mid to high tide can be found online.

The following series of short walks are the highlights along the coast and avoid any areas made difficult by tides or tricky coastal conditions. These can be combined into longer walks to suit.

36. Hillsborough Cemetery and Grannys Bay

 Sea, bush and a fascinating old cemetery

 Moderate ~ 50 minutes

 How to get there: Taylors Bay, Frederick Street, Hillsborough.

There are numerous entries to this loop walk, but this description starts from Taylors Bay where there is parking, toilets and picnic areas. Even better, all the uphill walking is done first.

Walk along a bay reserve for about 100m metres to a set of steps up to Frederick St where you will cross the road and take the path into the Belfast Reserve. Initially the walking is easy, through pleasant bush and along a small street, but gradually the climb becomes steeper with a number of short flights of steps up to Hillsborough Cemetery, which opened in 1916 to service an ever-expanding city. At the cemetery wend your way up through the graves to the top at Hillsborough Road where there are great views over Onehunga, the Mangere Inlet, Mangere Mountain and South Auckland with the Hunua Ranges in the far distance. From the top, walk down Clifton Road to the end and take the track marked Grannys Bay. After walking five minutes the track splits and here take the path to the right down to Grannys Bay. Reaching the water's edge take the track to the left along the coast with views through ancient pohutukawa down to the water. Eventually the track emerges on to Bagley Street where it is a short walk via Hoskins Ave and Frederick Street and back to the start.

37. Waikowhai Park, Hillsborough

 Established in 1914, this loop walk combines bush, beach and native birds

 Medium ~ Captains Bush Loop: 45 minutes return

Waikowhai Bay: 30 minutes return

 How to get there: The park is on Waikowhai Road, well signposted off Hillsborough Road.

Waikowhai Park, established in 1914, lies at the heart of the 10-kilometre Waikowhai coastal walkway and takes its name from the many kowhai trees that grow along the coast.

The park is the best starting point for two short loop walks. The first walk is an easy stroll to the east through Captains Bush down to Wesley Bay, a pleasant combination of bush and beach. While there are a number of old kowhai, the dominant tree here is kohekohe, a tree of tropical original with large bright green leaves. At low tide you can walk along the water's edge to the lower carpark and back up the road. Keep a sharp eye out for fossilised crabs along the rocky shore at Wesley Bay.

The second walk to the west is shorter and drops down to the sea at Waikowhai Bay, with longer options to Cape Horn and Wattle Bay. While the tracks are in very good condition, there are several steep sections with many steps.

There are two car parks, one down by the sea at Faulkner Bay and the main car park further up the hill. Parking is limited by the sea where there is a lovely picnic area, but no toilets. The tracks begin up the hill where there is good parking, toilets, a playground and very sturdy picnic tables.

Leigh Harbour Walkway - NORTH #5

Historic Northcote Point Walk - NORTH #38

Oakley Creek Walk - CITY #8

Panmure Basin Walk - CITY #27   *Credit: Jonathan Pierce*

Old Onehunga Walk - CITY #32

All Saints Anglican Church on the Old Howick Walk - EAST #3

Tawhitokino Regional Park - EAST #11

SS Wairarapa Graves, Whangapoua Beach - ISLANDS #1

Tiritiri Matangi Island Loop Walk - ISLANDS #12

Awhitu Regional Park - SOUTH #20

Hunua Falls - SOUTH #21

Wairoa Loop Walk - SOUTH #23

Rimmer Road Beach Walk - WEST #3

Muriwai Gannets - WEST #5

Bethells Beach - WEST #9

38. Cape Horn Lookout

 Lovely vista from atop high cliffs

 Easy ~ 30 minutes

 How to get there: The track is clearly marked for the lookout on Cape Horn Road, off Hillsborough Road. Parking on the road is very limited near the lookout, more parking 50 metres further along at the end of the road

True to its name, Cape Horn Lookout is situation on a high dramatic bluff that offers marvellous vistas to the south and west. These cliffs, composed of Waitemata sandstone with bands of siltstone, were once part of the seabed. The view is partially obscured by old pine trees which, like other exotics in these coastal parks such as gum and wattle, are either being removed or are dying out, gradually being replaced by native trees.

39. Manukau Domain

 Expansive westerly views from high above the Manukau

 Easy ~ 45 minutes return

 How to get there: The Domain is on Halsey Drive near the intersection of Godwit Place.

From a high grassy park there are fabulous views over the Manukau Harbour, out to the heads and in the distance, the Awhitu peninsula. Located on the lookout point is the sculpture Open Stone by Japanese artist, Hiroaki Ueda, erected in 1972. From the lookout two walks drop down through the domain to the coast, the shortest one is steep with many steps while the longer track is easier and leads down to Wattle Bay, a deep inlet off the harbour with a small wetland and surrounded by lush regenerating bush. There is a small picnic area at Wattle Bay.

40. Gittos Domain

 Hidden bays on the north shore of Manukau Harbour

 Medium ~ 40 minutes return

 How to get there: Gills Crescent, Blockhouse Bay. Street parking only which is busy weekdays as it is next to a school.

Set aside as a reserve in the early twentieth century, the Gittos Domain has a network of short tracks though mainly regenerating bush, but closer to the water are several very impressive pohutukawa and puriri trees. A track meanders down the slope to the optimistically named Sandy Bay and on to Flounder Bay. Some of the paths are partly sealed and treacherously slippery when wet.

41. Blockhouse Bay Beach Reserve to Green Bay Beach Reserve

 A peaceful stroll through lovely native bush with views over the harbour

 Easy ~ One hour return

 How to get there: At the end of Endeavour Street, Blockhouse Bay where there is a small carpark and steps down to the shore. There is also street parking at the end of Blockhouse Bay Road.

Blockhouse Bay Beach Reserve was set aside as a park in 1870 and today a coastal walkway known as Te Ara O Tiriwa, The Pathway of Tiriwa, wends its way through mixed bush that includes huge pohutukawa, puriri and kowhai.

From the beach climb the short path up to Taunton Terrace where the track is clearly marked off to the left. The path follows the line of cliffs - there are endless glimpses of the harbour through the trees - with a short side track down to a tiny rocky beach. Like all the walks along this coast, the track is in excellent condition, but it is undulating with several hilly sections that include steep flights of steps. Very good tree identification signage makes this walk especially enjoyable.

After reaching the small beach at Green Bay return via Taunton Terrace from where there are even better views over the Manukau. Good swimming at Blockhouse Bay and Green Bay at high tide, though in recent years there have been some issues with the water quality at Green Bay.

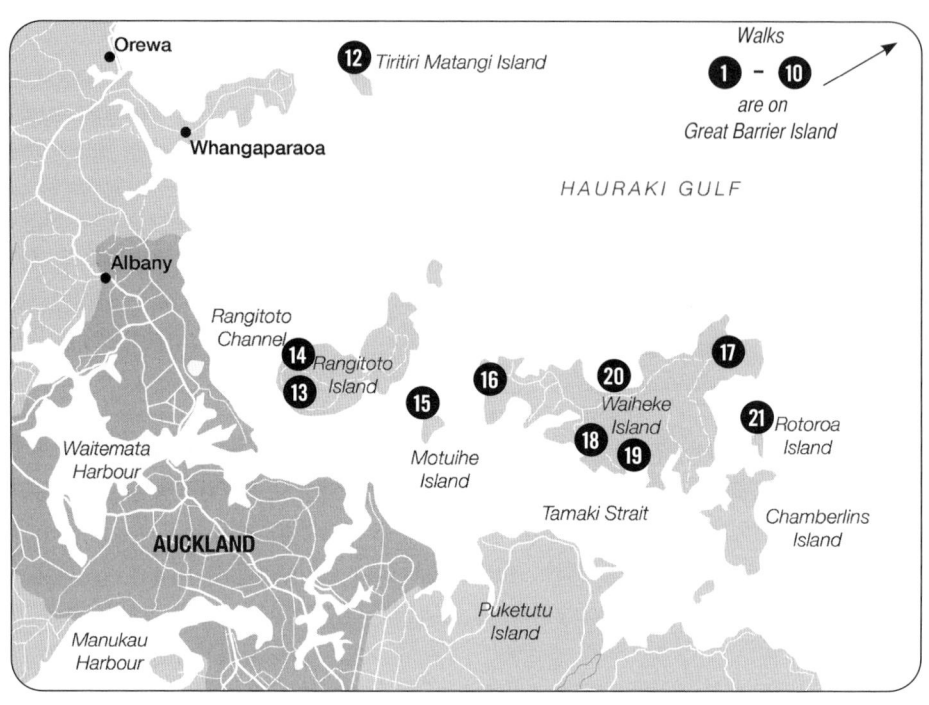

ISLANDS

1. SS Wairarapa Graves, Whangapoua Beach
2. Warren's Creek Track
3. Old Lady Track Lookout
4. Windy Canyon Track
5. Haratonga Coastal Loop Track and Beach
6. Kaitoke Hot Springs
7. Te Ahumata Track
8. Station Rock Lookout
9. Dolphin Bay Track
10. Whaler's Lookout and Johnson's Bay Walk
11. Copper Mine Walk, Kawau
12. Tiritiri Matangi Loop Walks
13. McKenzie Bay and Lighthouse
14. Rangitoto Summit
15. Motuihe Island Loop Walk
16. Matietie Historic Reserve Walk
17. Stony Batter
18. Cascades Loop Walks
19. Pa and Rua Tracks Loop walk
20. Little Oneroa to Palm Beach Coastal Walk
21. Rotoroa Island Loop Walk

Hauraki Gulf

Lying to the north and east of Auckland, the Hauraki Gulf contains over 50 islands, though many are little more than rocky outcrops. Easy access by sea meant that the islands were readily settled by both Maori and Pakeha resulting in substantial human impact on the environment of all the islands. Exceptions are the rugged Little Barrier Island, which was set aside as a wildlife reserve in 1895, and Rangitoto which was impossible to farm or cultivate. However, in recent years the important conservation role of islands has led to several islands playing a vital role in the preservation of native flora and fauna. The gulf also has five marine reserves. This section includes walks on the islands of Great Barrier, Kawau, Tiritiri Matangi, Waiheke, Motuihi, Rangitoto, and Rotoroa.

Great Barrier Island

Lying 100km to the northeast of Auckland, Great Barrier Island/Aotea is the largest island in the Hauraki Gulf. When sea travel was more common, the island was readily accessible and has a long history of Maori and Pakeha occupation. No untouched wilderness, having been ruthlessly stripped of its timber, today 60 percent of the island is conservation land. Having never had goats, stoats, deer, hedgehogs or possums, the island is a stronghold of several rare birds including the kaka, brown ducks and New Zealand dotterels. Kaka in particular are very common all over the island.

Tradition holds that the discovery of this island gave this country the name Aotearoa, 'land of the long white cloud'. Kupe's wife on the Aotea waka, after the long journey from their Pacific homeland in Hawaiki, saw a long cloud on the horizon and cried out 'He ao, he ao', 'a cloud, a cloud.' From her call, Kupe named the island Aotea. Later when the mainland was discovered, the name was extended to Aotearoa. Curiously Maori never had a single name for the entire country, and Aotearoa referred to the northern part of Te Ika A Maui (the North Island.) When Europeans arrived, they used the old Dutch name New Zealand, but many people sought a distinctive local name. During the nineteenth century Maoriland was widely used, but was gradually overtaken by Aotearoa so today that name is accepted as the Maori name for the entire country.

There is both air and ferry services to the island and for up-to-date information visit www.greatbarrier.co.nz

1. SS Wairarapa Graves, Whangapoua Beach

 Lonely graves on a lovely beach

 40 minutes return ~ Easy

 How to get there: On Mabey Road, 10km from Aotea Road at Okiwi. The road is mainly gravel.

Just a few minutes after midnight on October 29th 1894, in dense fog and darkness, the SS Wairarapa carrying 235 passengers and crew slammed into the rocks at Miners Head. In the darkness and confusion more than 120 people died, of which a number were buried on the island. There is something still deeply sad and melancholic about these graves. It is uncertain how many are buried here and there is no usual list of names, so presumably no one knows just who these lost souls are. Possibly there is some consolation that they lied buried in such a beautiful spot.

Whangapoua is a magnificent long sweep of untouched beach sheltered by Arid Island not far to the east. A brightly painted sign by the local Okiwi School ask visitors to share the beach and stay below the high tide. In spring and summer you will certainly see the endangered New Zealand Dotterel scurrying along the beach warning you off their flimsy nest just above the high water mark. Open and exposed, there is little shade here, apart from a handful of pohutukawa trees near the graves.

Well-marked from the car park, the walk is flat and easy.

2. Warren's Creek Track

 A pretty waterfall trickles down into a wide pool

 To the Waterfall: easy, 40 minutes return

Loop Walk: easy, one hour return

Port Fitzroy Store: easy, one hour 15 minutes one way

 How to get there: The entrance is opposite Akapoua Bay Camping Ground on the Aotea Road, just beyond Port Fitzroy

Following Warren's Creek upstream, the track is mostly flat all the way, though it does cross the stream several times so come prepared for a bit of rock hopping or getting your feet wet. When you arrive at the first swimming hole, the track to the waterfall skirts along the rocks for another 70 metres on the left-hand side of the creek. Here, a narrow stream of water drops 15 metres down a rock face into a perfect circular pool. The pool is not obvious at first and you need to scramble up a small rock face taking care to get a good footing and a firm grip on the tree roots.

From the waterfall you can continue up the steps and return to the road via the Bridle Track where you will emerge about 300 metres from the start. From this point you can also continue along the Bridle Track which reaches Aotea Road directly opposite the Port Fitzroy Store. Of course, you can also start the walk from the store.

3. Old Lady Track Lookout

 A wide panorama over Rarohara Bay and Port Fitzroy Harbour

 45 minutes return ~ Hard

 How to get there: Glenfern Road, Off Aotea Road, Port Fitzroy

No one is sure how this track acquired its name, but it is either a joke or named after one very tough old lady. From the road the track drops down and crosses a small stream and from here it is all uphill to the rock at the top. Just past the creek, the track climbs up several flights of stairs and after a few hundred metres branches off to the left. It is a steady rather than steep climb, but it is a trudge, and right at the end there is a rocky scrabble to the top.

Directly below is the tiny settlement of Port Fitzroy and beyond is a magnificent vista directly down Rarohara Bay to Port Fitzroy beyond. Return the way you can and if you are in the mood for a longer walk, the main track runs more or less parallel to the road finally emerging from the bush at Karaka Bay Road where you will need to walk 2.5km back to the start if you haven't organised transport. This section of the walk will take a further 50 minutes.

4. Windy Canyon Track

 A rugged volcanic canyon high on Mt Hobson with great views

 Medium ~ 30 minutes return

 How to get there: The walk is clearly signposted from the summit of Whangapoua Hill on Aotea Road. Parking is opposite the entrance to the walk

The rugged outcrops of Windy Canyon are testament to the volcanic origins of Mt Hobson/Hirakimata, as the track picks its way through a dramatic canyon. Keep an eye out for the glass-like obsidian embedded in the rocky breccia walls and the Great Barrier tea-tree and daisy, both found only on the island. The views from the top are fantastic and true to its name it is very windy up here (if you spot my cap in the bush below, I would like it back).

A popular short walk, the track is in excellent condition and starts off through attractive bush. While there are lots of steps, they are only right towards the end with plenty of spots to take a breather. The top is crowned by a large rocky outcrop and if this looks a bit daunting to climb at the base of the rock to the left in a very narrow track to the top which is much easier.

The hike to the top of the mountain is more demanding and takes five to six hours return.

5. Haratonga Coastal Loop Track and Beach

 Coastal bush, an old pa site and a stunning small beach

 Medium ~ One hour return

 How to get there: Begins at the Haratonga Camping Ground, at the end of Harataonga Road, 2km from the Aotea Road, north of Claris. The last section from the road down to the camp is narrow and bumpy.

This track begins at the lovely Harataonga Camping Ground with markers through the camp clearly indicating the start of the Harataonga Coastal Walkway. Walking through regenerating bush, the easy walk initially follows the coastal walkway and then veers off to the right. Now the track follows a coastal ridge towards the sea, with some steep but not difficult sections. Once reaching a high point with coastal views, the track then climbs again to an old pa site with extensive vistas north and south along the coast and to Arid Island just offshore.

From this high point the track drops steeply, and you will have to hang on to the fence to maintain your footing, finally emerging through a small gate, not far from the camping ground. If you want to go directly to the beach turn to the left and follow a clear track through the paddock to a stile. Over the stile you will need to wade through a shallow stream to the beach (there is no way of keeping your feet dry.) Alternatively, you can loop back through the camping ground, cross over the bridge and go to the beach that way which will take another five minutes, but your will have dry feet.

Haratonga beach is not large but is just gorgeous, protected from rough weather by several small offshore islands and only accessible on foot.

6. Kaitoke Hot Springs

 Water from a natural hot spring mingle with the cooler Kaitoke Stream.

 Easy ~ 2 hours return

 How to get there: The track begins on the right on Whangaparapara Road four kilometres from the intersection of the main north/south road.

One of the most popular destinations of the island, natural hot spring wells up from subterranean depths to mingle with the cooler waters of the Kaitoke Stream.

Dead flat, this easy track initially follows a small shallow stream through handsome bush and then skirts the huge Kaitoke swamp, the largest wetland on the island and home to the elusive fernbird and enigmatic bitten. Boardwalks cross sections of the wetland and then enters more typical Barrier bush dominated by large manuka.

The springs themselves are along a shallow section of the Kaitoke Stream where it is joined by a small side creek. The water is not deep, frequently murky and often crowded; the experience is more enjoyable away from the main holiday period. Along both the main stream and the side creek are numerous small pools that can accommodate two or three people. There is a toilet, but no changing rooms.

Just uphill from the pools, via a long flight of steps is a lookout over the swamp in one direction and in the other, the jagged volcanic peaks around Mt Hobson.

7. Te Ahumata Track

 Not as hard as it looks, high bluffs in the heart of an old gold field afford fantastic views.

 Medium ~ Two hours return

 How to get there: Entrances off both Whangaparapara and Blind Bay Roads.

From a distance the tall bluffs of Te Ahumata (398m) looks like a daunting hike, but in reality, the excellent track is a steady, rather than steep climb and well within the reach of anyone of moderate fitness.

Te Ahumata was once the centre of bustling gold fields that operated here from the 1890s through to the 1930s. On the Whangaparapara Road are the concrete foundations of a stamper battery, all that remains of the gold town of Oroville that sprang up here in 1900. On Blind Bay Road is a short walk (10 minutes) to the main entrance of the Iona Mine which worked for just four years from 1902 to 1906.

Starting from the saddle on the Whangaparapara Road, the track begins on an easy grade through regenerating bush. After 30 minutes the track to the summit veers off to the right and the next 400m is much rougher, though not difficult and the track then improves with a steady climb to the summit with just a few short steeper sections. From this junction the vegetation is merely waist height, kept naturally short and well-trimmed by wind and the shallow soil and allowing endless views in all directions.

At top a maze of narrow tracks wind around the summit crowned by a telecommunications tower. A short track leads to a lookout point with a wonderful panorama over Medlands Beach.

8. Station Rock Lookout

 Marvellous views of the southern part of the island

 Easy ~ 30 minutes return.

 How to get there: On the summit of the road between Medlands Beach and Gooseberry Flat. The entrance to the track is easy to miss but it right as the summit of the road.

As this track begins right on the summit of the rock, you have already done the hard climbing in the car so why not take the advantage and do this short walk to a marvellous viewpoint. The track begins through lovely bush and is flat at first but then starts to climb (including a series of short steps), finally emerging through a small grove of tall hebes to the lookout. Panoramic views to the north encompass vistas over Medlands Beach and beyond to Kaitoki Beach and to the south over Tryphena Harbour and in the distance Coromandel Peninsula.

9. Dolphin Bay Track

 Bush fringed bay encloses a boulder beach with startlingly clear water

 Medium ~ Two hours return

 How to get there: From Shoal Bay, turn into Cape Barrier Road. The track is 1.5km on the right. The road is both sealed and gravel, parking is limited

Don't be put off by the notice board stating 'tramping track' at the start of this walk. In reality this is an excellent track, well-marked and the steeper sections made easier by steps. The first section of the walk winds up and down a long ridge, through tall manuka with just the occasional glimpse of the sea both north and south. After about 30 minutes the track passes through a wonderful grove of ancient pohutukawa trees and nikau palms. From here the track drops down to the left, winding down through bush to the sea.

Dolphin Bay is a beautiful small bay, only accessible by foot and fringed by trees. To the south looms the Coromandel Peninsula and just offshore is Motu Tohora island. Overhead kaka swoop and chatter noisily in the trees. The water is beautifully clear, and although the shore is covered in smooth boulders, the rocks are not sharp, so it is not difficult to go swimming.

Now for the bad news: it is all uphill back to the ridge track, but there are no very steep sections, so take your time, it's not that difficult.

10. Whaler's Lookout and Johnson's Bay Walk

 Coastal and Coromandel views from Cape Barrier

 Medium ~ 50 minutes return

 How to get there: From Shoal Bay, near Tryphena, take Cape Barrier Road to the end (around 5km).

Whaling conjures up an image of nineteenth century sailing ships hunting whales from flimsy rowing boats, so it comes as a surprise that this whaling station operated in the 1950s, finally ceasing operations in 1962. The whalers targeted mainly humpback whales which migrated north between May and July and then south again during September and October. Once a whale was spotted the lookout alerted the whaling station in the bay below.

The walk begins steeply downhill to Johnson's Bay, a picturesque boulder beach with views to Coromandel Peninsula and beyond. Just offshore is tiny Motu Tohora (Whale Island.) From the bay the track climbs steadily uphill to a headland, open to the elements and with glorious views east to Te Pani Island, south over Coromandel and beyond to the Hunua Ranges. Take a breather on the sturdy seat boldly engraved with "Whalers Lookout." If you are lucky you might just spot a Brydes whale, a species which permanently live in the Hauraki Gulf.

The road to the track is narrow, winding and mostly gravel. Take your time. At the end a large sign advises "Recommended for 4WD only" and although the road beyond is narrow and a bit rough, it is comfortably managed by the average car. The second sign states, "Stop Private Road" and here there is a small carpark on the right. Barrier folk are super sensitive about privacy and if you wander on to private property don't expect a friendly reception. From the carpark, walk down the road for 150 metres to the beginning of the track. The track is in good condition, but there are steep sections with stairs.

Kawau Island

The original house on Kawau Island was built in 1845 for the manager of the nearby copper mine. In 1862 George Grey (Premier of New Zealand 1877–79) purchased Kawau Island for 3,500 pounds, and over the years greatly expanded the house, planted exotic trees, and stocked the island with an array of animals including monkeys, zebras, kookaburras and wallabies. Many of the trees remain, and there is still a colony of kookaburras on the mainland. The Parma wallaby from Australia is now extinct in that country, and wallabies from Kawau (where they are a pest) have been shipped home.

11. Copper Mine Walk

  Easy ~ One and half hours return

  How to get there: Kawau Cruises, Sandspit Wharf, End of Sandspit Road, Sandspit, www.kawaucruises.co.nz, 0800 111 616, Ph (09) 425 8006.
There is a fee for the car park near the wharf.

From the wharf at Mansion Bay take the Coach Road directly behind the Mansion House. This wide track is also a 4WD road, leading through tall old pine trees with an understorey of manuka and tree ferns and it is along this road you are likely to see both wallabies and weka. Several side-tracks are closed due to the danger of toppling trees and breaking branches.

Copper mining began on the island as early as 1844 with the mine shafts going deep under the sea below the engine room. Today all that remains is part of the engine room with its impressive 20-metre brick chimney and several mine shafts. One of the shafts is accessible for about thirty metres with the entrance streaked with the vivid green of oxidised copper. Another low tunnel cuts through the bluff (watch your head), from where you can clamber along the rocky shore to Dispute Cove, perfect for a picnic on the grass under shady trees.

From Dispute Cove follow the track to the lookout point where it rejoins the Coach Road back to the Mansion House. If you are keen on a swim, the best options are Miners Bay near the copper mine or Ladies Bay a short distance from the wharf.

The Mansion House has variable hours, so you need to check that the house is open if you intend viewing the interior. The 10.30am sailing is also the Mail Boat Cruise which calls at other stops before arriving at Mansion House. When boarding the sailing double check the time the ferry arrives at Mansion House as you will need two hours to comfortably walk to the copper mine and back.

Tiritiri Matangi Island

For those familiar with New Zealand's native bush, the one thing most noticeable on arriving at Tiritiri Matangi is the sound of birds. Most of our native forest has been silenced by the voracious appetite of introduced predators, but here the bush is alive with sound: chattering kakariki, raucous tui, melodic korimako, noisy tieke and the whistles of hihi. Not only is the bush alive with bird call, but everywhere birds flit and swoop, many of which were on the edge of extinction a mere few decades ago.

Tiritiri Matangi Island is both an inspirational conservation story and the country's most accessible bird sanctuary.

Maori legend has it that Tiritiri Matangi island, like all the other islands of the Hauraki Gulf, is one of the floats of a huge fishing net and the name of the island very appropriately means 'tossed by the wind.' The main pa on the island was known by the same name.

Both Maori and European settlers reduced the island natural bush cover to just a few coastal and gully remnants on this small, relatively flat island of only 230 hectares. The bird population was decimated and even the hardy puriri was reduced to just two mature trees. When the island returned to crown management in 1970, it was assumed that the bush would naturally generate from the surviving trees, but the dense grass and bracken prevented any significant comeback for the plants.

In a bold move the Department of Conservation embarked on a programme not only to replant the island, but also to develop it as an open sanctuary with easy access for the public. Equally importantly it was decided to involve the public in tree planting, particularly school children, in the massive operation to plant over a quarter of a million trees between 1984 and 1994. The result has been an overwhelming success and led, not only to a haven for endangered birds, but also to this island being used as a model for many other such reserves around the country.

Once the predators were removed and some cover established, recovery of birdlife was spectacular and over 70 species of bird have been sighted on the island of which 11 were relocated here. The birds include takahe, hihi, little spotted kiwi, pateke, kokako, tieke, korimako and kakariki, many of which are now very common on the island, especially around the bird-feeding stations. The bird feeding stations are critical to the survival of a substantial bird population as the island lacks enough mature trees to provide a food source all year round. Many of the bird populations quickly reached their maximum for the island and now Tiritiri is a major source of birds for relocation elsewhere. Tuatara have also been reintroduced to the island and are breeding slowly.

There is no food available on the island, though cold drinks and small gifts are for sale from a shop below the lighthouse. Toilet facilities are available in several places. Bunkhouse accommodation is available and bookings are through the Department of Conservation: **www.doc.govt.nz/tiritiribunkhouse.**

For first time visitors the guided tour led by Supporters of Tiritiri Matangi is an excellent introduction to the island. Bookings are essential Ph 09 307 8005.

360 DISCOVERY runs ferries to the island from downtown Auckland and Gulf Harbour; Sailings are such that you will need to plan to spend the best part of a day on the island. Winter and summer sailings may vary. Phone 09 307 8005 **www.360discovery.co.nz.**

As the number of visitors per day are strictly controlled, it pays to plan ahead especially in summer.

12. Island Loop Walks

 New Zealand's most accessible bird sanctuary, preserving some of the country's most endangered species.

 Island Loop Walk: Easy, three hours

Lighthouse Loop Walk: Easy one hour

Tiritiri Matangi has a maze of excellent walking tracks of varying length. The walk from the wharf to the lighthouse will take about 50 minutes return while a walk around the island can take up to 3 hours. The island terrain is rolling, and none of the tracks are difficult. At various points small shallow ponds have been created for the shy and endangered pateke. You are most likely to see the rare takahe near the historic lighthouse. Although not native to the island, this predator-free habitat is a haven for this endangered species and takahe are now not the slightest bit afraid of people, to the point that they will steal any unguarded food.

The oldest surviving puriri, as well as a massive pohutukawa estimated to be 800 to 1000 years old, are located on the Kawerau track. The Wattle and Kawerau tracks have excellent tree identification signage for those needing to brush up on their tree identification. One tree not found on Tiritiri is kauri as there is no evidence that kauri ever grew on the island

Most people confine their visit to the southern part of the island which has more bush and birds, but the north and east has spectacular views and is more open with birds flitting above the low vegetation. Along the east coast are dramatic cliffs, peppered with sea caves and beautiful coves overhung with ancient pohutukawa. The limited number of people on the island at one time ensures that Tiritiri is never overrun with visitors.

Sandy Hobbs Bay, a five-minute walk from the wharf, is the best swimming beach, though North East Bay is more sheltered and is good at high tide.

Rangitoto Island

How to get there: Fullers runs a regular ferry to the island from downtown Auckland, some with a stop in Devonport. Winter and summer timetables vary so check the website. (**www.fullers.co.nz**, phone 09 367 9111)

Take care not to miss your ferry back as there is no overnight accommodation on the island and alternative transport to the mainland is expensive.

Despite appearing at a distance to be entirely bush covered, Rangitoto has an impressive volcanic landscape ranging from broad swathes of raw lava to mature forest. There is some uncertainty just when Rangitoto first exploded out of the sea, but the last eruption on the lower slopes was around 600 years ago and large areas of the island are still barren lava. The rock here is mainly a'a lava, which is formed by a crust of cooling lava solidifying over still liquid lava beneath which then breaks the surface into jagged blocks. It is very difficult to walk across the broken lava fields on Rangitoto.

The full name of Rangitoto is Te Rangi i totongia a Tamatekapua, 'the day that the blood of Tamatekapua was shed'. This refers to a battle around 1350 in which the crews of the waka Te Arawa and Tainui clashed on the island and Tamatekapua, the captain of the Te Arawa, lost the fight and presumably was injured.

The loose volcanic rock is slowly being colonised by the toughest of plants including pohutukawa, griselinia and astelia. The forest cover on Rangitoto is dominated by just a few species, and the most abundant, pohutukawa is forming the largest forest of this species in New Zealand. Adapted to withstand salt-laden winds, dry soil and harsh sun, pohutukawa easily handles the island's tough environment. Although there are a few places where mature pohutukawa grow up to 20 metres high, most trees are small and often quite stunted. A peculiarity of Rangitoto is that pohutukawa and northern rata freely hybridise and most of the pohutukawa on the island are in fact hybrids. The nectar of the tree is a vital food source for tui and also provides a much sought-after honey for apiarists.

While the terrain is exceedingly free draining making it difficult for most plants, Rangitoto does receive a good rainfall and the low trees and shrubs are festooned with lichens and mosses. Another oddity of the island is that the moss Racomitrium lanuginosum, usually found growing high in the mountains, grows at sea level on Rangitoto.

Contrary to expectations the densest forest is around the summit and is more typical of New Zealand's lush bush and includes some very large trees. It is here you are likely to encounter tui and tieke, the latter bird introduced to the island. The island does not attract many forest birds as it lacks fresh water and a continual food source, but one bird you will find all over the island is the friendly piwakawaka.

Although little altered by Maori and Europeans, Rangitoto flora and fauna suffered tremendously with the introduction of rats, possums, cats, stoats and even wallaby. After a huge pest clearing campaign, both Rangitoto and Motutapu were declared pest free in 2011. Since then native birds such as takehe, kiwi and tieke have been reintroduced to the islands and some birds including korimako and kakariki have made their own way over from Tiritiri Matangi not far to the north.

While forest birds are scarce, sea birds abound. The rocky shore is perfect habitat for the blue penguin, the world's smallest penguin, while along the shoreline near the wharf is New Zealand's largest colony of native black-backed gulls.

Most visitors arriving on the ferry head straight for the summit so if you have time it is a more pleasant and quiet walk to head for Islington or McKenzie Bay first, walk up to the summit from there and then come down the main track. There is a small sand/rock beach at McKenzie Bay where you can swim and swimming off the wharf is great, though not when the ferry is arriving.

Unlike most tracks in New Zealand, mud is unheard of on Rangitoto, but the loose scoria gravel can be very slippery especially when walking down hill, so visitors need shoes with a good tread. For those less mobile or short on time, there is also the option of the 'road train', the Volcanic Explorer Tour run by Fullers which goes to the summit and McKenzie Bay.

While there are toilet facilities at the wharf, on the summit and at McKenzie Bay, there is no café, food or water and you must bring (and take back) everything you are going to need, including sun block and a hat in summer.

13. McKenzie Bay and Lighthouse

 A historic lighthouse sits just off Rangitoto's only sandy beach.

 Easy ~ Two hours return

 How to get there: The McKenzie Bay Track leaves from the wharf

From the wharf the coastal track leads through raw lava fields and pohutukawa forest to Rangitoto's only sandy beach. The concrete lighthouse was first built in 1882, but it took over 20 years to sort out a dispute between the Auckland Harbour Board and the Marine Department before the lighthouse finally began operation in 1905. The track passes several of Rangitoto's famous baches (small holiday houses.) In the 1920s and '30s Aucklanders built baches on public land at Rangitoto Wharf, Islington Bay and McKenzie Bay. Most have now been removed, but around 30 baches have been kept as examples of the innovative do-it-yourself beach culture of the period.

14. Rangitoto Summit

 A magnificent vista not only of the island but also of the entire Hauraki Gulf, Waitemata Harbour and Auckland city.

 Medium ~ Two hours return

 How to get there: The Summit Track begins from the wharf

The walk to the summit (259 metres) is a steady climb on a well-formed path and leads to a magnificent view over Auckland and the Hauraki Gulf. A side track just below the summit (20 minutes return) leads to extensive lava caves, some collapsed and some intact. It is not difficult to scramble through the caves and, while possible without a torch, it is a more pleasant experience with one.

While you can return the way you came, there are two other return routes. One is to the west via McKenzie Bay, the island's only sandy beach, and then back along the coast to the wharf. The other is via Islington Bay which is very close to Motutapu Island. Both will take around 1½ hours so make sure you time the ferry return correctly.

Near the wharf are two short walks, one through a small kowhai grove and the other through a glen of kidney fern, an extraordinary plant that has perfectly adapted to Rangitoto's hot dry climate.

Motuihe Island

Devastated by the arrival of humans, the native flora and fauna on Motuihe was reduced to tiny bush remnants and only the very toughest birds survived. Extensively farmed and at one time a prisoner of war camp, navy base and quarantine station, the island has made a remarkable recovery. Volunteers have planted 350,000 native plants and while most of the vegetation is only a few metres tall, 80 per cent of the island now has bush cover. With the removal of predators, the little spotted kiwi, kakariki, tieke and tuatara have all been reintroduced to the island and are flourishing.

Motuihe is a popular destination for Auckland boaties, mainly attracted by the island's two beaches, one facing north and the other south which means that one beach will always be sheltered from the wind. The beaches are good swimming in all tides but best mid to high tide.

On the island there is basic camping, toilets and information and in the summer a small kiosk selling a simple range of food and drinks.

Transport to Motuihe has been erratic over the years with a ferry service off and on. Check the Fullers website first to see if a regular ferry is running. The alternative is water taxis or charter, both of which can be expensive depending on numbers.

15. Motuihe Loop Walk

🚶 Easy -- Two and half hours

The island divides into two halves with the beaches in the middle and in total covers 179 ha with the highest point just 63 metres. The southern part of the island is the longer walk and this will take you through the regenerating bush and past small bays. It is here that you will see most birds. The northern part of the island focuses on the human history as this is the location of the settlement and the quarantine station. The entire circuit will take no more than two and half hours on good tracks. The signage is a bit erratic, though it doesn't matter too much as you won't get lost.

Waiheke Island

No one knows where the name Waiheke, 'cascading water' originated. Some say it's a joke – no rivers or waterfalls remotely qualify. Others say a surveyor asked a local Maori the name of the island, but the man thought he was asking the name of the stream by which they were standing. Taimoana Turoa, in Te Takoto o te Whenua o Hauraki, says when the chief Kahumatamomoe came ashore from the waka Te Arawa, he desperately needed to urinate – take your pick.

While Waiheke is the gulf's second largest island, it was intensely farmed and urbanised so today very little bush remains, though development has been largely confined to the western side of the island.

With the numerous wineries on the island, along with its pretty beaches and the proximity to downtown Auckland, Waiheke has gone from a bucolic island culture to a bustling tourist destination with cafes, restaurants, accommodation and good transport.

Fullers run a ferry to the island (**www.fullers.co.nz**, phone 09 367 9111) just 30 minutes from downtown Auckland with some ferries stopping at Devonport. From the wharf there is an excellent bus service around the western side of the island include a "Hop-on, Hop-off" bus.

16. Matietie Historic Reserve Walk

 Coastal views of Auckland and the Gulf, old pa sites and a close-up peek at some rather amazing houses.

 Loop walk via Cable Bay: Medium 1 hour 10 minutes

Loop walk via Owhanake Bay: Medium two hours

 How to get there: The walk begins and ends from Matiatia, the main Waiheke wharf. The start of the walk is via the shoreline beyond the Matietie Reserve sign to the left of the car park.

Ideal for those who are going to Waiheke for the day on the ferry and do not want to venture too far afield on the island, the walk follows the coast around to Cable Bay and then returns inland to Matiatia. The walk begins to the north of the car park by the wharf; if the tide is right in, the first part of the walk is a scramble over rocks and tree roots for about 100 metres. This is by far the most difficult part of the track. From the small bay just beyond the wharf the walk then follows the markers around the coast. Here the track winds its way through open grass, and links rocky headlands with small gravel beaches easily accessed by short side-tracks. The wide views include downtown Auckland and the islands of the inner Gulf: Rangitoto, Motutapu, Motuihe, The Noises, Tiritiri Matangi and, in the far distance, Little Barrier. As an extra bonus, this track passes close to some of Waiheke's most expensive houses and parts of the walk are like strolling through the pages of a design magazine.

On the headland the terraces of an old pa site are clearly visible (in pre-European times Waiheke was home to around 1,000 Maori), and old pohutukawa cling to rocky cliffs.

At Cable Bay, easily identified by the triangular cable sign, turn right uphill until you hit the road, then turn left and continue down the road to the track which leads off to the right just past the locked road gate. This takes you back to Matiatia. For those wanting a longer walk, from Cable Bay continue along the steep track uphill and on to Owhanake Bay, then turn inland where the track takes you back to the road leading to the wharf. This longer walk will take about two hours.

17. Stony Batter

 Excellent views of the Hauraki Gulf from this extensive and well preserved Second World War fortification.

 Easy ~ 45 minutes return

 How to get there: At the end of Stonybatter Road off Man o'War Road on the eastern side of the island, 25km from the ferry terminal.

One of the most impressive remains of New Zealand's coastal defence system, this complex was begun in 1942 to protect the northern approaches to Auckland from the Japanese. However, the batter was not completed until 1948, well after the war was over, and the guns were never fired in defence. While very little exists above ground, the underground rooms are largely intact and surprisingly fresh in appearance. Closed for safety reasons in 2017, the underground installations are currently closed.

From the end of the public road, the walk is along a gravel farm track with the red tinge of the road hinting at the area's geological origins. Passing olive groves, grape vines, and small patches of coastal bush, the track winds past open paddocks with distinctive rock formations, and the open and lofty location gives excellent views over the Gulf.

Reaching the batter, most visitors do the short loop walk, missing out on the spectacular 360 views from the ridge just above the track. Instead of walking to the left, hop over the stile to the right and walk the short distance up hill on the track to Opopo Bay to take in spectacular views of the whole island and the gulf. Walk along the ridge for 100 metres and drop back down to the road and then do the loop walk in reverse.

Few visitors give much thought to the distinctive rock formations that give the hill its name. Waiheke Island is primarily composed of greywacke sandstone, but the fluted shaped boulders are of andesitic breccia and the only remnants of two ancient volcanoes that erupted over eight million years ago. During that period, Waiheke was part of a wider volcanic field that included the present-day Coromandel Peninsula and Great Barrier Island which were all connected by dry land.

If you are up for a much longer walk, two tracks, one north to Hooks Bay and the other south to Opopo lead to small gravel beaches and will add an extra hour to the walk.

There is no public transport to the reserve, though rental cars and bikes are available at Matiatia Wharf. However, if you are cycling you need to be fit as is it a long and very hilly bike ride with the last 7km gravel road.

Whakanewha Regional Park

Located on the southern side of the island, this small regional park of 270 hectares was opened in 2007 and preserves an area of mature and regenerating bush, including fine stands of kohekohe and taraire, two trees that prefer the warmer northern climate. Located on a large tidal bay, swimming is best at high tide.

How to get there: On Gordons Road, off O'Brien Road, Rocky Bay. The walks are described from the Sculpture carpark which is by the beach with a large picnic area, toilets and information.

18. Cascades Loop Walks

 Nikau groves, attractive bush stream and great views

 Cascades via Nikau and Central Tracks: Easy, One hour

 Park Walk, via the Cascades, the Tarata and Kowhai Tracks and Dotties Lane: Easy One hour 45 minutes.

These walks start directly over the road from the carpark and while the walk is uphill, the slope is very gentle with a few steps towards the end. Aptly named, the Nikau track passes through a series of magnificent groves of nikau palms ranging from seedlings to trees five or six metres high. The regenerating bush is predominately manuka, with larger trees on the higher slopes. The Nikau Track joins the wide Central track and just a few metres to the left, another track leads to the Cascades. This loop walk will take around 15 minutes and follows a modest stream (best after rain) down a series of small falls and rocky pools.

Returning to the Central Track you now have two options. You can return to the carpark via the Central Track which will take around 30 minutes. Otherwise retrace your steps back down the Nikau Track for a few hundred metres to the junction of the Tarata track which you will have passed earlier. Take the Tarata Track to the right which follows the hillside with the best bush in the park and great views over the bay and to downtown Auckland.

Eventually the Tarata Track meets the Kowhai Track on the left which in turn leads downhill to Gordons Road. At this point cross the road and walk a short distance down the access road opposite until you meet Dotties Lane, which will lead you back to the carpark. Dotties Lane (named after the endangered New Zealand Dotterel), was specifically developed to pass through low coastal vegetation, taking walkers away from the beach, and thereby leaving the low dunes and tidal margins to rare wading birds. The sculpture of a dotterel guardian by the carpark is a collaborative work between local artists and Waiheke High School students.

19. Pa and Rua Tracks Loop Walk

 An old pa site, a gentle coastal walk and fine old pohutukawa

 Easy ~ 25 minutes

From the car park, walk along the wide grassy picnic area to the headland and scramble around the rocky point (can be tricky right on high tide) to the camping ground. Walk through the camping ground hanging to the left where the Pa Loop Track enters the bush. From here it is a modest uphill walk, past several gnarled old pohutukawa to the pa site, though very little evidence remains.

At this point the Pa Loop Track meets the Rua Loop Track which leads straight ahead past a series of old kumara pits. Originally much larger and covered, the precious kumara crop would have been stored within the protective palisades of the pa. Continue along the track to the lookout point where the track then drops steeply down to the carpark.

20. Little Oneroa to Palm Beach Coastal Walk

 Five small bays, coastal bush and amazing views

 Medium ~ One and half hours

 How to get there: Little Oneroa Beach, Goodwin Ave, off Oceanview Road, 3km from the Matiatia Wharf.

Encompassing five of Waiheke's most attractive small bays and several reserves, this is very much a local walk. The signage is sparse, and visitors will need a good map and frequently check their location to avoid getting lost. While there are steep sections, lots of steps and paths are uneven in places, this is a great walk to discover a lesser known corner of this island.

Beginning at Little Oneroa, the track quickly climbs up from the beach and dips up and down along above the shore with great views over the Oneroa Bay. After about 10 minute the track leads off at right angles and it is easy to miss, but don't worry, you can then turn right at Newton Road and be back on track. Beyond Newton Road, the track continues and drops down some steep stairs to Fishermans Rock. You cannot get around the rocks to Hekerua Bay from this point so if this detour appeals, you will have to return to Newton Road.

From the end of Newton Road, turn left into Queen's Drive where after 200 metres there is a clearly marked track on the left down to Hekerua Bay. Only accessible on foot, Hekerua Bay is a small, sheltered gravel beach ideal for swimming. Drop down to the beach and walk for about 20 metres where the track is to the right and goes over a headland with fantastic views and down to tiny Sandy Bay. Do not walk up the Te Aroha Ave Track; it is steep and takes you in completely the wrong direction.

From Sandy Bay walk along Great Barrier Road to Enclosure Bay which as the name suggests is almost enclosed by rocky outcrops and is perfect for swimming. Now walk up Empire Avenue, which although not marked, is the narrow gravel road directly opposite the bay. At the end of Empire Ave are five tall pou, painted strikingly in black and marking the entrance to McKenzie Reserve. A local initiative, this hillside has only recently been replanted in native trees and shrubs and at its heart is a unique semi-circular seating arrangement along with detailed information about the reserve.

Continue uphill to Great Barrier Road and walk up to Coromandel Road where you will turn left. The next intersection is Hauraki Road where you will turn left again and walk a few hundred metres to Cory Road where a marked path drops down to Little Palm Beach, a clothing optional bay. Walk along this bay, over a low rocky point to Palm Beach, named after the large phoenix palms at the far end.

Palm Beach is a glorious small sandy bay, considered by many to be the best on the island. If you don't fancy walking back along the road, the good news is that a regular bus service will take you back to Little Oneroa beach or to Matiatia wharf.

Rotoroa Island

How to get there: 360 DISCOVERY runs ferries to the island from downtown Auckland stopping at Waiheke Island (Orapiu) and Rotoroa on the way to Coromandel. Sailings are such that you will need to plan to spend the best part of a day on the island. Winter and summer sailings may vary. Phone 09 307 8005 **www.360discovery.co.nz**.

Purchased by the Salvation Army in 1908, for over 100 years Rotoroa was an alcohol and drug rehabilitation centre for men (the women were on nearby Pakatoa Island.) Intensely farmed and developed, very little of the island's native vegetation survived with the exception of a few large pohutukawa clinging tenuously to the cliffs. Rotoroa Island today is a very different place, a precious wildlife sanctuary run by the Rotoroa Island Trust together with the Auckland Zoo and the Department of Conservation.

Over half of the island has been replanted with more than 400,000 native plants. Although most are just a few metres high, common and rare native birds are making a comeback in this predator-free environment.

Weka are everywhere, roaming the lawns around the administration buildings or on the beach feeding on sandhoppers; it is one bird that survived the earlier bush clearances. Tieke, kiwi and a pair of takehe have been reintroduced to Rotoroa and a small gannet colony is being encouraged. New Zealand dotterel nest on the beaches, though they need some protection from the weka. There are not too many places in New Zealand that visitors can get up close to a pair of takehe out feeding with their chick. In particular, the kiwi programme has been very successful, so much so that birds from Rotoroa are now being rehomed in other predator-free locations. In addition, a number of special ponds have been created for the shy, nocturnal pateke.

Once rare on Rotoroa, the shore skinks rapidly recovered once rats were eradicated.

While there are toilets, picnic areas, water, hostel and holiday home accommodation, there is neither a shop nor a café so you need to bring anything you want for a day out.

21. Rotoroa Loop Walk

 A new wildlife sanctuary in the Hauraki Gulf

 Easy ~ Two hours

Two hours is plenty of time to cover the entire island on both the north and south walking circuits from where there are endless panoramic views over the gulf, the long, rugged hills of the Coromandel Peninsula and nearby Ponui and Waiheke islands. Several beaches are ideal for swimming, the best of which are Ladies Bay and Mens Bay – neither are far from the wharf.

The takehe are likely to be seen around the information centre, but all the birds are easy to see as the vegetation is mostly no more than a few metres high

An excellent information centre tells the history of the island when it was an alcoholic and drug treatment refuge.

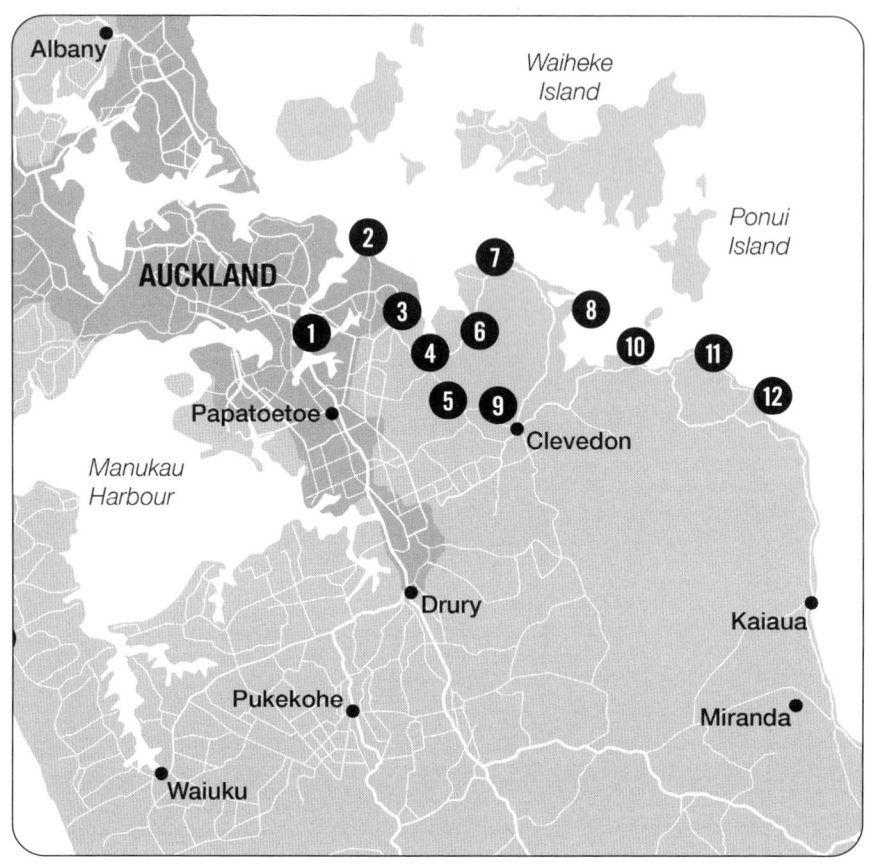

EAST

1. Rotary Walkway, Panmure Basin to Pigeon Mountain/Ohuiarangi
2. Musick Point Reserve/Te Naupata
3. Old Howick from Howick Beach to Stockade Hill
4. Mangemangeroa Reserve
5. Point View Reserve
6. Whitford Path/Wade Walkway, Whitford
7. Maraetai Coastal Walkway and Omana Regional Park
8. Duder Regional Park
9. Clevedon Scenic Reserve
10. Waitawa Regional Park
11. Tawhitokino Regional Park
12. Tapapakanga Regional Park

1. Rotary Walkway, Panmure Basin to Pigeon Mountain/Ohuiarangi

 Popular walk along the estuary of the Tamaki river and up to the low peak of Pigeon Mountain

 Easy ~ Two hours one way

 How to get there: Numerous entrances but this walk is described from Kerswill Place off Pakuranga Road near Panmure Bridge

Not the most pristine of waterway and only 15 kilometres long, the Tamaki River snakes deep into the Auckland isthmus. Characterised by deep tidal creeks, this walkway follows the eastern shore of river as it dramatically broadens north of the Panmure basin as it merges into the Hauraki Gulf. While the usual starting point is the Rotary Reserve on Pakuranga Road, opposite the Pakuranga Mall, starting by the Panmure Bridge makes for a much more interesting walk.

The first few hundred metres of the walk feature several information panels detailing the history of the three bridges that spanned the Tamaki River at this point, the first a highly unusual swing span bridge opened in 1865. Prior to the bridge the important Mokoia pa occupied the high ground on the western bank.

Winding along the shore, the broad, mostly concrete pathway offers bucolic vistas of the river as it quickly widens into a broad estuary. At several points information panels draw the walker's attention to seemingly ordinary banks of white crumbly soil, but which illustrate an incredibly violent chapter in Auckland's geological history. Known as ignimbrite, this soil originated from an eruption several hundred thousand years ago in the central North Island, an explosion so powerful that it left a layer of fine pumice so thick that even today it is several metres deep. This enormous cloud of pumice and ash swept across the island at such a speed that it would have taken just 60 minutes to reach Auckland and was so hot that it left a layer of charred vegetation below the ash.

At the Wakaaranga Creek, the walkway follows a tidal inlet, thick with mangroves and home to wading birds, to Pigeon Mountain/Ohuiarangi.

After crossing Prince Regent Drive, the track skits a small restored wetland and enters sports fields. Just 55 m high, the volcano erupted over a long period forming a series of craters most of which are now obscured by urban development and quarrying which began as early as the 1840s. Little also remains of the pa which originally crowned the summit. Somewhat neglected with all the older trees recently cut down, a rough track leads to the top from which there are expansive views over the surrounding suburbs and the Hauraki Gulf. The high ugly fence on top marks the edge of an abandoned quarry with a very steep drop off.

Most of this popular walkway is also a cycleway and while most cyclists are very considerate, always be prepared to move quickly out of the way.

It's a long way back to the beginning and it is best to return along the walkway than to walk along the busy and noisy Pakuranga Road. An alternative is to catch a bus back to Panmure from stops on Pigeon Mountain road or from nearby Highland Park Mall.

2. Musick Point Reserve/Te Naupata

Rugged cliff tops offer fantastic vistas over the gulf

From carpark: Easy, 20 minutes return

Coastal low tide route: Medium, One hour one way

How to get there: Short Walk: From Musick Point Road take the road through the Howick Golf Course to the carpark at the end.

Coastal Walk: From the north end of either Bucklands Beach or Eastern Beach

Long occupied by Ngai Tai, the Te Waiarohia pa covered the very tip of the long peninsula known as Te Naupata. The pa was encircled by a series of defensive trenches that protected the pa from attack from the land and even today these ditches are particularly clear near the end of the point. However, the defences were no match for Ngapuhi invading the Waitemata in 1821 and in the face of an enemy heavily armed with muskets, the pa was abandoned and never reoccupied.

Now known as Musick point, the English name is not a spelling mistake but the surname of pioneer flying boat aviator Captain Edwin Musick. The short track, which is quite rough in places, begins behind Musick Point Air Radio Station and winds around the point with a flight of steps leads down the cliff for those keen on further exploring the rocky shoreline or to access the popular fishing spot on the large flat rock at the base of the cliff. There are excellent view of the inner Gulf islands and especially the volcanic cone of Brown's Island, which lies just offshore.

At mid to low tide is it easy to walk right around the point from either Bucklands or Eastern beaches although you need to have a good sense of balance to negotiate some of the more slippery sections.

The high cliffs are typical of the cliffs that make up much of Auckland's coastline. The soft cliff rock, known as Waitemata Sandstone, frequently breaks away from the cliff face. Here at Musick point the soft rock is a combination of sandstone and mudstone, the layers of which are clearly visible at the shoreline.

3. Old Howick from Howick Beach to Stockade Hill

 Stroll through history at one of Auckland's oldest Fencible settlements

 Easy ~ 40 minutes

 How to get there: Howick Beach, end of Selwyn Road

Long settled by Maori descendants of the Tainui waka, the European settlement began when the ship Minerva arrived at Owairoa (Howick Beach) on November 15th, 1847. The ship carried retired English soldiers, known as Fencibles, who were given land in exchange for light military duties, in this case to protect the Auckland settlement from Waikato tribes. Local Maori built simple huts by the beach until more substantial accommodation was built. Once a distant and separate town accessible by sea, Howick is now a suburb of Auckland.

Begin this walk right down by the beach where once a substantial wharf provided easy access by sea to central Auckland and now there are wide views out to the islands of Waiheke, Motuihe, Motutapu and just off shore tiny Motukaraka Island.

From the beach walk up Selwyn Road noting two old beach houses at number 112, built in 1900 and at 102, built in 1910. Further up the road on the left is Shamrock Cottage, easily recognisable with its long veranda and shingle roof. One of Auckland's oldest buildings, the cottage dating from 1847 was originally built as a liquor store and soon after became the Royal Hotel. Now a popular tea rooms, the building retains many of its original features including the old scrim wallpaper.

Continue up the road to Howick's most notable building, All Saints Anglican Church. Prefabricated at Kohimarama, the church was largely erected before the Minerva arrived with the first service held on Christmas Day 1847, though at the time the church was minus its roof. Surrounded by old headstones, the church has been little altered in the intervening 170 years.

Directly across the road, just discernible are the traces of the main door of the stylish Spanish Mission Monterey Theatre built in 1929.

Continue up the main street to the Prospect of Howick Hotel, built in 1930 to replace the older 1906 Marine Hotel which burnt down in 1925. The story goes that the fire started when a maid left on an electric iron being unfamiliar with the workings of this recent invention. The blaze was impossible to contain as, at the time, Howick had neither a fire brigade nor a public water supply.

Nearly half of the 770 Fencibles were Irish and over to the right on the corner of Park Hill Road is the old graveyard of the Catholic Church, Our Lady Star of the Sea, replaced by a new building in 1960.

Directly ahead is Stockade Hill with superb views over the Hauraki Gulf and west as far as the Manukau Heads. In 1863 a simple blockhouse was erected on the summit as part of the string of such defences to protect Auckland from attack by Waikato Maori, though today only part of the earthworks still remain. Old oak trees compliment the First and Second World War Memorials and at the base is an information board featuring excellent photos of Howick in 1863.

From this point cross Ridge Road to Howe Street which was originally the main street of settlement prior to 1900. Continue down to Abercrombie Street where number 34 is the last remaining recognisable Fencible cottage in Howick. Cross over Cook Street into Sale Street and at the corner of Tanglewood Place (under the tall palm) is MacDonald House, built in 1859 as a Fencible officer's house for Captain Alexander MacDonald. Continue down Sale Street and back to Howick Beach.

4. Mangemangeroa Reserve

 A tidal creek is flanked by magnificent native trees

 Easy ~ Somerville Road Loop Walk: 30 minutes return

Hayley Lane: One hour return

 How to get there: Loop Walk: From 108 Somerville Road, Howick (next to the Somerville Barn),

Hayley Lane: From the roundabout on Whitford Road turn into Point View Drive and drive 1.5km to Hayley Lane on the left. There is no parking at the beginning of the walk at the bottom of the lane so park at the top.

At first glance from the car park high on Somerville Road, this small reserve running along the Mangemangeroa Creek isn't especially inviting and the initial impression is reinforced as the loop track drops down through grassy paddocks and into low replanted native trees. However, as the track nears the tidal creek, the bush quickly changes with numerous large native trees of a surprisingly wide variety of species. Totara, nikau, karaka, puriri, tree ferns, mapou, kohekohe taraire and mahoe can all be found here. Excellent signage is perfect for those wanting to brush up on plant identification, while other information boards detail Maori and European history.

Bird life, both native and introduced is prolific. Piwakawaka, kereru, tui, pukeko, heron and ruru are all common, while the dense vegetation on the fringes of the waterways is the preferred habitat of the banded rail.

The access to the reserve is via the Rotary Loop Walk. However, for a longer walk start at the end of Hayley Lane from where it will take about 30 minutes to reach the reserve and loop walk. This section of the walk follows the stream along a deep bush clad valley.

5. Point View Reserve

 Endless views from the hangout of the long-tailed bat

 Easy ~ 40 minutes

 How to get there: Caldwells Road, off Point View Drive, Botany

Most visitors to this 29-hectare reserve only walk as far as the lookout by the trig and very few continue on to the pleasant loop walk through grassy areas and a deep gully along the Mangemangeroa Stream, the home of native marine life such as eels, koura and banded kokopu. The panorama from the trig is magnificent. Far to the west is the Manukau Harbour and Takapuna Beach to the north. The view to the east is a good deal more bucolic, with rolling farmland and gullies.

Tui, piwakawaka, kereru and riroriro are all found here, but of special interest is a small colony of the rare native long-tailed bat that make their home in the reserve.

The bush is mainly generating forest with a few large trees, but you are most likely to have the tracks to yourself making for a pleasant quiet walk (the loop walk takes about 30 minutes). Other short tracks lead to entrances on Caldwells Road and Gracechurch Drive. For a longer walk, one of the tracks leads on to the adjoining Gracechurch Reserve. Parts of the reserve are closed to protect the kauri trees.

The New Zealand long-tailed bat / pekapeka (Chalinolobus tuberculatus) is one of just two surviving native bat species – the other is the short-tailed bat (Mystacina tuberculate). The long-tailed bat is closely related to other long-tailed bats in Australia, New Guinea, New Caledonia and Norfolk Island and is thought to have arrived in New Zealand within the last two million years. These bats are aerial feeders, catching insects on the wing and are likely to roost in the many old pine trees in the reserve. Flying up to 60 kilometres per hour, the long-tailed bat has a very large home range of around 100 square kilometres.

6. Whitford Path/Wade Walkway, Whitford

 Ruins of an old wharf and a bucolic stroll along a deep tidal creek

 Easy ~ One hour return

 How to get there: Whitford Village Green, on the left just past the Whitford Roundabout

Once connected to Auckland by a regular ferry, Whitford lies well up stream on the tidal Wade River. The Whitford Path begins in the large park known as Whitford Green and after crossing the park go over the bridge and up Whitford Wharf Road to the roundabout, taking time the way to view the remains of the original town wharf and to scamper up a few steps to a low lookout over the river.

From here walk up to the roundabout and turn right and 50 metres on, again to the right is the Wade Walkway. The easy track follows the river downstream where it quickly widens to a broad estuary, the shallows thickly crowded with mangroves. The importance of river transport in the Auckland region quickly becomes apparent as by sea, central Auckland is a short, comfortable boat ride away, whereas by road travel would have been both difficult and slow. The walk is more interesting at low tide as the river empties, revealing broad banks of thick mud deeply divided by narrow river channels and a small abandoned yacht illustrates the perils of miscalculating the tide.

Thickly planted in native trees and scrubs the pathway runs out at the end of Wades Road.

7. Maraetai Coastal Walkway and Omana Regional Park

 A gentle beach walk and with outstanding views of the inner Hauraki Gulf from coastal bluffs

 Easy ~ One hour 30 minutes return

 How to get there: Begin at Maraetai Wharf, Maraetai Coast Road, Maraetai

From the Maraetai Wharf follow the coast north through Maraetai Park and the Maraetai Beach Boating club to a wide well-formed path that skirts a rocky shore broken by small sandy coves and over hung with old pohutukawa. After about 10 minutes the path continues past seaside houses and then climbs up to the low cliffs of Omana Regional Park. Within the park are several easy walks, the longest of which The Perimeter Walk will take one hour.

Although the landscape has been considerably altered by both Maori and Europeans and much of the park is still farmland, Omana has a diversity of habitats that attracts many bird species. Ragged, crumbling cliffs of Waitemata sandstone face Waiheke, Ponui and Rangitoto islands and offer magnificent vistas over the Hauraki Gulf, with downtown Auckland in the distance. Ancient, twisted pohutukawa cling to the cliff tops creating bright splashes of red when flowering in summer, while below a wide sandstone rock platform is exposed at low tide. The brackish Te Puru creek runs along the western boundary of the park and then curls inland to a small wetland dense with raupo, oioi and water loving plants.

These diverse habitats are home to sea and wading birds including pukeko, shags, kingfisher, plovers, and stilts which freely roam the creek and shoreline, while forest birds such as tui, kereru, warblers and fantails are common in the bush. The exposed seabed at low tide attracts gulls, oyster catchers and in the summer migratory birds. The open grass paddocks suit paradise duck, one of the few native birds that have benefitted from the destruction of native forest.

Regenerating bush runs the length of the park along the Whitford/

Maraetai Road and here you will find titoki, kohekohe, kahikatea and rewarewa. Omana Beach near the main car parks as well as Te Pene Beach are safe swimming at high tide.

8. Duder Regional Park

 Magnificent views of the Coromandel Peninsula, Firth of Thames and the islands of the inner Gulf, and a historic landing site of the waka Tainui.

 Easy ~ Two hours

 How to get there: From SH1 travel towards Whitford and on to Maraetai, then follow the coast south to Umupuia Beach. From the southern end of Umupuia Beach turn right into North Road. The entrance to the park is on the right a short distance down this road. Facilities: Off road car parking, toilets and information boards

Duder Regional Park occupies the Whakakaiwhara Peninsula and is currently almost entirely farmed with just a few tiny patches of bush. Some very large puriri have survived in the gullies along with matai, kahikatea and kowhai. They provide a home for the more common native birds such as piwakawaka, kereru, ruru, tui and riroriro. Tidal mudflats, saltmarsh and shell banks on the south coast of the peninsula attract migratory and wading birds.

Around AD 1300 the waka Tainui anchored at very end of the peninsula while sheltering from a storm and is remembered in the place name Te Tauranga o Tainui. Whakakaiwhara pa was strategically located at the very tip of the peninsula, and terraces, kumara pits and defensive ditches are still visible today. The Duder family purchased the land in 1866 and continued to farm it up to 1994 when it was sold to the Auckland Regional Council for a park.

The farm loop walk is best undertaken anticlockwise following the south coast of the peninsula. This gives a comfortable steady hill climb to the trig point, which has grand views over the Firth of Thames, the Gulf islands of Waiheke, Ponui, Browns and Rangitoto, and to the east the blue-tinged Coromandel Peninsula. A further track leads out to the point; this will add another 50 minutes.

9. Clevedon Scenic Reserve

 Expansive vistas of South Auckland from the summit of this bush-cloaked hill

 Medium ~ One hour return

 How to get there: Thorps Quarry Road, off North Road, just east of the Clevedon-Kawakawa Road intersection, Clevedon. Facilities: Car park, toilets and a large picnic area

Set aside as a reserve in 1930, the 100 ha Clevedon Scenic Reserve had previously been part of William Thorp's farm, an enthusiastic conservationist who was keen to see that the bush was preserved. Luxuriant bush clings to the steep slopes including puriri, totara, taraire, kahikatea, kohekohe, rimu, karaka and even a fine stand of kauri. Birdlife includes kereru, tui, riroriro, piwakawaka, with shining cuckoo visiting in summer, and even the occasional kaka.

The Taitaia stream runs through a small wetland near the car park from where tracks rise up to a summit of 225m. The views from the top are stunning; east to the Hauraki Gulf and the Coromandel Peninsula, south over the Clevedon Valley and the Hunua Ranges, west over the Manukau Harbour and north to Auckland City and Takapuna Beach. There are two tracks to the summit which together form a loop – the Totara track to the left is shorter, but steeper and the Puriri Track to the right is a more gradual climb. At the base of the hill a short side track leads into a small wetland in the old quarry, abandoned in 1957, with water trickling down the rock face thickly encrusted with mosses.

10. Waitawa Regional Park

 Views over the Hauraki Gulf and whales off shore

 Medium ~ One hour

 How to get there: From Clevedon take the Clevedon-Kawakawa Road for 13 kilometres to the park.

This large sprawling park was only established in 2014 and still is in a fairly raw state, but will be a magnificent park for future generations. Previously farmed, only small areas of mature bush survived in steep gullies, but now huge areas have been planted in native trees and shrubs. Two old pa sites can be found in the park, and from the high hills, there are marvellous views of Waiheke and Ponui islands, which lie just a short distance away. As well as mountain bike tracks and horse-riding trails, the old wharf at Waitawa Bay is a magnet for recreational fishers, while the sheltered, north-facing Mataitai Bay offers good swimming at mid to high tide and is ideal for kayaks.

Around twenty species of whales and dolphins have been recorded in the gulf, most of which are seasonal visitors. However, a group of around 50 Bryde's whales (named after Norwegian Johan Bryde and pronounced 'brooders') have established a resident population, a rare occurrence for this species. If you are lucky you might just spot these whales offshore.

All four loop walks start from the main parking area at the Mataitai Bay where there are toilets and picnic areas. The longest track, steep in places, skirts the perimeter, dipping down to the coast at varying points and traversing bushy gullies. However, the tracks are all linked so can be easily shortened if you prefer a shorter walk.

11. Tawhitokino Regional Park

 A beautiful stretch of beach fringed by pohutukawa and safe for swimming at all tides.

 Easy ~ 1 hour return

How to get there: How to get there: From Kawakawa Bay, follow the coast road for four kilometres east to Waiti Bay to the car park at the very end of the road. The last section of this road is narrow and cars frequently park on the verges so take it slowly.

This little-known bay is a gem on the Firth of Thames coast. Its long sandy beach, fringed by pohutukawa trees, is pleasantly empty even on a hot summer's day. It is safe for swimming at all tides (clothing optional) and has an uninterrupted view of the Coromandel Peninsula. The beach is fringed by old pohutukawa and in the small reserve behind the beach are handsome kowhai and rewarewa trees. Although not common, weka are occasionally found in the area between Tawhitokino Bay and Kawakawa and after several years of increasing numbers, in more recent times the weka population has inexplicably dropped.

The walk to Tawhitokino takes about 30 minutes and starts from the beach at Waiti Bay (not up the hill) and follows the shore around the rocky headland to Tuturau Bay which can be little tricky at high tide (best at low tide). From this bay, the track climbs over ridge through regenerating bush.

12. Tapapakanga Regional Park

 Beautiful coastal scenery with views over the Firth of Thames to the Coromandel Peninsula

 Moderate ~ Two hours

 How to get there: The park is on Deery's Road off the Orere-Martingarahi Road, which is the main road along the Firth of Thames.

Tapapakanga Regional Park, a mixture of farmland and coastal bush which opened in 1995, overlooks the waters of the Firth of Thames. Within the 120-hectare park, the fenced off bush remnants are flourishing with fine specimens of taraire, tanekaha, tawa and rewarewa. Around the old Ashby homestead (1900) there are several magnificent old pohutukawa while just to the south of the main car park is a small grove of taraire.

The Firth of Thames is the large bay at the mouths of the Waihou and Piako rivers at the southern end of the Hauraki Gulf and it is flanked on the east by the Coromandel Peninsula and to the west by the Hunua Ranges. Originally the Waikato River flowed through the Hinuera valley, entering the sea at the Firth of Thames. The river carried huge amounts of pumice from eruptions in the central North Island as well as depositing enormous quantities of gravel, mud and sand creating the flat Hauraki Plains. Twenty thousand years ago debris from a large and violent volcanic eruption forced the river to change to its present course, discharging into the Tasman Sea. The shoreline was once much further south and has gradually extended north over time.

There are a number of walks through the park and one mountain bike track, but the most appealing walk in the park is the coastal loop track, which as the name suggests hugs the coastline to the south and then loops steeply uphill before dropping back to the car park. The views are simply superb. The beach is more boulders than sand and not that great for swimming, but the old trees provide plenty of shade for a summer picnic and there is also camping at the northern end of the beach.

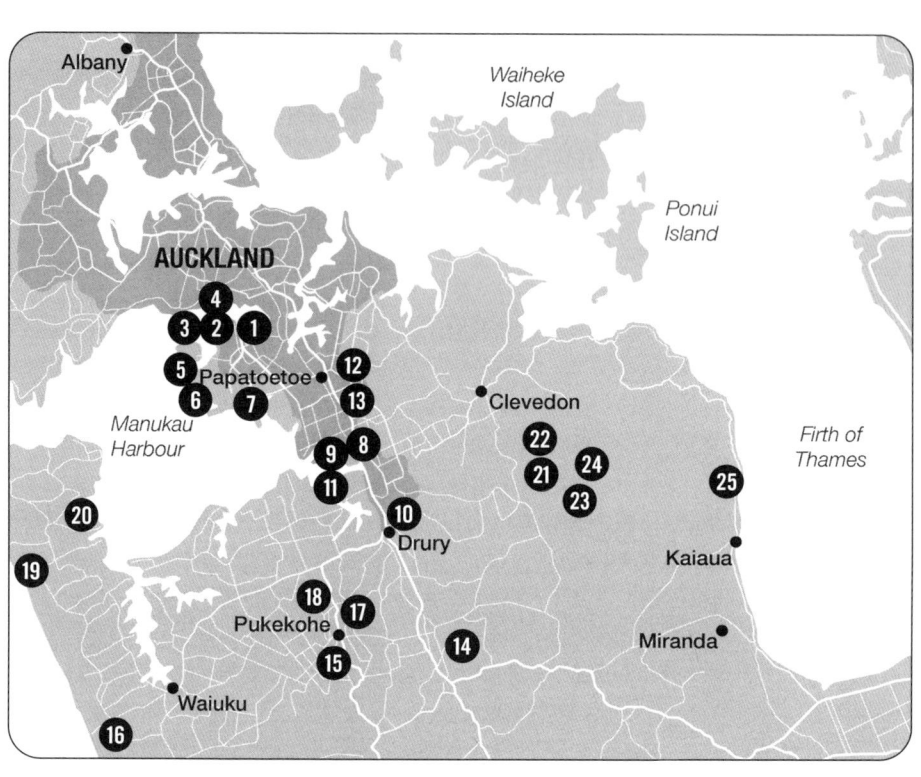

SOUTH

1. Mangere Mountain
2. Mangere Lagoon
3. Ambury Park
4. Kiwi Esplanade
5. Watercare Coastal Walkway
6. Otuataua Stonefields
7. Puhinui Reserve
8. Otara Creek Reserve, Ngati Otara Park and the Otara Markets
9. Weymouth Walkway
10. Pahurehure Inlet Walkway
11. Conifer Grove Walkway
12. Murphy's Bush Scenic Reserve
13. Auckland Botanic Gardens and Totara Park
14. Mt William Scenic Reserve and Walkway
15. Harker Reserve and the Vivian Falls
16. Port Waikato Sand dunes.
17. Cape Hill Walk, Pukekohe
18. Henrys Scenic Reserve and Te Ara O Whangamarie Walkway
19. Hamiltons Gap
20. Awhitu Regional Park
21. Hunua Falls
22. Cosseys Reservoir Loop Walk
23. Wairoa Loop Walk
24. Wairoa Suspension Bridge Walk
25. Waharau Regional Park

Mangere Walks.

Although described separately, all the following six walks are very close together and can be combined to create walks of varying lengths.

1. Mangere Mountain

 The largest and most original volcanic cone on the Auckland Isthmus

 Easy ~ One hour

 How to get there: Main entrance at the end of Domain Road, off Coronation Road, Mangere Bridge.

One of the largest and least modified of Auckland's 50 volcanic cones, Mangere Mountain is a quiet haven compared with the better-known volcanoes. Auckland volcanos behave very differently from the volcanoes in the central North Island. Fuelled by lava from basaltic magma from deep in the earth's core, the eruptions are relatively peaceful as they generate lava fountains and flows rather than huge explosions. These lava flows can be very fluid and travel for long distances and such flows are common on the Auckland isthmus.

Mangere has two distinct large craters, one of which has a lava dome or tholoid in the crater formed by the upward pressure after the main vent has become blocked.

The rich volcanic soils sustained a large Maori population in pre-European times, growing kumara and taro, with easy access to seafood in the Manukau Harbour. Maori land boundaries indicated by low stone walls fan out from the base of the mountain, and kumara pits and house sites are clearly visible inside the craters. There are excellent views out over the Manukau Harbour from the top. The track follows the rim of the craters, but as the whole park is open grass, you can just stroll anywhere. The Visitor Centre on Coronation Road is an alternative starting point, though the displays are mainly geared to schoolchildren.

2. Mangere Lagoon

 Restored volcanic crater on the edge of the harbour
 Easy ~ 40 minutes
 How to get there: Main parking area, Creamery Road off Kirkbride Road

In contrast to the twin cones of the adjacent Mangere Mountain, Mangere lagoon was an explosive volcano that erupted some time before the creation of the mountain itself. The lagoon was created 7,000 years ago when the warming climate caused sea levels to rise and fill the crater with sea water, leaving the crater dome as a small island in the centre.

The twentieth century was not kind to the lagoon starting in the 1930s when the crater wetland was drained for pasture. In the 1950s the lagoon was turned into the sludge ponds for the city's sewerage which also saw the removal of the crater dome. When in the 1990s, Watercare completely updated the sewage system, things finally improved and by 2003 the lagoon was completely restored along with its iconic island. Native coastal vegetation is gradually replacing the grass and pine trees and today a track, ideal for walking and cycling encircles the lagoon and is linked to the longer Watercare Coastal Walkway.

3. Ambury Park

 Wading and migratory bird paradise on a special lava flow
 Easy ~ One hour
 How to get there: At the end of Ambury Road, Mangere Bridge (off the South Western Motorway.)

Best known as a farm park, Ambury Park sits on a wide ash-covered lava flow from nearby Mangere Mountain. The flow is exposed on the coastal margins and there are excellent examples of rough and broken a'a lava. Between the lava are saltmarshes, shell banks and saline herb fields. The broad intertidal mudflats adjoining Ambury Park and the adjacent Kiwi Esplanade are one of the most important wading bird habitats in the

Auckland region. Low tide exposes vast areas of seabed, ideal feeding ground for thousands of endemic and migratory aquatic bird species. Along with wrybill, knots, godwit, shags and heron, the area is a vital winter roost for the South Island Pied Oystercatchers.

A number of tracks cross the flat farmland and a loop walk that encircles the entire park will take less than an hour. Children will enjoy the opportunity to get up close to docile farm animals. There are also excellent toilet and picnic facilities.

4. Kiwi Esplanade

 Birds, lava flows and a historic church

 Easy ~ One hour return

 How to get there: Kiwi Esplanade runs along the shore at Mangere Bridge and starts at the northern end of Coronation Road.

Kiwi Esplanade, which runs for 2.5 kilometres along the Mangere Inlet, has been designated as an area of significant conservation value, not only for its bird life, but for New Zealand's best example of pahoehoe lava flows. The esplanade is mostly grass with some modest sized trees and, at low tide, a vast area of rocks, reefs and mudflats are exposed.

Two of the three main types of lava can be found here: pahoehoe and a'a (pronounced ah-ah.)

Pahoehoe lava is formed when molten lava breaks through the congealed surface crust and is characterised by billowy, smooth or rope-like surfaces. By continually advancing out in front of the lava flow, this billowing movement creates weird and wonderful shapes sometime referred to as lava sculpture. These lava flows are often very thin from just 10 centimetres through to a metre thick and, in this fashion, can advance up to 50 kilometres. Pahoehoe is a Hawaiian word which means 'smooth unbroken lava'.

In contrast a'a is where a lava flow is both cooling and expanding, constantly breaking through the solid surface and twisting the solid lava in jagged blocks. The surface of a'a is very broken and rugged making it very difficult to walk on.

Hard though it is to imagine, Allan Park on the foreshore was the site of one of Auckland's hottest nightspots, the Oriental Rendezvous Cabaret which operated here from 1923 until burning down in 1940.

Rather than walk back all the way along Kiwi Esplanade, detour by Boyd Avenue and into Church Road and down to St James Anglican Church. Construction began sometime between 1855 and 1857 on a permanent church to serve the local Maori community using stone cut from nearby Mangere mountain. The church finally opened in 1859, and this historic urupa next to the church is known as Mangere Piriti Urupa.

Continue down Church Road to the roundabout and turn left into Coronation Road. If you are feeling hungry the lively Mangere Bridge town centre is also on Coronation Road just to the right.

5. Watercare Coastal Walkway

 Walk (or cycle) through the restored shoreline, now home to migratory birds

 Easy ~ One and half hours

 How to get there: There are numerous entry points to the walkway but the most accessible with parking and toilets is from Ambury Park at the end of Creamery Road, Oruarangi Road and at the Ihumatao Stonefields at the end of Ihumatao Quarry Road.

On the upper eastern reaches of the Manukau Harbour, New Zealand's largest marine restoration project began with the radical upgrade of the Mangere water treatment plant that originally covered 500 hectares. Begun in the mid-1990s and opened in 2005, the project significantly restored 13 kilometres of the Manukau Harbour coastline. Over a quarter of million nature trees were planted along with the creation of numerous small beaches. In addition to giving the public easy access to the coast, the Watercare project protected and restored vital habitat for birdlife. Today the rich shallow waters of the harbour host tens of thousands of migratory birds and is home to many coastal and wading birds.

The wide and flat track suitable for walking and cycling runs seven kilometres from the Stonefields to Ambury Park and from Ambury Park it easy to continue on through to the Onehunga Lagoon.

6. Otuataua Stonefields

 Easy ~ 30–40 minutes

 How to get there: From George Bolt Drive (the road to the airport) turn right into Ihumatao Road, right again into Oruarangi Road and finally left into Ihumatao Quarry to the carpark at the end.

While undoubtedly an area of significant historical and archaeological importance, to the untrained eye the Otuataua Stonefields are difficult to make sense of. Settled originally by Te Wai o Hua, and covering 100 hectares, the stone fields highlight the importance of kumara and taro to early Maori.

Despite this country's equitable climate and rich soil, there are few edible native plants; and even those such as fernroot and karaka berries take a huge amount of preparation before they are edible. On arrival from their tropical homeland, the first Polynesian migrants found that the crops they had carried with them were drastically restricted by climate and only kumara and taro grew successfully. This had a significant impact on where Maori could live and the pre-European Maori populations were largely restricted to the warmer northern parts of the country and to coastal areas further south.

Both taro and kumara need a long period of warm sunny weather to mature. One method of maximising the heat required by these delicate tropical plants was to plant the crops very close to rock walls or in a small circle of rocks, thereby taking full advantage of the sun's heat reflected off and held by the rocks. Here at Otuataua, what appear to be merely random stone piles are in fact the remains of carefully constructed walls and mounds designed to enhance the growth of these two vital crops. The site also contains the Otuataua pa, although this pa is difficult to spot compared to those on the volcanic cones.

The stonefields also contain Auckland's smallest volcanic cone - merely 30 metres high. Puketaapapa, might be small, but it is perfectly formed and complete with its equally small crater. The volcano is immediately to the right of the car park with the loop track also leading to the right from the main entry point.

The other volcano in the reserve, Otuataua, is not much larger and both erupted around 20,000 years ago. From the slopes of Puketaapapa, the broad lava flow west to the Manukau Harbour is clearly visible. A third volcano, Mangataketake, has been completely quarried away. The shoreline to the west of the Otuataua Stonefields is one of the most important habitats for shore birds including migratory bird such as the Eastern curlews, wrybills, godwits and knots.

An easy walk through rocky outcrops and farmland, this walk is enhanced by the excellent information, certainly helping to interpret what at first glance appears to be a landscape without much form.

7. Puhinui Reserve

 An exceptional reserve protects rare flora and fauna

 Easy ~ Two hours

 How to get there: End of Price Road, off Puhinui Road, Wiri

Covering almost 200 hectares, this reserve established in 1991 occupies most of the Puhinui Peninsula between the Puhinui Stream and Manukau Harbour. Much of the reserve is in farmland and is used as an equestrian centre, but there are considerable areas along the stream and shoreline that have been replanted in coastal native trees and shrubs.

The margins of the reserve along the harbour and the stream are an exceptionally important wildlife refuge – this is the largest area of original salt marsh and coastal vegetation remaining on the Manukau Harbour foreshore. The tidal flats along the harbour's edge are an important feeding ground for numerous migratory birds including lesser knots and godwits. Such is its importance that 40 hectares on the harbour side have been designated a conservation area with no public access, though there are several points where there are a good views over the protected coastline. Predator free, black stilt, wrybill, fernbird and New Zealand dotterel are just some of the rare birds found in this area. However, it is not just birds that need protection, but also unusual and endangered native plants such as the native musk and the sea primrose.

A section of the Puhinui Stream has been designated as the Puhinui Stream Wildlife Refuge which attracts huge numbers of wading birds while upstream, it is believed to contain the oldest and largest mangroves in the Auckland region. The other side of the stream is protected by the Weymouth Walkway. In addition to protecting plants and bird, the reserve also preserves three small volcanic craters.

The reserve does not draw many visitors, so the flat tracks are ideal for both walking and mountain biking including family groups. The easy tracks are simple to follow as they are all through open pastureland. A combination of farm tracks and informal paths, the walks can be muddy in parts and don't forget to close the gates behind you.

8. Otara Creek Reserve, Ngati Otara Park and the Otara Markets

  A tidal creek, a spot of Rugby League, an historic school and finally food and shopping

  Easy ~ One hour

  How to get there: East Tamaki Road 400 metres from the intersection of Bairds Road, Otara. This area is very busy on a Saturday and it might be best to park on the other side of the creek and cross back over the small bridge.

Otara Creek Reserve is a sprawling park of over 200 hectares on both sides of the tidal inlet near the Otara shopping centre. Not exactly pristine, local community groups are endeavouring to restore the area, but old habits die hard and along the way you are likely to encounter old mattresses, a bit too much litter and the occasional shopping trolley. It is best to follow the western side of the creek as the track is not continuous on the opposite side. Starting from East Tamaki Road enter Otara Creek Reserve and follow the meandering stream, thick with mangroves, through Mayfield Park and on to Ngati Otara Park. Passing through wide grassy fields, the tree-lined path can be very muddy in places.

At Ngati Otara Park stop and watch local teams, supported by enthusiastic parents, playing Rugby League; you just might spot a future star here. From this park walk back down Otara Road to the Otara market, passing on the way the historic Dingwall building on the Manukau Institute of Technology Campus.

This heritage listed building opened in 1916 as Dilworth Ulster Institute School of Agriculture, designed by the architect Richard Atkinson Abbott who was also responsible for Auckland Grammar School. The school and farm were not a success and closed in 1919.

Next stop is the Otara Market, one of Auckland's oldest and most vibrant markets. This is not a tourist attraction but caters for the local population with a strong emphasis on Polynesian and Asian food. Here you are guaranteed to find the cheapest fruit and vegetables in Auckland, along with tasty food treats that you will find nowhere else in the city.

9. Weymouth Walkway

 A foreshore walkway with views over the harbour to the Manukau Heads.

 Easy ~ 45 minutes

 How to get there: There are numerous entrances to the walkway but the entrance off Pitt Avenue is recommended as it has an off street car park and picnic areas.

Over the years the eastern shores of the Manukau Harbour had become a convenient dumping ground for industrial and human waste and in the 1960s a huge area was reclaimed for the Auckland International Airport. The mangrove forests were frequently turned into farmland or worse rubbish dumps as they were considered swampland and of little economic value. In recent years both the local council and the residents around the eastern shores have been actively preserving and improving the health of the harbour. Huge numbers of native trees and shrubs have been replanted, the water quality of the tidal creeks and estuaries has been vastly improved and increasing numbers of migratory and wading birds have returned to this area of the harbour. As a consequence, this once forgotten face of Auckland is rapidly attracting an increasing number of visitors to its parks and reserves.

One such area is Weymouth where urban Auckland pushes hard up against the Manukau harbour. While not a large area, the reserves, through which the Weymouth Walkway runs, are an important buffer zone between industrial and urban sprawl and protect a long stretch of the upper harbour.

The walkway rambles along creeks, over low cliffs, through grassy parks and along a shelly beach with expansive views over the entire harbour and out to Manukau Heads. Much of the walkway is planted in natives and side tracks at various points lead down to the water's edge. At mid to low tide huge areas of the seabed are exposed attracting wading birds in their thousands.

Officially the walkway begins off Hanford Place, though this is the least attractive stretch of the walkway and it is not unusual to see all manner of domestic rubbish thrown down the bank into the creek. The access points of Burundi Street and Pitt Ave are much better starting points. The walkway is concreted so is ideal to walk and bike in any weather.

10. Pahurehure Inlet Walkway

 Dramatic restoration of this tidal inlet

 Easy ~ 40 minutes return

Facilities: Street parking on Wharf Street and off street parking and toilets in Prince Edward Park

 How to get there: Park by the Counties Manukau Badminton Club in Ray Small Park, Elliott Street, Papakura

The Pahurehure Inlet adjoining Papakura is hardly pristine. However, local action to improve the natural health of the inlet is indicative of a

change of attitude to the tidal waterways of the upper Manukau Harbour. The construction of the Southern Motorway in 1963 cut two arms of the inlet off from each other and dramatically confined the water flow to the two inlets, Pahurehure Inlet No 1 to the north and Pahurehure Inlet No. 2 to the south (both are clearly marked and visible from the motorway.)

With the restricted water flow, sediment built up over the years allowing the rapid expansion of mangroves. Recently Inlet No 2 has been largely cleared of mangroves, an action that has stirred up considerable controversy.

Over the last century, as the harbour was both reclaimed and polluted, the waters became increasingly silted up and, consequently the native mangrove flourished. Beaches and tidal flats, previous clear of mangroves became dense forests with only the very deepest of channels remaining open water. At the same time the shallow mangrove swamps were reclaimed or just became dumping grounds for rubbish. Now the mangrove swamp is recognised as a vital habitat for juvenile fish, shrimp, crabs and molluscs, while their extensive root system stabilise the coastal margins and prevent erosion. In other areas beaches, sandbanks and open tidal shores have completely disappeared under the relentless advance of the mangroves and, in the process, important feeding grounds for wading birds have been lost. In some areas these mangroves are being removed, not without opposition, but as a result the aquatic bird life has increased considerably.

While it will take some time for the Pahurehure Inlet to recover, the return of bird life to the now open shores has been impressive. The godwits have returned as have the stilts, royal spoonbills and, large numbers of white-faced heron. Even the shy banded rail has found a home in the margins of the lagoon.

The walkway has also been upgraded with a substantial boardwalk at the beginning and extensive replanting of native trees and shrubs.

This walk starts at the Ray Small Park on Elliott Street by the Counties Manukau Badminton Club as this is the beginning of the boardwalk and from there the path follows the shoreline along Prince Edward Park via Gills Avenue to Youngs Beach Reserve on Cliff Road.

11. Conifer Grove Walkway

 A broad walk crosses over saltmarsh and through mangrove forest

 Easy ~ 30 minutes one way

 How to get there: Several entry points but the most convenient is the Walter Strevens Reserve, off Walter Strevens Drive which runs through the heart of Conifer Grove.

This walkway along a northern branch of the Pahurehure Inlet links three coastal reserves, the Walter Strevens Reserve, Conifer Grove Esplanade Reserve and the Brylee Drive Reserve. The highlight of the reserve is an 800-metre boardwalk through the mangroves and saltmarsh with a lookout for birdwatching. Wading and aquatic birds feed on the tidal flats and a small the rocky reef.

The easy path and boardwalk are ideal for walking and cycling.

12. Murphy's Bush Scenic Reserve

 A virgin kahikatea forest in South Auckland

 Easy ~ 40 minutes

 How to get there: Murphy's Road, Flat Bush, South Auckland

The largest remaining lowland bush in Auckland, the 26 hectares of Murphy's Bush was gifted to the Manukau District Council in 1981 by the family of local farmer Conway Murphy, who had taken great care to preserve this remnant of forest.

True to its name kahikatea is the dominant tree and it is easy to see why early European settlers called the tree white pine as kahikatea forest has the feel of a pine forest rather than the more tropical feel of New Zealand bush. However, there is more to Murphy's Bush than kahikatea with mature rimu, puriri and totara, including one extremely large totara tree, estimated to be hundreds of years old. A small stream curls through the flat reserve which is very easy walking and, although there is little signage it is hard to get lost for long. The reserve has a number of walking tracks through the bush that take from 10 minutes to one hour and are suitable for wheel chairs.

13. Auckland Botanic Gardens and Totara Park

 A large open garden combining formal gardens with more open park-like grounds and short bush walks through adjoining Totara Park.

 Botanic Gardens: Easy, one hour

Totara Park: Medium, one hour

 How to get there: Botanic Garden Entrance: Hill Road, Manurewa, signposted off the Southern Motorway. Totara Park Entrance: Wairere Road, Manurewa.

Opened in 1982 on 64 hectares in Manurewa, the gardens may lack old-world garden charm but this is more than made up for by the fascinating range of plants not possible in confined older city gardens. The gardens are ideal for a long ramble through a diverse array of over 10,000 plants in 24 collections ranging from formal flower beds (the dahlias are incredible) and rose gardens through to the more exotic South African collection. Entrance to the gardens is free and there is an excellent café in the smart new Visitor Centre.

Running along the bottom of the gardens is the Puhinui stream and beyond that the dense bush of Totara Park which is connected by path to the gardens.

Covering 216 hectares, Totara Park is a combination of recreational spaces, farmland and the original broadleaf and podocarp bush. As the name clearly suggests the totara trees are a feature of the park but the variety of large native trees is impressive, and include kohekohe, tawa, kauri, rimu, matai, kauri and kahikatea with a dense understorey of nikau and tree ferns. Along with the trees, many with identification signs, come the native birds such as piwakawaka, riroriro, shining cuckoo, tui, kereru and even kaka.

Running north to south from the main carpark on Wairere Drive is a broad access road off which branch two loop walks to the east and west, both of which will take about 30 minutes each. The loop to the east is a more gentle grade, while that to the west is surprisingly rugged with numerous steps. These two loop tracks are for walkers only, while the tracks on the farmland are also used by mountain bikers and horse riders so you need to keep your wits about you.

Near the entrance is a swimming pool (summer only), tennis courts and off the central track is an adventure playground.

14. Mt William Scenic Reserve and Walkway

 Two choices of farmland or bush to the top of Mt William for fabulous views over Auckland and the Waikato

 Mt William from Puketutu Road: Medium, 1 hour 45 minutes return

Mt William from McMillan Rd to Puketutu Road: Hard, Two hours one way

 How to get there: Puketutu Road is off Razorback Road easily accessible from the Ridge Road exit of the Waikato Expressway, SH1 at Bombay.
McMillan Road is off Irish Road which is off SH2 just east of Pokeno.

Mt William is a distinct pyramid shaped hill easily visible from the Southern Motorway east of Bombay. This peak at 373 metres, together with nearby Puketutu at 376m (recognisable by the cell phone tower) are two of the highest points in the Auckland region. What makes them attractive as a walking destination is that they are in open farmland with astonishing vistas in every direction. To the north lies the city of Auckland with Rangitoto glimpsed on the horizon, while to the south and west are views over the lower Waikato with Mt Pirongia easily visible. Over to the east is the Firth of Thames and the Coromandel peninsula.

Definitely a track of two halves, a decision needs to be made just what sort of walk do you want as the two entrances are quite a distance apart (not walkable). From Puketutu Road, the track meanders over rolling grass hills with a short climb at the end and this is a comfortable walk of less than an hour suitable families and the moderately fit. The access from McMillan Road is very different. Here the track is in poor condition, very muddy with steep slippery sections and you will need tramping boots (the mud is deep) and a good level of fitness. This track is best tackled during a dry spell in summer. However, the bush is very attractive with a variety of good-sized trees including kahikatea, rimu, totara, matai, tawa, miro, puriri, karaka and kohekohe. Unusually, the reserve contains a grove of kauri, tanekaha and hard beech, the latter tree is not so common this far north. The rare king fern is also found in the reserve.

15. Harker Reserve and the Vivian Falls

 A picturesque waterfall in a handsome bush reserve

 Easy ~ One hour 30 minute return

 How to get there: From the village of Tuakau take River Road to the bridge over the Waikato River. After crossing the bridge turn left and then right into Onewhero Road. After 1.5km the reserve is on the right.

Unlike most reserves, the Harker Reserve is a 25 ha area of bush protected by the Harker family under a Queen Elizabeth covenant and generously made available to the public. Little known outside the local district and attracting few visitors, the reserve itself is in two parts and the waterfalls are in a small separate patch of bush to the west of the main reserve.

Situated in a deep valley, the reserve is a combination of regenerating bush and much older trees in the steeper sections. An excellent track runs the full length of both reserves with a short loop track meandering through the older growth. Most people skip the loop track which is a pity as the bush here is very attractive and dense, and as the loop track runs virtually parallel to the main track, it only adds another 10 minutes to the walk, though the track itself is a bit more basic.

The falls drop 12 metres in single drop into jumble of limestone rocks in a deep gully surrounded by old nikau palms and regenerating bush.

The track to the falls can be slippery and wet, especially the last section down a small flight of stone steps. Known in Maori as Te Wai heke a Maoa, excellent information boards tell the story of the warrior Maoa and his connection with the waterfall.

16. Port Waikato Sand dunes.

 A wild beach walk at the mouth of the Waikato River

 Easy ~ Three hours

 How to get there: Sunset Beach, Ocean View Road, Port Waikato

While not far from Auckland (an hour's drive), Port Waikato feels like a place time forgot, so best not to come expecting beach umbrellas and designer stores. However, if wild lonely beach walks are what you crave, this is the place for you.

Below the bridge over the Waikato River near Tuakau, the river begins to fan out into a wide delta of low islands and multiple streams. However, near the mouth, the river reforms into a huge shallow lagoon, protected from the open Tasman Sea by a wide spit of sand dunes.

Huddled along the southern shore of the lagoon and behind the sand dunes is the small beachside settlement of Port Waikato and the mostly small old-fashioned baches hunker down away from the wind in the broad flat behind the dunes and high hills. It is hard to believe that this was once a lively port originally called Putataka (still the name of the high hill above the town), established as a base during the New Zealand Wars and it was from here that gunboats moved upriver to bombard Maori pa with devastating effect.

Between the broad river estuary and the turbulent Tasman Sea is a substantial area of dunes built up by river and sea currents and moulded by the fierce westerly wind. At first glance this looks like a short beach walk, but the area is much bigger than it looks and a walk from the surf club at Sunset Beach around to Maraetai Bay on the estuary will take around 3 hours. If it is very windy you won't last long on the open beach and swimming is only advisable directly in front of the surf club or in the lagoon. The land is part public land, DoC land and Maori trust land so stick to the coastline or the formed tracks which cut across the dunes.

17. Cape Hill Walk, Pukekohe

 Get acquainted with the ancient Franklin Volcanic Field

 Easy ~ Twenty minutes

 How to get there: Brownlee Place off Reynolds Road, Pukekohe.

Not a long walk but Cape Hill offers an excellent view over the thriving town of Pukekohe and a simple lesson in local geology. While the area is famous for its market gardens on rich red soils, it is not easy to see where the volcanic soils actually came from.

The Franklin Volcanic Field is much older than the Auckland Volcanic Field erupting between 500,000 and one million years ago. Covering an extensive area, the field contains no fewer than 80 craters, though many are small and have substantially eroded. Pukekohe Hill is the largest and youngest of the volcanoes in this field. The field extends from Red Hills in the north, down to Mercer and Pukekawa in the south, Waiuku in the west and out to Hunua in the east.

The Waikato River cuts through the heart of the field and the Southern Motorway passes through two craters, one at Pokeno and the other just north of Bombay. The most visible crater is just east of Pukekohe where the best views are from the historic church on Runciman Road near the intersection with Pukekohe East Road.

The walk begins through the Settlers Walkway, a small area of replanted native bush with individual totara trees dedicated to early European settlers. After zigzagging your way through the trees, the track leads up to a small pavilion at the top of the hill. From here the cones of the old volcanos, dating back as far as one million years are clearly visible, and the hill you are standing on is also one of those old volcanos. Return the way you came and instead of going back down hill, walk straight ahead to a small patch of bush. On your left is a small exposed section of volcanic rock easily recognised by its red colour and distinctive layers. In the bush is a fine grove of tall totara and down the bottom of the hill is a boardwalk over a tiny wetland.

Return to Brownlee Place passing several attractive small ponds alive with ducks.

18. Henry Scenic Reserve and Te Ara O Whangamarie Walkway

 Pretty cascading waterfall in a hidden reserve

 Easy ~ Henry Reserve: 20 minutes

Henry Reserve and Te Ara O Whangamarie Walkway: One hour

 How to get there: Henry Reserve is Hunter Road, off the Patumahoe Road, 1.5km from Patumahoe. Te Ara O Whangamarie Walkway is off Clive Howe Road, Patumahoe

Little known these two small reserves linked by a track through farmland are well worth visiting if you are in the area. Henrys Reserve is the pick of the two with a small waterfall and fine bush. A short loop walk circles through handsome native bush, primarily of taraire along with tawa, pukatea, rimu, kahikatea and totara. Just 15 metres high, what the waterfall lacks in height track it makes up for in style with the rushing water cascading down through moss-encrusted volcanic boulders reminiscent of a perfect Japanese garden.

The Te Ara O Whangamaire walkway leads to another small reserve. Here a basic loop track meanders through regenerating bush and then up a short steep hill to the road.

19. Hamiltons Gap

As wild as it gets along the Awhitu Peninsula

Easy ~ Allow one to two hours

Facilities: Large parking area, toilets and a picnic area

How to get there: West Coast Road off Awhitu Road, just north of Pollok. The road is sealed except for a small stretch near the end.

At Hamiltons Gap a small stream cuts through the old and very steep dune country built up over millennia by the constant winds off the Tasman Sea, creating the only public access point along this long coast. The dramatic and wild landscape is well worth the detour off the main road. Rugged cliffs of golden sandstone shaped by the endless winds rise above the black sand beach while serried banks of wild rollers pound the wide beach creating magnificent vistas north and south. In the small dunes around the mouth of the stream, visitors can find the native pingao grass that has been replanted. While getting to the coast is not so easy, visitors can walk long distances in either direction on the wide sandy beach.

Hamiltons Gap is an excellent place to get a grasp on the geology of the Awhitu Peninsula. In contrast to the ancient, rugged and rocky Manukau North Head and the Waitakere Ranges, the Awhitu Peninsula is a geological baby and is largely composed of consolidated sand underlaid by ancient volcanic rock.

During numerous ice ages, the sea was much lower and, at that time, the Manukau Harbour (and the Waitemata) was a wide tree-covered river valley. Gradually as the climate warmed and the sea rose, the whole basin became one vast bay. Inland eruptions then swept huge quantities of sand and pumice down the Waikato River, which in turn were swept north by the prevailing currents. In addition, the same northerly currents dragged black sand from the Taranaki eruptions and together all this material first formed a long sandbar and then gigantic sand hills. As various times ash deposits from various volcanic eruptions and swamp formations have added more material and these appear in the sand hills as dark horizontal lines. Over time the consolidated sand hills supported a forest which, since the arrival of humans, has largely vanished.

There is always a catch and here that snag is the weekend dirt bike riders who race at high speed along the beach and on occasion blatantly ignore the signs to stay off the dunes. Best visited on weekdays. The toilet, fashioned from driftwood, is worth a visit in its own right.

20. Awhitu Regional Park

 A coastal gem on the shores of the Manukau Harbour

 Easy ~ One and half hours

 How to get there: From Waiuku, drive north along the Awhitu Peninsula to Matakawau. Two kilometres past Matakawau, turn right into Brook Road which leads to the park.

Nestled on the sheltered eastern side of the Awhitu Peninsula on the Manukau Harbour, this attractive park is a lovely combination of beach and wetlands. On either side of the headland are two long sand/shell beaches best for swimming at high tide. Behind the beaches are long, low sand dunes, behind which are two substantial wetlands, surprisingly free from mangrove and home to shy and elusive fernbirds, bitterns and banded rails. Regenerating native bush encircles the wetlands and pohutukawa trees adorn the headlands and beaches. The area is very tidal and more appealing to visit closer to high water, though the open flats do provide an important feeding ground for birds including godwits. Offshore is tiny Kauritutahi Island.

At the heart of the park is the 19th-century Brook Homestead, typical of the comfortable farm villas of the day and set among fine old trees on headland overlooking the harbour. Just in front of the homestead is a small roughly built cottage which initially housed the family until sufficient money was available to build a more substantial home.

Both wetlands are encircled by easy walking tracks, well-marked and with good signage. To cover the whole park would take no longer than two hours with numerous shorter options in between. The park also has excellent facilities with good parking, toilets, information boards, and picnic areas with tables and barbecues.

Hunua Regional Park

Covering 14,000 hectares, the Hunua Ranges are primarily a major water catchment area for the city of Auckland, but also preserve important native flora and fauna. Rising to a high point of 688 metres at Kohukohunui, the ranges are the largest forested area in the Auckland region, even though the area was thoroughly milled for timber in earlier times. The landscape is surprisingly rugged with dense bush and on the high peak, Kohukohunui, there is a rare area of sub-montane forest. Over 450 native plants have been recorded here and while tawa dominates, there are fine stands of rimu, kauri, matai, kahikatea and rata.

Hochstetter's frog is found deep in the Hunua Ranges, which is also home to Auckland's only population of kokako. A 600-hectare area of the ranges has been intensely managed to control predators, and the kokako population has now risen from four pairs in 1994 to over 60 pairs. North Island robin, long extinct in the ranges, have been reintroduced to the kokako management area.

Large areas of the park have been closed in an effort to control kauri dieback disease.

21. Hunua Falls

 Striking 30-metre waterfall and short bush walks

 Easy ~ 30 minutes

 How to get there: One kilometre north of Hunua, turn right into White Road and after one kilometre, turn right again into Falls Road for a further two kilometres.

The Wairoa River follows an old fault line until it reaches the hard basalt core of an ancient volcano where the river tumbles 30 metres over a cliff as the Hunua Falls. Basalt is formed during volcanic eruptions and makes up 90 per cent of all volcanic rock. Dark coloured and fine grained, basalt in its liquid lava form can flow for very long distances. Once solid it is very hard and does not erode easily. Especially impressive after heavy rain, the falls attract many visitors with the many pleasant picnic spots along the stream and the huge pool at the base of the falls.

Most visitors just do the short five minute walk to the falls but a longer walk over the steam gives a much better impression of these attractive falls. From the carpark, cross over the bridge and head uphill for about 300 metres. Take the track to the right and walk up to the high lookout point over the falls. From the lookout point return to the track, turn right and take the lovely bush walk along a small stream dense with parataniwha back down to the falls. Return to the carpark along the lower track.

The pool at the base of the falls is a popular swimming spot, but it is deeper and less benign than it first appears. A number of people have drowned here so be careful if you enter the water.

22. Cosseys Reservoir Loop Walk

 The pick of the walks in the rugged Hunua Ranges

 Medium ~ Cosseys Reservoir: One and half hours return

Loop Walk: Two and half hours

 How to get there: One kilometre north of Hunua, turn right into White Road and after one kilometre, turn right again into Falls Road for a further two kilometres.

From the Hunua Falls carpark, cross over the bridge and follow gentle uphill track up and over a low ridge down to Cosseys Creek. This requires a bit of nimble rock hopping to cross and can be slippery when wet. The path initially follows the stream and then comes the hard part, a long steep climb with lots of steps. The good news is that is all the hard climbing is done and the remainder of the walk to the reservoir is much easier as the track continues through the thick bush high above the stream.

The 42-metre-high earth dam was opened in 1955 with an average capacity of 14 billion litres of water and covering 121 hectares. There are toilets, a shelter and picnic areas at the reservoir.

From the reservoir the track climbs steadily up to the high point of the walk at the junction of the Massey track. Just below this junction is an excellent viewing platform over the lake, while just beyond is a glimpse of a small grove of large kauri, though access is now limited for obvious reasons.

Now on the Massey track, the walk is pleasantly all downhill back to the falls which will take about an hour. Though there are no views on this part of the trip, the bush here is denser with many large trees including rimu, kahikatea, tawa and kohekohe, while the understory is thick with nikau palms.

Most visitors do the walk anti clockwise, but if the weather is hot consider doing the walk in reverse and spend some time in the swimming holes along Cosseys Creek near the end of the trip.

23. Wairoa Loop Walk

 Handsome bush walk above the Wairoa Reservoir

 Loop Walk: Medium, two hours

Lookout: Medium, 50 minutes from the first carpark, 40 minutes from the carpark by the locked gate.

 How to get there: From Hunua Village head south along Hunua Road for six kilometres and turn left into Moumoukai Road. After 1.5 kilometres, where the road divides, take the left-hand road to Wairoa Dam.

The track begins to the right about 500m past the locked gate and from there it is a steady uphill passing through attractive bush with large trees. While it is all uphill, including several short flights of stairs, the grade is not difficult or too steep. After 20 minutes the track reaches a detour off to the left ending in a wooden platform overlooking the reservoir and the thick bush clad Hunua ranges. This detour will take about 10 minutes.

Returning to the main track continue uphill for five minutes to the telecommunications tower, and now, all the hard climbing done, the track becomes a wide access called the Repeater Road. Passing through pleasant bush there is an excellent lookout point over upper reaches of the Wairoa reservoir in the valley below.

After about ten minutes the track drops into dense bush to the right. This is by far the most attractive part of the walk as the track follows the ridge, meandering gently downhill through dense bush. Keep an eye out for miromiro / tomtit, a striking small bird easily recognised by its distinctive black and white colouring. About halfway down, the track meets a small bush stream, tumbling down through rocky cascades and follows this waterway back to the carpark.

At the carpark a rough unmarked track drops down to the stream below where there is a waterfall and small waterholes perfect for a dip on a hot day.

24. Wairoa Suspension Bridge Walk

 A dam, reservoir lake and a swing bridge over a bush stream

 Bridge Walk: Medium, One hour, 30 minutes

Dam Walk: Easy, 40 minutes

 How to get there: From Hunua Village head south along Hunua Road for six kilometres and turn left into Moumoukai Road. After 1.5 kilometres, where the road divides, take the left-hand road to Wairoa Dam.

It's hard to resist a walk that starts off over a suspension bridge, but enjoy it while you can, once across the deep gully it's a solid uphill climb made a little easier by flights of steps. Once you reach the ridge, there is a window of a view through the bush over farmland to the south. A few minutes after the view, the track drops down to the right and to the dam (the original track to the upper lookout is now closed to prevent the spread of kauri dieback). After 10 minutes walking downhill, the track reaches a wooden platform with views over the dam and the reservoir surrounded by thick bush.

Supplying around 65 per cent of Auckland's water, there are five earth dams in the Hunua Ranges with reservoir lakes that reach deep into the rugged ranges, including the Wairoa Dam built in 1975. Once you reach the dam it is a 25-minute walk to car park. If you are in the mood for more, the track to another lookout branches off the road back

(see previous entry.)

If you just want to walk up to the dam, it will take about 20 minutes from the locked gate, where there is a toilet and picnic area at the base of the dam.

25. Waharau Regional Park

 Rich native bush combines with views over the Firth of Thames

 Waharau Bush Walk: Easy, 40 minutes

Waharau Ridge Track: Medium, Three hours

 How to get there: The park is on the East Coast Road, 8km north of Kaiaua

This small, 170-hectare coastal park touches the coast at Waihihi Bay and then extends inland into the foothills of the Hunua Ranges protecting a diverse native forest of towai, tawa, hinau, totara, rimu, kauri, beech, rewarewa and tanekaha. The small coastal section of the park has puriri, kowhai and karaka. The park has excellent facilities including the lovely Blackberry Flats camping ground, along with extensive picnic areas.

Located at the entrance to the park, the Waharau Bush Walk is on a very good track linking several small gullies, though there are some short steeper sections with steps. Along the bush track are a smattering of identification signs for those wanting to brush up on their knowledge of native trees.

The longer loop track is a long, steady uphill climb with some steps to a ridge. The track then cuts along the ridge and from this high point there are great views over the Firth of Thames, to the Hauraki Plains and the Coromandel Peninsula and this is a great spot for a lunch break.

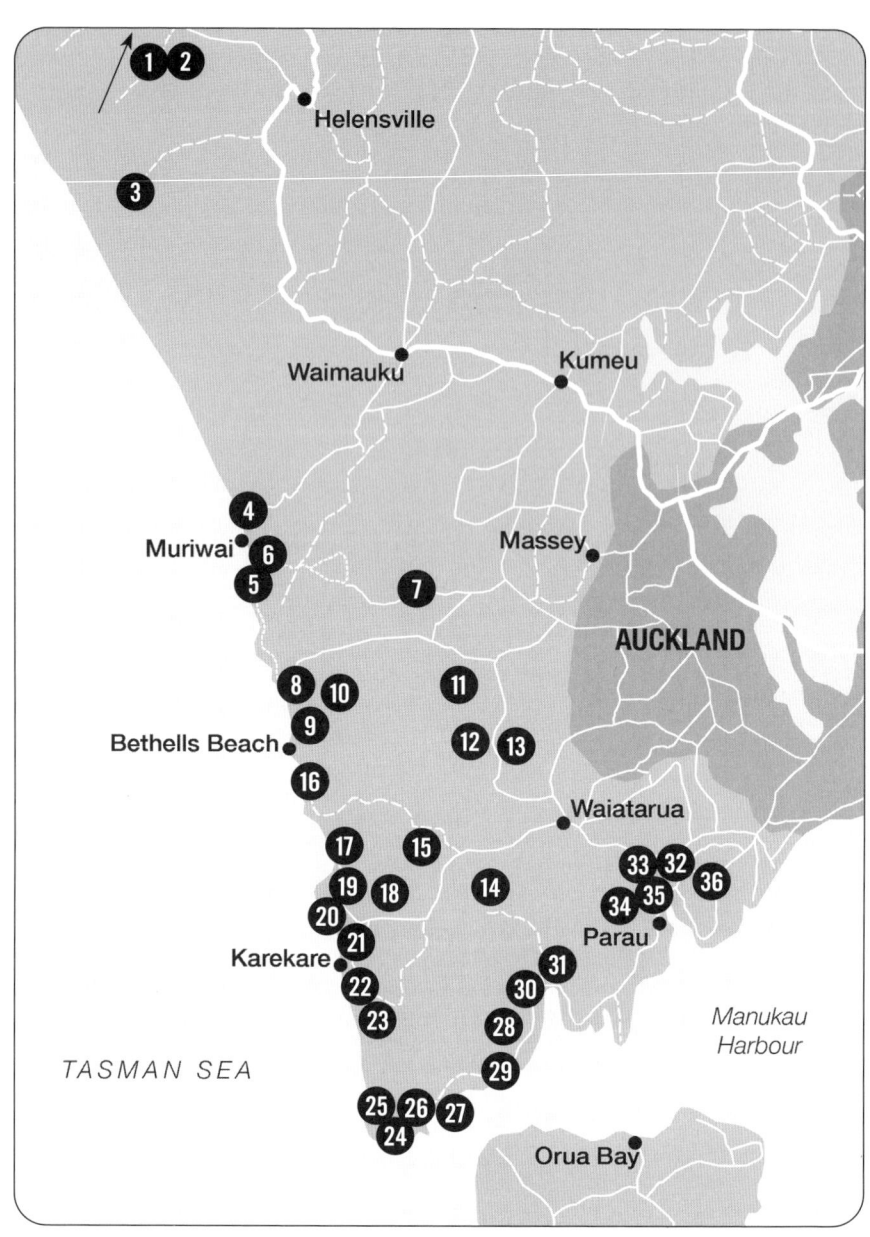

WEST

1. Waionui Inlet and South Head
2. Te Rau Puriri Regional Park
3. Rimmer Road Beach Walk
4. Okiritoto Stream Walk, Muriwai
5. Muriwai Gannet Colony
6. Muriwai Lookout
7. Mokoroa Falls, Goldies Bush
8. O'Neills Bay, Te Henga
9. Te Henga/Bethells Beach and Dune Loop Walk
10. Lake Wainamu Walk
11. Pae o te Rangi Farm Regional Park
12. Waitakere Dam
13. Spragg Bush Loop Walk
14. Upper Nihotapu Dam
15. McElwain Lookout
16. Anawhata Beach
17. Whites Beach, Piha
18. Kitekite Falls
19. Tasman Lookout, The Gap and Lion Rock
20. Te Ahua Point
21. Coman's Track
22. Karekare Falls
23. Tunnel Point and the Pararaha Valley, Karekare
24. Whatipu to Karekare Beach Walk
25. Whatipu Caves
26. Ninepin Rock and Paratutae
27. Omanawanui Track
28. Mt Donald McLean
29. Manukau Bar Lookout
30. Karamatura Falls and Valley
31. Lower and Upper Huia Dams
32. Arataki Nature Trail
33. Arataki Loop Track/Slip Track, Pipeline Road and the Beveridge Track
34. Beveridge Track, Arataki Centre
35. Exhibition Drive Walk
36. Zigzag Track, Atkinson Park, Titirangi

1. Waionui Inlet and South Head

 Bird paradise on vast tidal lagoon on the Kaipara harbour

 Easy ~ Two and half hours return

 How to get there: 39km north of Parakai. At the junction of South Head and Trig Road turn left into Trig Road even though South Head Road appears to be the main road. From this point the road is gravel and the final section passes through forestry land, which can be rough and bumpy especially towards the end. There are no petrol stations or shops beyond Parakai, though there is a café at Shelley Beach.

Waionui Inlet is as far north as you can go on the south head of the Kaipara Harbour and the lack of any facilities (other than a few old shady pine trees) deters many visitors (especially during the week) and gives Waionui a wonderful feeling of isolation.

A vast tidal lagoon, ringed by golden sand hills of the Papakanui Spit, shelters the inlet from the worst of the westerly winds and beyond the spit the high sand hills on the other side of the harbour entrance are clearly visible.

This area is one of this country's most important coastal habitats and a destination for birds seasonally migrating between the northern and southern hemispheres. A mixture of salt marsh, mangrove forest, tidal sandbanks and dunes, it is not surprising that the Kaipara Harbour attracts over 30,000 migratory birds. At low tide, 80 percent of the inlet is above water, making this an ideal feeding ground. Godwits, knots, banded dotterel, Pied Stilt, Far-Eastern Curlew, Oystercatcher, Caspian tern, Turnstones, Fairy Tern, Pacific Golden Plover, Variable Oystercatcher and Whimbrel can all be found here.

The sheltered waters of the lagoon are popular with kayakers and at low to mid-tide, visitors can walk on wide sand flats out to the lagoon entrance and out to South Head. From the carpark follow the 4WD track to the right along the southern shore. After 30 minutes the track narrows but continue walking for another 10 minutes to where the lagoon empties into the harbour. Here at low tide you can venture out on low dunes and sandbanks to bird watch but take care you are not cut off by the tide. If you want to make to South Head continue along the shore to the low 50 metre bluff a little further south.

It is best to come three hours before low tide as this will give you a comfortable six hour window in which to walk. At high tide, the water laps right up to the shore, but you won't be cut off, though you might have to walk through shallow water at various points.

Keep an eye out for fallow deer which roam the coastal area between Muriwai and South Head. If you don't see any animals, you will certainly notice their tracks.

2. Te Rau Puriri Regional Park

 Marvellous views of the Kaipara and a delightful harbour beach

 Easy ~ One and half hours return

 How to get there: South Head Road, 30km north of Parakai. The sign for the park is quite small and the off-road parking is easy to miss as the entrance is alongside a cattle yard. Going north the turn into the parking area is on a very sharp bend so extra care is needed.

Established in 2005, Te Rau Puriri Regional Park covers almost 250ha of rolling hills down to, and along the Kaipara Harbour, and includes the long sand and shell beach at Waipiro Bay. The park is largely farmland and a walking track forms a long loop down to the coast and back. On the way to the beach take the track downhill to the right; it takes longer, but has continuous harbour vistas all the way. On the return trip follow the track that leads up the valley, where a short steep climb at the end takes you back to the carpark.

The beach is a lovely spot (best for swimming at high tide), and doesn't attract many visitors, so there is a good chance you will have this place all to yourself. The coast is favoured by wading birds with heron, black swan, stilts and pied oystercatcher all common here, often in large numbers.

There are patches of regenerating bush in the gullies, home to tui and kereru

3. Rimmer Road Beach Walk

 The ultimate long and lonely beach walk

 Easy ~ Allow at least an hour

 How to get there: From Helensville head south on SH16 for four kilometres and then turn right into Rimmer Road and continue 6 kilometres to the end of the road. This is a forestry road and mostly rough gravel, but comfortably managed in an average road car. The forestry gates are open from 7:00am to 6:00pm.

If it is long, lonely walks along the beach you pine for, then the northern end of Muriwai beach is as wild as it gets - even the pines of Woodhill Forest, struggle in the constant salt-saturated winds. The only access to this stretch of coast, windblown dunes pile up close to the beach, the rumble of the pounding surf is unrelenting and pure air flows off the endless Tasman Sea.

The Tasman Sea, Te Tai-o-Rehua, more commonly referred to by Australians and New Zealanders as 'the ditch', covers around 5,600,000 square kilometres and drops to a maximum depth of 5,200 metres. The sea appeared between 55 and 85 million years ago as Australia and New Zealand separated during the breakup of the super southern continent of Gondwana. Exposed to the constant and vigorous westerly wind of the 'roaring forties', the Tasman has a reputation for stormy waters.

Few people come here as it is mainly used as a 4WD entrance to the beach and it is highly likely you will have the place to yourself. It's up to you whether you want to walk for 30 minutes or for 3 hours.

4. Okiritoto Stream Walk, Muriwai

 A sandy tidal creek flowing into the huge sweep of Muriwai Beach

 Easy ~ 40 minutes return

 How to get there: From Muriwai, turn north and drive to the end of Coast Road where there is a carpark, toilet and information board.

Muriwai is a huge expanse of beach, but most people visit the gannet colony and the short section of the beach directly below the gannet colony in front of the surf club. However, if you after a quieter stretch of the beach then head off to Okiritoto Stream, where you can wander along the stream and down through the wild dunes to the beach.

Once at the beach you can head south along the stretch of beach where 4WD vehicles are banned (they can use the beach to the north). The tracks here are pretty informal, but apart from stunned pohutukawa and karo, the vegetation is mainly dune grasses and it is impossible to get lost.

Black sand, known as titanomagnetite sand – a feature of this entire coast – originated as volcanic ash from Taranaki and was swept north by the tide and current. High in iron content, it is difficult to walk barefoot on a hot day. Facing the restless Tasman Sea, the beach here is frequently windy and exposed, but the sheltered stream has a number of sandy swimming holes, ideal to cool off in.

Like most west coast beaches, Muriwai can be treacherous for swimmers and it is highly advisable to enter the water in the patrolled area in front of the Muriwai Surf Lifesaving Clubhouse.

5. Muriwai Gannet Colony

 Close-up views of a thriving gannet colony, a secret cave and old pa sites

 Easy ~ Gannet colony: 20 minutes

Gannet colony from Muriwai Beach: 50 minutes return

Maori Bay: 30 minutes return

 How to get there: Take Motutara Road through Muriwai township and near the beach turn left up Waitea Road to the carpark. The track to the gannet colony exits from this carpark and the track to the lookout is 100 metres down the road on the right. This car park is frequently full and if that is the case return to Motutara Road, turn left and park down by the beach.

Long occupied by Maori, who were attracted to the area by the fur seals on Oaia Island just off shore, there were once two pa on the northern slopes of Otakamiro Point. The seal colony on the island still exists and seals can occasionally be spotted on the beach at Maori Bay, just to the south of Otakamiro Point.

Early in the 20th century Australasian gannets began establishing nesting sites on Oaia Island (which lies 1.5km offshore), then on Motutara Island, and in 1979 they established themselves on Otakamiro Point, one of only two mainland nesting sites in New Zealand. Now each year, from August to April, over 1200 pairs nest here and the proximity of the nesting birds gives the public easy and close access.

Related to shags and pelicans, the Australasian gannet / takapu (Morus serrator) is a very elegant seabird with beautiful white and yellow colouring and a streamlined shape, perfect for diving into water from a height in order to catch fish. Just one species breeds in New Zealand, and nearly 30 breeding colonies are scattered around New Zealand, mainly on offshore islands. The best time to see the chicks is November and December. White-fronted terns also nest in large numbers on the steep sections of the cliffs where these small graceful birds seem to just float in the air regardless of wind strength.

The track to the colony begins from the carpark and weaves over the cliff tops to various lookout points offering close views of the birds both on their nests and flying overhead. While the birds are an attraction by themselves, the views along the coast are spectacular. To the north the 50 kilometre stretch of beach disappears into the horizon, while to the south are dramatic coastal cliffs of dark volcanic stone.

Just below the gannet colony is Maukatia Bay (locally known as Maori Bay) and along these cliffs are internationally recognised examples of pillow lava which can be found for a one-kilometre stretch south of the car park. Pillow lava is formed by underwater eruptions and the rapid cooling effect of the water which caused the lava to billow out and then cool in rounded pillow shapes. It is not uncommon to see seals on the beach.

At low tide a secret cave under the gannet colony is accessible from the beach. The cave is not visible from above so go down to the beach and walk to the right where you will find a split in the rock. Enter the narrow cave and walk through to the open ocean, it's especially impressive in rough weather.

Most visitors only go to the upper car park and stroll out over Otakamiro Point to see the gannets. However, it is really worth the effort to begin your visit by walking up from the lower car park by the beach at the end of Motutara Road (just past the café). From here the walk up to the gannet colony is less than 10 minutes. The track winds through lovely coastal bush and old pa sites with amazing coastal views. This is a very popular spot for both bird watchers and surfers and the top car park is frequently full.

6. Muriwai Lookout

  A lovely climb up through superb native bush to wide coastal views

  Easy ~ 40 minutes return

  How to get there: Waitea Road, 220 metres on the left from the intersection with Motutara Road.

Located high above Muriwai, the lookout is on the north-eastern lip of the ancient volcanic rim that makes up the Waitakere Ranges. From here, the dune country runs all the way to Manganui Bluff north of Dargaville, created by volcanic sand swept down the Waikato River and then driven north by currents and wind.

The great views over the beach are reward in themselves, but the track up to the lookout is through very handsome native bush, passing through several jungle-like groves of nikau palms, along with huge pohutukawa, puriri, taraire and kohekohe and an understorey of kawakawa. Near the entrance off Waitea Road are clumps of the native Renga Renga lily, a popular garden plant, but not so common in the wild.

The Lookout Track is well maintained and is a steady rather than steep climb. At the first junction, turn left following the sign to Domain Crescent and not the sign to the right marked Lookout Track. You can either continue down to Motutara Road (the main road into Muriwai) or return the way you came.

If parked at the top car park (the one closest to the gannet colony), the track begins 100 metres down Waitea Road on the right. From the bottom car park by the beach, the track is about 100 metres up the Motutara road on the left.

7. Mokoroa Falls, Goldie Bush

 A double waterfall in coastal forest.

 Waterfall lookout: Easy, 45 minutes return

Mokoroa Stream and Loop Walk: Medium, two hours return

 How to get there: End of Horsman Road, off Wairere Road from Waitakere township

The Mokoroa Falls are located in the 192 ha Goldie Bush Reserve, gifted to the people of Auckland by David Goldie, former Mayor of Auckland and Member of Parliament for West Auckland. He was also a prominent timber merchant and this reserve was thoroughly milled by Goldie before he gave it to the city in 1925. Today the native trees are slowly regenerating, and the bush is mainly dominated by kanuka and tree coprosma, though young kauri, rimu and tanekaha are beginning to break through the canopy.

There are in fact two waterfalls, the larger fall in volume (11 metres high) on the Mokoroa Stream and a taller falls on the smaller Houheria Stream. Both tumble over a cliff of volcanic stone 20 million years old. Together they merge into a single pool on the Mokoroa stream with a pleasant picnic spot at the bottom of the falls which is accessed via a steep side track just before the lookout. There are numerous swimming holes downstream but take care near the cliffs as a substantial rock fall occurred here in 2014.

The track to the falls, previously very muddy and slippery, has been substantially upgraded, though there is still a short muddy stretch near the beginning. While it is downhill to the falls and uphill on the return, the grade is gradual and not difficult.

For the more adventurous, there is a track along the bush-fringed stream, but this involves numerous stream crossings and is frequently unmarked, especially where the track follows the stream bed. It is much easier walking up stream so take the Goldies Bush Walkway (marked to the left not far from the entrance) down to the stream and then work your way up to the waterfalls.

8. O'Neills Bay, Te Henga

 A wild isolated bay enclosed by volcanic cliffs

 Easy ~ One and half hours return

 How to get there: From Ranui in West Auckland take the Swanson Road west. At the junction of Waitakere Road and Scenic Drive, veer left into Scenic Drive and continue for 3km, then turn right into Te Henga Road. After 4km turn left into Bethells Road and continue 6.5km until you cross over a one-way bridge just past Tasman View Road. The car park is immediately to the right after the one-way bridge.

O'Neills Bay is a wonderful, wild and windy beach that encapsulates the best the west coast can offer. Erangi Point and Kauwahaia Island at the southern end of O'Neills Bay offer some protection from the winds which have created a wide bank of sand hills behind the beach. As with all the west coast beaches, swimming is only to be untaken with great care.

The short easy walk on a good track (40 minutes one way) skirts Erangi Point with great views directly below over Ihumoana Island and Waitakere Bay and beyond that the long stretch of Te Henga Beach. The plants along the track are exposed to the constant wind; even tough manuka are shaped into low growing plants with an architectural beauty. On the slope down to the bay, the track passes through a lovely grove of mahoe or whitey wood which is recognisable by the white patchy trunks and the thick litter of papery leaves crunch under your feet. An old volcanic crater forms the northern part of the bay. The track is part of the longer Te Henga Walkway, though beyond O'Neills Bay the track becomes more difficult and more suitable for adventurous bushwalkers.

You can walk along Te Henga beach and over to O'Neills Bay, but this walk, while a bit longer, is both easier and has much better views

9. Te Henga/Bethells Beach and Dune Loop Walk

 Premier wild west coast beach

 Easy ~ 50 minutes return

 How to get there: From Ranui in West Auckland take the Swanson Road east. At the junction of Waitakere Road and Scenic Drive, veer left into Scenic Drive and continue for 3km and then turn right into Te Henga Road. After 4km turn left into Bethells Road and continue 7.5km to the car park at the end of the road.

Te Henga beach is a turbulent, wide beach enclosed by dramatic rocky bluffs. The unstable sand dunes formed by the driving westerly winds ensure that the small settlement is well back from the beach. In the deep hollows behind the beach pohutukawa, mahoe, flax and cabbage trees manage to thrive, though not above the height of the dunes. Golden native dune grass, pingao, is in abundance on the dune fringes. Originally this was a much deeper bay but over the past 6,000 years, sand has been driven inland from the ocean while silt has washed down the river gradually filling in the bay and, in the process, created the long stretch of sandy beach we see today.

From the carpark walk down to the beach along the edge of the Waitakere River as it spreads across the sand and empties into the sea. The river is the outlet for the both Lake Wainamu and the Te Henga swamp, the largest wetland in the Auckland region. You can cross the river at the mouth and walk along the dunes and over a low saddle to O'Neills Beach from this point, though this can be a bit tricky near high tide.

From here it is a 20-minute walk to the cliffs at the southern end of the beach which are mainly composed of pillow lava. There is also a large sea cave to explore at low tide and, if the sea is not wild, it is possible to walk out on to Raeakiaki Point. This coastline is infamous for unexpected large, rogue waves so don't take any risks if the sea is rough.

The rocky outcrops on the beach are excellent examples of volcanic breccia. Breccia refers to stone that has formed from other rock fragments cemented together with finer material. In the case of andesitic breccia, the base material is of volcanic origin which has been broken up and then, over a long period of time, reformed into hard stone. Here the finer material is partially eroded by the sea leaving the distinctive larger stones exposed.

From the southern edge of the beach retrace your steps for about 200 metres where there is wide gap in the dunes, often made clearer by foot tracks. Walk through this gap and into the dunes where a narrow track leads up over a grassy dune. From the top of this small rise, the extent of the dune country behind the beach comes as a surprise. Not only does this extend the whole length of the beach but is also a good 500 metres wide. Equally surprising is the profusion of plants that flourish in this exposed landscape. Near the beach the soft foliage of the kanuka is trimmed to precision by the salt-laden winds while further away from the sea, larger pohutukawa are gaining a firm foothold.

Meandering through the low vegetation, the track is easy to follow and eventually emerges on the road by the carpark.

10. Lake Wainamu Walk

 A deep, freshwater lake created by massive black sand dunes

 Easy ~ Lake edge: One hour return

Lake Circuit and dune: Two hours return

 How to get there: From Scenic Drive, turn right onto Te Henga Road and after four kilometres turn left in to Bethells Road and drive six kilometres to the carpark. The track begins on the left once you cross the bridge about one kilometre before Bethells Beach/Te Henga. There is limited parking at the beginning of the track, but there is more parking across the road at the start of the walk to O'Neills Bay.

Around 6,000 years ago, wind-driven sand from the beach created an enormous dune that today is around one kilometre long and 200 metres wide. Eventually the dune completely blocked the Wainamu Stream and in the process, created a long, deep lake. The dune is much bigger than it first appears and in a strong westerly wind the sand is whipped across the broad dune, like some desolate desert scene from a movie. Today the dune is mostly stable as the dune stabilisation project behind the beach has cut off the source of sand.

Native freshwater fish found in the lake include grey mullet, long finned and short finned eels, inanga, banded kokopu and common bully. The lake and stream margins are the favoured habitat of water birds such as shag, duck and swan.

The lake at the edge of the dune is particularly deep, making it an ideal swimming spot and children, and the young at heart, will have great fun sliding down the steep dunes along the stream.

The track to the dunes begins on the left once you cross the bridge over the Waiti Stream about one kilometre before Bethells Beach/Te Henga. Initially the track to the dunes follows the stream, but then diverts up across the dune. It is much easier to the walk in an anti-clockwise direction, crossing the dunes first as they are more extensive than at first glance, are slow going, and frequently very windy. It will take about 30 minutes to reach the lake. The track around the lake begins to the right, undulating through patches of bush with occasional steps, but nothing difficult.

At the head of the lake the Wainamu stream tumbles down a steep valley creating numerous rock pools perfect for a dip on a hot day and a handsomely carved pou whenua celebrates the connection Te Kawerau a Maki have with this land.

The track along the eastern shore is easier and more open and once back at the dunes, just follow the stream back to the car park. Similarly, if you are only going to the lake, on your return walk to the eastern edge of the dune and find the stream there. The stream bed is very shallow with a sandy bottom, so it is much easier walking in the stream than on the track and pleasantly cool on a hot day.

11. Pae o te Rangi Farm Regional Park

 City views from atop windswept farmland

 Medium ~ Long Road: 1hour 15 minutes return

Te Henga Road: 2 hours 15 minutes return

 How to get there: Te Henga Road entrance. Corner Bethells and Te Henga roads, 4km from Scenic Drive. Long Road entrance. From Te Henga Road turn left into Bethells Road and after 400m turn left into Long Road and drive 1km to the end.

A curious place, this is a park that divides into two distinctive halves. The lower part of the park (entrance off Te Henga Road) is given over to a disc golf course and horse riding, and is not appealing as a walk on its own. There are yellow and orange markers along the main track, but the signage by the parking doesn't explain what these markers mean. The yellow markers lead to a tiny basic camping ground which has a toilet and a tap, but oddly for a camping ground little flat ground. The orange markers are the walking track, which eventually leads via the Whatitiri connecting track to Long Road track and onto the upper section of the park.

The Long Road Track is a solid 20-minute uphill slog on gravel farm track which suddenly opens out into wide open grassy paddocks. Now you will understand why the park name means "the footstool of Rangi'. From this point it is an easy 15 minutes' walk to the summit, with glorious views east to Rangitoto and the central city, and west over the sea and coast. Most importantly you are now pleased that you decided to trudge all this way after all.

If the lower part of the park doesn't sound at all appealing, then drive to the top of Long Road and walk from there. You still have a solid uphill walk, but it certainly is a good deal shorter.

Waitakere Ranges Regional Park

Sitting between the city and the west coast is the Waitakere Ranges Regional Park which, like Hunua Ranges Regional Park, is a major water catchment area for Auckland City. More accessible than Hunua, this 17,000-hectare park is literally laced with walking tracks of every description ranging from sedate beach walks through to demanding tracks in thick bush and steep terrain. Much of the park was milled for timber in the nineteenth century and large areas were cleared for farming, but today the bush is regenerating steadily covering over old scars. Birdlife is notable by its absence, although the Ark in the Park project which covers 1000 hectares of the Cascades Kauri Park has seen the reintroduction of whitehead, North Island robin and hihi in the predator-controlled area.

Today most of the park is closed in a bid to prevent the spread of kauri die-back disease. Tracks are gradually being reopened and the ones included are open at the time of publishing. The Arataki Centre and the Auckland City website will have up to date information.

12. Waitakere Dam

 Sitting on top of a high bluff overlooking the Waitakere Valley, the dam gives excellent views over the ranges.

 Easy ~ One hour return

 How to get there: On Scenic Drive, 7km north of the intersection with Piha Road.

Built between 1905 and 1910, this was the first reservoir constructed in the Waitakere Ranges to replace the city's water supply at Western Springs. The area around the dam formed the nucleus of the huge Waitakere Ranges Regional Park, on the fringe of New Zealand's largest city. To assist in the construction of the dam, which at the time was in an isolated part of Auckland, a small tramway was built to bring materials to the site; and is still operating.

The dam itself is built across the Waitakere River on top of a high bluff and therefore has extensive views over the bush and the valley far below. There is a long flight of steps just to the right at the beginning of the dam and these lead down to the foot of the dam where a small bridge crosses the stream to a lookout.

While the access to the dam is on a sealed roadway, from the carpark it is all downhill and some of the steeper sections will have you puffing on the way back.

13. Spragg Bush Loop Walk

 An historic cemetery and dense native bush

 Easy ~ 45 minutes return

 How to get there: Not easy to find, the track begins at 699 Scenic Drive, 5.5 km north of the intersection with Piha Road, near Mountain Road. Parking is limited.

In 1901 Wesley Spragg purchased this land for a holiday home and in 1924 gifted the land to the city for a reserve. The cemetery, however, is much older and burials began during the 1860s until it was closed in

1906 and added to the Spragg Bush Reserve in 1929. Most of the graves belong to the local Bethell, Russell and Colebrook families.

From the carpark on Scenic Drive the track immediately plunges into thick bush and not far along the track is the historic cemetery. The track runs parallel to Scenic Drive and after about 15 minutes a short track leads off to the left and back to Scenic Drive. Take the right-hand track through the bush to Turanga Road and walk back down the road (there is no footpath but it is not busy) almost to the end where another track goes off to the right, through the bush and back to the beginning.

14. Upper Nihotapu Dam

 Engineering history combines with a glorious bush walk

 Easy ~ 1 hour 40 minutes

 How to get there: On the Piha Road, 1.5km from the intersection with Scenic Drive, Waitakere

Opened in 1923, the Nihotapu Dam is the second oldest of the five reservoirs in the Waitakere Ranges which still supply Auckland City with 20% of its domestic water supply. Located high on the rugged ranges, the concrete dam was an outstanding feat of engineering in very difficult terrain so it is not surprising that it took eight years to build.

Leaving the Piha Road, the excellent track runs through regenerating bush almost parallel with the road until it joins with the service road to the dam. A feature of this section is the numerous young rimu trees with distinctive weeping branches that makes them very easy to identify. Gradually dropping downhill, the road runs along the Nihotapu Stream as it tumbles downhill into a deep gorge. Finally, the stream drops over a 10 metre high waterfall into the placid waters of the reservoir. From this point the track meanders along the edge of the small lake and the bush here is older and more luxuriant with tall northern rata and kauri trees breaking the skyline on the ridges. Built across a narrow gorge, from the dam the southern shores of the Manukau Harbour are clearly visible through the trees. A handy shelter has excellent information on the statistics of the reservoir along with construction details.

A further 10 minutes on is a small picnic area and a siding of the tramway used in the construction of the dam. From here you can follow the railway and the pipeline to the base of the dam. Return the way you came.

15. McElwain Lookout

 Now you know why people get lost in the Waitakere Ranges

 Easy ~ 20 minutes

 How to get there: Anawhata Road, 2.5km from the Piha Road turnoff. The sign for the lookout is tucked away on the left and is easy to miss.

In contrast to the dramatic coastal vistas along the Anawhata Road, the view from the McElwain lookout is altogether different, and in fact the sea is barely glimpsed at all. A short easy walk leads to a wooden platform that rises above the low bush and the view from the top is a graphic reminder on just how large and rugged the Waitakere Regional Park really is. Ridge after bush-clad ridge stretch away in every direction obscuring both the sea to the west and the city to the east and it is easy to see why visitors occasionally get lost in the park despite being so close to New Zealand's largest city.

The bush here is regenerating slowly, but nonetheless lush with ferns, astelia, mountain cabbage tree and five finger with rewarewa thrusting up through the low vegetation. Particularly attractive are the distinctive long weeping branches of the young rimu, a form they lose as they grow taller.

Piwakawaka and miromiro / tomtit flit among the lower branches feeding on insects disturbed by passers-by.

Tomtits are one of the most widely distributed of our small native birds and are found on both main islands, Stewart and Chatham Islands the sub-Antarctic Snares and Auckland Islands. Highly territorial they have adapted to regenerating bush and exotic scrubland, though they prefer habitat with large mature trees. Some variation in colour occurs regionally but general the females are mostly brown and white and the males black and white.

16. Anawhata Beach

 Isolated beach with a backdrop of dramatic cliffs and rocky headlands

 Medium ~ One hour return

 How to get there: Take the Piha Road and turn off onto the gravel Anawhata Road which is narrow and winding for all of its ten kilometres so take it easy.

A magnificent wild beach flanked by rocky headlands, Anawhata is only accessible by foot so it is never crowded. The beach is split by a rocky outcrop of Parera Point along which a small stream runs down to the wide-open expanse of sand that is constantly pounded by the surf. Behind the beach, the small dunes are the breeding grounds of the endangered New Zealand dotterel, while white-fronted terns and pied oyster catchers are common on the open sand. Rising above the open bay are barren dark volcanic cliffs broken here and there by tough coastal plants battered into shape by the strong winds. The kowhai in this area are notable for their smaller than usual leaves, a variation is found only on this stretch of the coast.

The track down to the beach is steep so think twice about bringing little ones as you might be carrying them on the way back up the hill. Initially the track follows a gravel road but then becomes steep and rough as it drops off into the gully leading to the beach. Sheltered from the wind this gully is thick with ferns, nikau palms and young trees and, at one point, visitors must bend down to go under a huge pohutukawa that has toppled over the path and then continued to grow.

17. White's Beach, Piha

 Only accessible on foot, this beach is surrounded by steep bush-clad hills

 Medium ~ 50 minutes return

 How to get there: The track begins at the very end of North Piha Road, Piha

Like Anawhata Beach just to the north, White's Beach is only accessible by foot, but is worth the effort for those who enjoy a wilder, unspoiled landscape. The track to the beach winds up over the headland of Te Waha Point through low bush of manuka, karaka, rangiora, hebe, kawakawa and pohutukawa. From the top there is a great view over White's Bay. The track down to the beach is steep and rough and needs a bit of care. The small beach is backed by dunes covered in marram grass and, like elsewhere on this coast, even on a good day the surf is rough and unpredictable so great care should be taken when swimming. As with other bays on this coast, White's Bay was formed by a volcanic eruption 16 million years ago.

The track to White's Beach from North Piha is hard to find. From the car park drop down to beach and walk north past a number of shallow sea caves (little blue penguins nest here so dogs are prohibited). Above the beach is a single power line supported by wooden poles. Walk to trees at the left of the last pole and the start of the hidden track will become obvious.

18. Kitekite Falls

 The Glen Esk stream tumbles down a series of cascades into a pleasant bush-lined swimming hole.

 Easy ~ One hour return

 How to get there: At the bottom of the hill to Piha turn immediately right into Glenesk Road. The track begins from the car park at the end of this road.

This is the quintessential Waitakere walk. From the car park the broad track follows the picturesque Glen Esk stream through luxuriant bush steadily uphill to the falls. In this sheltered, warm and wet valley, native plants of every type flourish from large kauri through to miniscule mosses and lichens. Along the Glen Esk Stream and thriving in conditions that are constantly damp is parataniwha (Elatostema rugosum), an attractive native ground plant with wide nettle-like leaves. This plant is only found in the North Island and thrives in wet, deep shade. Its leaves in certain seasons turn from green to shades of light pink, rust brown and deep red. While common in the bush, it is notoriously difficult to grow in cultivation.

The three cascades that make up Kitekite Falls are best seen from the viewpoint above the valley just before the end of the track. The track also offers views back down the valley over the tops of regenerating kauri. The lower falls drop into a small pool suitable for swimming, and the broad rocky area right by the falls is a good, if lumpy, spot for a picnic.

After crossing over the stream at the waterfall, the track continues downhill and re-joins the main track just before the car park. This is justifiably one of the most popular walks in the Waitakere Ranges Regional Park and attracts large numbers of visitors. For a less-crowded experience, try to visit on a week day.

The name of the falls is not so pleasant, however: it commemorates an intertribal massacre of Maori visiting from South Kaipara.

19. Tasman Lookout, The Gap and Lion Rock

 Several lookout points offer dramatic coastal views over one of West Auckland's most popular beaches.

 Medium ~ First lookout: 20 minutes return

Tasman Lookout and the Gap Loop Walk: 40 minutes return

Lion Rock: 20 minutes return

 How to get there: At the bottom of the hill to Piha turn hard left into Beach Valley Road then, just before the beach, take the left fork into Marine Parade. The track begins at the car park at the end of the road.

This coastline is famous for its dramatic seascape. The wilder the weather, the more spectacular the experience along this walk. The first part of the track leads uphill with lots of steps to a T intersection where you take the right-hand track to a lookout high above Piha, with excellent views along the beach to Lion Rock and the coast to the north. Retrace your steps and this time go straight ahead and downhill to a second lookout above The Gap, a narrow sandy strip between the mainland and Taitomo Island (Camel Rock.) According to Maori tradition, The Gap was once the lair of the fearsome taniwha Kaiwhare. Taitomo Island itself is privately owned Maori land and the land beyond the beach is also privately owned.

Continue down the easy path to a small sandy cove and while the sea pounds through the narrow gap, the beach below is surprisingly sheltered. From the beach you can return to Piha along the beach and rocky shore. Not so long ago this was not accessible at high tide, but in a short space of time huge quantities of sand have built up the beach to a point where it is a comfortable walk in any tide. However, this coastline is notorious for rogue waves that wash people off the rocks, often to their death, so don't walk back along the shore if the waves look dicey. Note, too, that dogs are banned from this part of the beach, on account of nesting little blue penguins.

Ten minutes' walk away is iconic Lion Rock, known as Te Piha in Maori, which refers to the wave pattern breaking against the rock. The remnants of an old volcanic plug, there are a steep set of steps which lead up to a platform about halfway up and this is a high as you can go. At the platform is a stone seat and a carved pou of Ngati Tangiaro Taua who also loved to sit in this very spot. The steep climb made this the perfect location for the important defence pa Whakaari.

20. Te Ahua Point

 Dramatic sea cliffs dropping hundreds of metres into the wild ocean combine with spectacular coastal views.

 Easy ~ 50 minutes return

 How to get there: The track begins at the end of Te Ahu Ahu Road/Log Race Road, which turns left off Piha Road just before the road descends into Piha.

Situated between Karekare and Piha beaches, Te Ahua Point is a superb lookout atop towering volcanic cliffs that drop hundreds of metres into a wild sea. To the south, the view is along the coast to the dangerous bar that marks the entrance to the Manukau Harbour. Jutting out to sea far to the south is Mt Karioi near Raglan. To the north, the entire coast from Piha beach to the Muriwai coast stretches out before you. The salt-lashed and wind-sheared vegetation surprisingly supports stunted kowhai trees easily recognised by their fine foliage.

The dramatic cliffs of Te Ahua Point are the lip of the ancient Waitakere volcano. Erupting about fifteen million years ago, the volcano was active for about six million years and at its greatest extent had a diameter of 50 kilometres. The centre of this gigantic volcano was 20 kilometres to the west, but over a period of five million years, constant wave action completely eroded all trace of the volcano above sea level. Further earth movements tilted the eastern rim causing it to rise again above the sea and forming the present Waitakere Ranges.

The full name of Ahua Point is Te Ahua O Hinerangi and is named after the beautiful chieftainess Hinerangi who climbed to this headland and pined away waiting for her husband, who had drowned in the sea below.

The track is well formed and well-marked and the grassy knoll at the turnaround point is a good place for a break, though is frequently windy. For those wanting a longer walk the track continues downhill to Karekare beach.

21. Coman's Track

 It's a hard climb but the views are worth it

 Hard ~ Coman's Track and Mercer Bay Loop Track: Two hours return

Lower Lookout: 30 minutes return.

 How to get there: At the end of Watchmans Road, 200 metres north of the main Karekare Beach carpark

There is no two ways about it, the Comans Track is all uphill with lots of steps. However, it is in excellent condition so if you take your time it is comfortably managed by those of moderate fitness. The reward is a walk along one of Auckland's most spectacular coastlines.

Climbing quickly up from the beach, the track climbs through attractive bush, then follows a narrow coastal ridge with no shortage of spectacular views south over Karekare beach, the Manukau Bar and on a good day as far south as Karioi mountain near Raglan. Equally impressive are the volcanic cliffs that drop hundreds of metres into the sea. Eventually the track meets the Mercer Bay Loop track which continues on to a superb grassy point with even better views.

Of course, if you have transport organised you can have someone pick you up at the end of Te Ahu Ahu Road (see the previous entry.) If you only do this one way, oddly enough it is better walking uphill as the views of the coast are gradually revealed as you climb.

22. Karekare Falls

 Water fans over volcanic rock into a sheltered swimming hole

 Easy ~ 30 minutes return

 How to get there: Begin at the main parking area at Karekare beach and then walk up Lone Kauri Road for about 300 metres to the track on the left. It is difficult to park at the start of the track.

An easy stroll, suitable even for small children, the path drops down from the road, crosses over the Opal Pool stream and winds through attractive bush to the picturesque Karekare Falls. Known as a 'horsetail waterfall,' water fans out and cascades 30m down dark volcanic rock into a wide swimming hole. Named by AA Directions magazine as New Zealand's best swimming hole, the water flow is generally low so the pool is safe for all ages.

23. Tunnel Point and the Pararaha Valley, Karekare

 Wild beach, an old bush railway tunnel and a wetland valley

 Easy ~ Tunnel Point: One hour return

Pararaha Valley: One hour 30 minutes return

 How to get there: Karekare is well sign posted on the Piha Road about five kilometres from Piha. From here it is three kilometres to the beach and, although this road is sealed, it is very steep and narrow so drive carefully.

From the carpark, walk down to the beach through the pohutukawa glade, a good spot for a picnic if it is very windy on the beach. Once on the beach head south where you immediately enter the Whatipu Scientific Reserve. It is unusual to have such easy access to a scientific reserve as most are closed to the public, but no dogs are allowed.

The track is a bit tricky to find. About 500m past the Scientific Reserve where a wide stretch of flat, open ground reaches to the base of the cliffs, veer off to the left and keep your eyes open for a pink marker in the dunes to the right. Once you find the track then is very easy to follow and from this point the tunnel is about 10 minutes walking. The tunnel and the steam engine are all that remains of the bush tramway ran along the coast to a wharf on a sheltered cove just inside the entrance to Manukau Harbour. Just beyond the short tunnel is a small camping ground.

Continuing south a short distance from the tunnel you have a choice. You can veer to the right and walk down to the beach and return to Karekare or you can continue ahead to the Pararaha Valley which will take about 45 minutes to explore.

A long boardwalk leads from the dunes across deep ponds and into a deep valley enclosed by volcanic cliff. Sand blown up from the beach has blocked the stream, creating deep dune ponds. Aquatic bird life flock to the safe haven of the wetland and overhead kahu, the native hawk circles looking for a quick meal.

You will need to return from the valley the same way as the longer connecting tracks are now closed. Do not try and cross the dune country unless on a very clearly marked track. It is much more difficult than it looks with dense vegetation and deep ponds, and you will be disturbing the wildlife in the process.

Of course, you can do the walk along the beach first, but it surprisingly difficult to find the track as there are no markers up from the beach and most of the promising looking tracks have a tendency to just run out in the scrub.

At Karekare there is plenty of parking and toilets, but no shops, cafes or petrol, though on a sunny summer afternoon the car park can get crowded.

24. Whatipu to Karekare Beach Walk

 Easy. ~ Three hours

 How to get there: Karekare: The beach is well sign posted on the Piha Road about five kilometres from Piha. From here it is three kilometres to the beach carpark on a steep, narrow road.

Whatipu: Take the road through Titirangi to Huia on the northern side of the Manukau Harbour. From Huia the road to Whatipu is narrow, winding and unsealed.

Karekare is wilder and more dramatic than Piha Beach and considerably less developed with just a handful of holiday houses clustered in the bush, avoiding the prevailing westerly wind. Featured as a setting for the film, The Piano, steep cliffs drop into the sea at the northern end of the beach while to the south black sand stretches all the way to Whatipu. The northern and middle sections of the beach are the remains of a crater from a smaller eruption on the eastern edge of the gigantic Waitakere volcano and the Watchman rock formation in the middle of the beach is a lava dome within that crater.

Although the area around Karekare was heavily milled for timber, the native forest on the steep hills above the beach is making a steady comeback and includes the largest taraire forest in the regional park.

Whatipu on the north head of the Manukau Harbour is windswept and wild and pummelled by the thundering seas of the Manukau Bar. The highest wind gust in the Auckland region was recorded along this coast at the Manukau Heads on 21 February 1992 measuring 204 kilometres per hour. Over the past century the shoreline has changed dramatically with powerful westerly storms and savage tides moving huge amounts of sand from season to season. Even on a moderately good day, surf pounds the shoreline (swimming is not recommended), and salt-laden winds whip up the black sand along this exposed coast.

The wetlands, between the caves and the beach, is an important habitat for water birds including bittern, little blue penguin, fernbirds, New Zealand dotterel, shags and oystercatchers. Do not try to cross the wetlands – aside from disturbing the birds, the vegetation is impossible to walk through without a track with hidden and deep dune ponds.

Overlooking the bar are two islets, Ninepin Rock (the rock with the lighthouse) and Paratutae, the much larger island at the entrance to the harbour. Below Paratutae lie a few weathered beams, all that remains of the wharf from where kauri was formerly shipped in vast quantities to Onehunga. A tramline once ran from the wharf to Pararaha Valley to the north, though very little of the track now remains.

Now with all that information off you go for a spectacular beach walk with views far to the south where Mt Karioi near Raglan juts out to sea, while to the north is Piha beach and the Muriwai Coast. In all seriousness it is very exposed and wild, and you must be prepared for very dry and windy conditions. It is usually easier to walk from Whatipu to Karekare with the wind at your back and you will need someone to pick you up as you won't want to do a return walk.

25. Whatipu Caves

 Several large sea caves huddle behind sand dunes.

 Easy ~ 30 minutes return

 How to get there: From Huia, take Huia Road then continue on Whatipu Road. The trip is 9.3 kilometres, but the road is narrow and winding and the last 5km is gravel road.

The walk begins on the same track as the Gibbons track (which leads inland and is currently closed), but then branches off to the left and skirts the bottom of the cliff face leading to several large sea caves and a small camping area. Shaped by years of wave action, the caves are now a considerable distance from the sea as the marshy area between the cliffs has built up since 1940. The largest of the caves was once used for dances, though sand has now raised the floor level of the cave by five metres. Although the caves are substantial, torches are not necessary.

From a distance, the wetlands do not look difficult to cross but trying to walk through them will turn into a nightmare. Return to the car park to get down to the beach.

26. Ninepin Rock and Paratutae

 The northern head of the Manukau Harbour is one of the wildest and most scenically dramatic areas of the west coast.

 Easy ~ One hour, 15 minutes

 How to get there: Start as for the Whatipu Caves walk, but from the carpark take the track over the bridge and follow the track to left.

The first part of the walk is through dune vegetation to the beach, which leads to Ninepin Rock, the rock with the lighthouse, and to Paratutae, the much larger island to the left. Even on a moderately good day, wild surf pounds the shoreline (swimming is not recommended!), and salt-laden winds whip up the black sand along this exposed coast. On 7 February 1863 the HMS Orpheus struck the Manukau bar while trying to enter the harbour. Of the 259 men aboard only 70 survived; this is still New Zealand's worst maritime disaster.

However, it is its very wildness that makes this area so appealing. Here, only an hour's drive from downtown Auckland, you can walk along a windswept beach that feels a million miles away from civilisation.

While it looks easy to climb Paratutae, it is a lot harder to find a way back down.

27. Omanawanui Track

 Dramatic coastal views and a historic signal house

 Hard ~ Omanawanui: Hard, Two hours one way

Signal House Track: Medium one hour return

 How to get there: Whatipu Road, on the left 1.5km past the intersection with the Donald McLean Road.

One of the more challenging short walks in the Waitakere Ranges, this track has been substantially upgraded recently with flights of steps replacing the more difficult steep sections.

Right from the start the track winds constantly up and down, occasional skirting cliffs tops with a direct drop into the water. After about 40 minutes you reach the top of Omanawanui with a view that will make your head spin. After a short rest head off steeply downhill and after 45 minutes you will reach another summit from where the view is down over Whatipu. Continue down to the Signal House Track which branches off to the left and it will take you 20 minutes' walk to reach the house aptly named Albatross Nest. It was here that Thomas Wing, pilot and harbour master lived with his family in the 19th century and it is said the house was chained to the ground to stop it being blown away by the wind.

Return to the Omanawanui Track where it is a 20 minute downhill walk to the road.

28. Mt Donald McLean

 Expansive views high above the Manukau Harbour and north over the Waitakere Ranges

 Easy ~ 30 minutes return

 How to get there: Take Whatipu Road then turn right into Donald McLean Road and drive right to the end. The Mt Donald McLean walk starts at the car park.

Rising 389 metres about the sea, Mt Donald McLean's wooden viewing platform offers unsurpassed views that are hard to beat. To the north are the bush-cloaked ridges and valleys of the Waitakere Ranges; to the west Whatipu and the churning waters of the Manukau Bar; to the south the sandy slopes below the lighthouse on South Head and beyond to distant Pukekawa. The whole of the Manukau Harbour spreads out to the east while the central city and Rangitoto can be clearly seen in the north east.

The short track is an easy gradual climb. Despite the exposed windy site, the bush is surprising lush with regenerating kauri, rimu, nikau, totara, tanekaha, lancewood, rewarewa and tree ferns. It is also home to Hebe bishopiana – which is only found in the Waitakere Ranges – and to Hall's totara, a plant usually found at higher, cooler altitudes.

For those wanting something a bit more challenging, the summit can be reached from Huia via the Fletcher/Mt Donald McLean tracks which are suitable for people of good fitness and experience.

29. Manukau Bar Lookout

 A high point overlooking the notorious Manukau Bar

 Easy ~ 20 minutes return

 How to get there: On the Whatipu Road on the left, 5km from the Huia store.

A viewing platform looks directly west down the harbour to the notorious Manukau Bay, the scene of New Zealand's worst maritime accident in 1863 when the HMS Orpheus ran aground on the Manukau Bar. Even in fine weather the bar is a lethal combination of open ocean swells, fierce westerly winds, a tidal variation of around four metres and a sandbank that is constantly changing, making crossing very difficult even for experienced sailors.

A short flat track follows a ridge of regenerating tanekaha mixed with kanuka to the viewing platform. On the coast below there is a small colony of the New Zealand fur seal.

30. Karamatura Falls and Valley

 Lush forest, scenic falls and valley vistas

 Easy ~ One and half hours return

Facilities: Off road car parking, good signage and a basic camping ground which can be reached only by foot.

 How to get there: From Titirangi take the Huia Road for 15km to Huia. At Huia cross over the one-way bridge at the Huia Stream and continue along the coast for a further 800 metres where the entrance to the car park and the track are to the left.

The Karamatura stream cuts deeply into the old stone of the Waitakere volcano and in the process has created sheer bluffs that rise high above a beautiful narrow valley. Although heavily milled for timber in the nineteenth century, today the regenerating forest is lush and as varied as anywhere around Auckland. Northern rata are thriving here (no doubt the possums are under control), on the higher ridges are groves of kauri, some of good size, and near the car park, manuka trees are alive with the sound of cicadas in the summer. The understorey is dense with nikau (some very old), ferns, kiekie, mosses and lichen and the three most common New Zealand tree ferns are all found here – mamaku, ponga and wheki. Parataniwha, which thrives in moist conditions, is found in great swathes higher up the valley.

The valley is a popular starting point for many longer tracks in the park (many of which are now closed) and also the easier and much shorter Karamatura Loop track. Although it has steeper sections and some steps, the track is in excellent condition and perfect for families. On the highest point of the track is a lookout with panoramic views over the thick bush and the rocky bluffs. From here, it is easy to spot the large rata trees rising above the surrounding bush.

Slightly beyond the loop track are the picturesque Karamatura Falls. Around 15 metres high, a narrow stream of water rushes down a rock face into a small pool perfect for swimming on a hot day. On the cliffs around the waterfall, rengarenga lilies seem to grow out of pure rock. The track to the falls can be a bit muddy and uneven in places and near the falls involves a bit of rock hopping over the stream. Just before the falls, are several shallow caves and here it is easy to see the composition of the rock known as volcanic conglomerate, common in the Waitakere Ranges. A type of breccia, this rock is formed by larger rocks, infilled with smaller gravel, stones and finer sand which, over time, compresses into solid rock.

31. Lower and Upper Huia Dams

 A good walk to stretch your legs along a reservoir lake and bush

 Easy ~ Top of the Lower Reservoir: Easy, 30 minutes return

Head of the Lower Reservoir Lake: Medium, One and half hours return

Base of the Upper Reservoir: Medium: Two and a half hours return

 How to get there: Take the Huia Road from Titirangi to Huia. 750 m past the Huia Store turn right into Huia Dam Road to the carpark.

In all honesty the main appeal of this walk is that it is one of the few longer track left open in the Waitakere Ranges, but that said it is a pleasant outing. Also the walking is along a gravel access road so this is a good winter walk to avoid slippery tracks and mud.

Beginning along a sealed road, the track follows the tidal Huia tidal stream to the base of the dam where there are toilets. From there a path leads up the face of the earth dam where you can walk across to an information board. Opened in 1971, the 40m high dam, covers 55 ha and holds six and half million litres of water.

From the dam an access road follows the western shore for a short distance and then climbs through low bush over a ridge to emerge at two narrow arms of water at the very head of the lake.

From here the road narrows but the bush is much more attractive beyond the lower reservoir as the Upper reservoir was completed in 1929 and the bush has been protected since that time. Following the Huia Stream, the track finally ends at the base of the dam to protect kauri. Return the way you came. Unlike the lower earth dam, the narrow upper dam is concrete.

32. Arataki Nature Trail

 An introduction to the New Zealand bush for locals and visitors alike

 Medium ~ 45 minutes return

 How to get there: Arataki Centre, 300 Scenic Drive, 5.5km from Titirangi

From the Arataki Centre, a short tunnel under the road leads a track which meanders through handsome native bush. Although typical of second growth bush, there are a good variety of plants and a sprinkling of larger native trees. The highlight of the walk is a small grove of large kauri which give visitors a glimpse of what a kauri forest must have looked like before Europeans arrived.

The signage is disappointing. Considering the number of older overseas visitors that do this walk, the information is sparse, basic and aimed at children. A side loop focusing on plant identification is much better, even though some of the trees and shrubs are very small.

If your own tree knowledge is reasonable, this is a good place to take overseas visitors. Although short, there are some steep sections with steps.

33. Arataki Loop Track/Slip Track, Pipeline Road and the Beveridge Track

 A good walk from the popular Arataki centre combining natural and human history

 Medium ~ One and half hours

 How to get there: Arataki Centre, 300 Scenic Drive, 5.5km from Titirangi

Beginning from the Arataki Centre, this track starts off promisingly through pretty bush, but in all truth, most of this track is pretty ordinary and the main attraction would be if you just needed a good walk or you had never done it before.

The bush track emerges on to a gravel access road and then goes steeply downhill for about half an hour before joining the Pipeline Road. This is definitely a walk you want to do anti-clockwise as it would be no fun doing a solid 30-minute uphill walk at the end. The Pipeline Road is just as the ticket says, a road with a pipeline and even that is oversold. A massive water pipe runs for about 200 metres and then suddenly dips underground not be seen again. After another 30 minutes this road meets yet another road which links the walk to the Beveridge Track and now things suddenly look up. To this point the walk is through regenerating bush, mainly of modest sized manuka and there are no views. On the positive side it is very likely you will have this walk to yourself.

At the junction of the Beveridge Track and Exhibition Drive finally there is a view from the famous "Stop. Mackies Rest" seat, named after a trader who delivered goods in this area and liked to stop at this point for a rest. Here the views are over the Upper Nihotapu Dam and beyond.

From there the walk markedly improves, with views along a winding track through handsome bush that takes about 30 minutes back to the Arataki Centre (See Beveridge Track entry)

34. Beveridge Track, Arataki Centre

 Glorious views and lush bush on this hilltop walk

 Medium ~ One hour return

Linking the Arataki Centre with the Exhibition Drive Track, this lovely walk is worth a visit in its own right and while mostly easy, there is one steep section that will get your heart rate up. Beginning from the Arataki Centre carpark, the first section of the track runs parallel to the road with helpful plant identification signs. Gradually the track winds downhill through handsome bush on an excellent track with breaks in the vegetation opening to expansive views over the Upper Nihotapu Reservoir, the Manukau Harbour and beyond to the Awhitu Peninsula. Where the track meets the Exhibition Drive Track, rest awhile at Mackies Rest while enjoying the views. Return the way you came or continue along the Exhibition Drive Track.

Adding to the appeal are information boards with historic photos telling the story of construction of track and road as well as honouring the memory of Bill Beveridge after whom the track was named.

35. Exhibition Drive Walk

 A lovely walk in any weather with a panoramic outlook at the end

 Easy ~ One and a half hours return

 How to get there: On the corner of Woodlands Park Road and Scenic Drive, one kilometre from Titirangi, next to the Nihotupu Filter Station.

Dead flat all the way, this walk follows the old road used to construct the pipeline from the Nihotupu Reservoir. A curious mixture, the first part of the road is still used to access houses some of which were built when the pipeline was constructed. Facing south, the bush is lush and damp and the pipeline itself adds to the appeal. Manufactured in Britain, the sections of cast iron pipes were hauled up from the harbour and neatly laid all the way to the city. Information boards with photos give a glimpse of the hard work and tough lives led by these workers in the wet bush. The walk terminates at Mackies Rest but it worth continuing up the Beveridge Track to Arataki. If you don't have anyone to pick you up at Arataki, it is better walking back the way you came rather than walking back via Scenic Drive as this road is very narrow, mostly without footpaths and frequently busy.

36. Zigzag Track, Atkinson Park, Titirangi

 Lush bush in a quiet hidden valley leads down to the sea

 Medium ~ Zigzag Track return 50 minutes, 40 minutes via the road

Titirangi Beach one-hour return

 How to get there: Park Road, off South Titirangi Road, Titirangi

Atkinson Park is named after Henry Atkinson (1838 – 1921) who gifted the park to the city in 1913. Atkinson is credited with the scheme to harness the deep valleys of the Waitakere ranges to provide a reliable water supply for the growing city. In 1915 he built a family holiday home on Paturoa Road and was an early advocate of protecting the environment. Atkinson's other passion for a canal to link the Manukau and Waitemata harbours was never realised. The statue of Henry outside Lopdell House, originally stood on the summit of Mt Atkinson but was moved after repeated thefts of the statue's nose.

The heart of the park is a very steep valley cloaked in luscious bush above a small stream and the Zigzag Track, appropriately named, cuts back and forth down the valley with lots of steps. Although milled for the best timber long ago, there are many good-sized trees including kahikatea, rimu, kohekohe and kauri. The track doesn't go all the way down to the beach, emerging onto Titirangi Beach Road about 300 metres from the sea.

It takes about 20 minutes to walk down the track and 30 minutes to walk back up, but walking back up the road is much easier and only takes 20 minutes. The road has no footpath and is narrow in places, so care is needed, but it is not so busy and is bush clad on both sides all the way back to the start so it is not an unpleasant walk.

A walk down to tidal Titirangi Beach has picnic areas, toilets and a playground and adds another 20 minutes to the trip.

GLOSSARY OF MAORI WORDS

All living languages are in a state of flux and that includes both Maori and New Zealand English. Since the arrival of Europeans and the domination of English in New Zealand, many Maori words continued in use especially for native trees and place names. In recent years, the use of Maori has increased and, in several cases, has completely displaced English names. Many New Zealanders wouldn't recognise parson bird, swamp hen, black pine or bush hen (tui, pukeko, matai, weka). In many other cases both English and Maori are readily understood; tieke, hihi, kahikatea, ruru, kiore, (saddleback, stitchbird, white pine, morepork, Polynesian rat). Very occasionally Maori and English combine as in Rengarenga lily and Hauraki Gulf.

This glossary is not a dictionary, but gives the Maori names for flora, fauna and occasionally place names referred to in this book with the English equivalents.

In addition to the mixture of English and Maori, there are also many regional variations in both Maori names and spelling (or both) and in order to keep the glossary simple and useable, only the words in common usage are given here.

Maori	English	Maori	English
Aihe	Common dolphin	Kareao	Supplejack
Harakeke	Flax	Karoro	Black-backed gull
Hihi	Stitchbird	Kawau	Shag, cormorant
Horoeka	Lancewood	Kekeno	Fur Seal
Inanga	Whitebait	Kereru	Wood pigeon
Kahikatea	White Pine	Kihikihi wawa	Chorus cicada
Kakariki	Red-crowned parakeet	Kiore	Polynesian rat
		Koura	Freshwater crayfish
Kanuka	Tea tree	Kotuku	White Heron
Karamu	Coprosma	Kotare	Kingfisher

Korora	Little blue pengui[n]	Tara-iti	Fairy tern
Kokako	Blue wattle crow	Taranui	Caspian tern
Koromiko	Hebe	Tarapuka	Black-bill gull
Kuaka	Godwit		
Mahoe	Whiteywood	Tarapunga	Red-billed gull
Mamaku	Black tree fern	Tawhairaunui	Hard beech
		Te Auaunga	Oakley Creek
Manawa	Mangrove	Te Maanuka o Hotu-nui	Manukau Heads
Manuka	Tea tree		
Matuku moana	White-faced heron	Te Ika-a-Maui	North Island
Matai	Black Pine	Te Moana-nui-a-Kiwa	Pacific Ocean
Maungarei	Mt Wellington		
Maungawhau	Mt Eden	Te Naupata	Musick Point
Miromiro	Tomtit	Te Tai-o-Rehua	Tasman Sea
Moko	Copper skink	Te Tai Tamatane	North Island West Coast
Namu	Sandfly		
Oioi	Jointed wire rush	Te Tai Tamahine	North Island East Coast
Owairaka	Mt Albert		
Pateke	Brown teal	Te Tatua-o-Riukiuta	Three Kings volcanos
Pekapeka	Long-tailed bat		
Pepeketua	Frog	Te Tokaroa	Meola Reef
Pipiwharauroa	Shining cuckoo	Tieke	Saddleback
Piwakawaka	Fantail	Ti kouka	Cabbage tree
Poaka	Pied stilt	Titiwai	Glow-worm
Ponga	Silver fern	Toetoe	Cuttygrass, pampas grass
Pou	Carved wooden post		
Pukeko	Swamp Hen	Tohora	Whale
Pupurangi	Kauri snail	Torea	Pied Oystercatcher
Putangitangi	Paradise duck	Tuna	Eel
Raupo	Bulrush	Tuturiwhatu	New Zealand dotterel
Riroriro	Grey Warbler		
Ruru	Morepork	Waiorea	Western Springs
Tamaki makaurau	Auckland	Wapi	Wasp
		Weka	Bush hen
Takapu	Gannet	Whai	Stingray
Tara	White-fronted tern		